FIRSTBORN

Center Point
Large Print

**This Large Print Book carries the
Seal of Approval of N.A.V.H.**

FIRSTBORN

TOSCA LEE

CENTER POINT LARGE PRINT
THORNDIKE, MAINE

This Center Point Large Print edition
is published in the year 2017 by arrangement with
Howard Books, an imprint of Simon & Schuster, Inc.

Map by Jeffrey L. Ward

The text of this Large Print edition is unabridged.
In other aspects, this book may vary
from the original edition.
Printed in the United States of America
on permanent paper.
Set in 16-point Times New Roman type.

ISBN: 978-1-68324-467-7

Library of Congress Cataloging-in-Publication Data

Names: Lee, Tosca Moon, author.
Title: Firstborn / Tosca Lee.
Description: Center Point Large Print edition. | Thorndike, Maine :
    Center Point Large Print, 2017.
Identifiers: LCCN 2017019372 | ISBN 9781683244677
    (hardcover : alk. paper)
Subjects: LCSH: Secret societies—Fiction. | Serial murderers—Fiction. |
Large type books. | BISAC: FICTION / Suspense. | FICTION / Christian
/ Suspense. | GSAFD: Suspense fiction.
Classification: LCC PS3612.E3487 F57 2017b | DDC 813/.6—dc23
LC record available at https://lccn.loc.gov/2017019372

For Wynter, Kayl, Kole, and Gage.
You fill my life with joy, hilarity, love . . .
and more laundry than I thought
humanly possible.

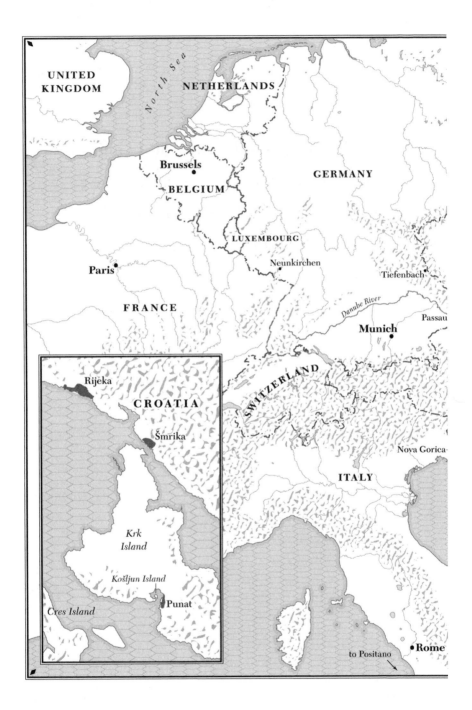

POLAND

UKRAINE

CZECH
REPUBLIC

Visnové

Trencín   SLOVAKIA

Cachtice

Bratislava

Vienna   *Danube River*

Györ   Budapest

AUSTRIA

Graz   HUNGARY

Maribor

Ljubljana   ROMANIA

Pristava

SLOVENIA   Zagreb

Trieste   Karlovac   CROATIA

Area of detail

Bucharest

BOSNIA
HERZEGOVINA   *Danube River*

Adriatic Sea   SERBIA

MONTENEGRO   BULGARIA

ALBANIA   © 2017 Jeffrey L. Ward

Nyirbator

Character List

PROGENY (ALSO KNOWN AS UTOD)

Anastasia: Elizabeth Bathory's illegitimate first child

Paul: Elizabeth Bathory's son

Audra Ellison: formerly Emily Porter (reported to have died in a car accident)

Eva: Audra and Luka's infant daughter

Tibor: Prince of the Zagreb court

Jester: French hacker/hactivist; Piotrek and Katia's half-sister

Piotrek: Claudia's protector "sibling"

Claudia: Piotrek's protector "sibling"

Nikola: Prince of the Budapest court (formerly Brother Goran); Amerie's former protector "sibling"

Amerie Szabo (aka Barbara Bocz): Audra's mother (deceased—possibly killed by Nikola)

Tamas Vargha: Audra's father (deceased—killed by hunter)

Ivan: Audra's former protector "sibling"; Tibor's biological brother (deceased—killed by hunter)

Katia: Piotrek's twin sister (deceased—killed by hunter)

Andre: Katia's lover (deceased—suicide)

Ana: Nino's protector "sibling" (deceased—killed by Nikola)

Nino: Ana's protector "sibling" (deceased—killed by Nikola)

Adran Horvat: (deceased—killed by hunter)

Analise: Arrick's lover (deceased—killed by hunter)

Arrick Drexel: former lover of Analise; not Progeny

SCIONS OF THE DISPOSSESSED (LIVING)

The Historian: leader of the Scions (identity unknown)

Luka Novak: Audra's former hunter, now husband, turned Scion traitor

Eva Novak: Luka's mother

Lazlo Becskei: Hungarian Curia president

Giada Borghi: Italian senator

Serge Deniel: French billionaire

Gerald Schelert: German banker

SCIONS OF THE DISPOSSESSED (DECEASED)

Cristian Alexandrescu: (a past Historian)

Attila Bertalan: (a past Historian)

Otto Errickson: (a past Historian)

Gregor: hunter killed days ago by heretic monk/ Scion Rolan Vasilescu

Franz Nowak: ancestor of Luka Novak
Tolvaj: one of the original twelve families
Me'sza'ros: one of the original twelve families
Samsa: one of the original twelve families

FRANCISCANS

Brother Goran: Nikola masquerading as a monk
  on Cres Island
Brother Daniel: curator of Progeny/Scion history
  at Kosljun Monastery, Krk Island
Rolan Vasilescu: member of heretic sect turned
  Scion

About Elizabeth Bathory

Hungarian Countess Elizabeth Bathory de Ecsed (1560–1614) is the most notorious female serial killer of all time. The exact number of her victims is unknown, though one witness testified at trial to a total of 650, as detailed in the countess's private diary.

Her accomplices were burned at the stake, but Bathory herself was spared execution. Instead, she was walled up in a set of rooms in Cachtice Castle (in present-day Slovakia), where she remained for four years until her death in 1614.

Known to be exceptionally educated, wealthier than the crown, and a doting mother to her children, the private life and sins of Elizabeth Bathory remain a mystery. History calls her a monster. Others, a victim of conspiracy and greed.

Legend knows her as the Blood Countess.

Before

Six weeks ago, I woke up in a cabin in the north woods of Maine with no memory of the last two years or any pertinent details of my life before. My real identity, for one, along with the names and faces of anyone I ever loved—all erased by an elective procedure I chose to undergo in a bid to protect a powerful secret.

Because when you're me, knowledge is dangerous. And my memory is deadly.

It took them one month to find me.

My name is Audra Ellison and I am twenty-one years old. I've spent the last two weeks on the run, chased across Eastern Europe, hiding in her underground. Piecing together the past I erased. Not knowing whom to trust.

I am a direct descendant of the "Blood Countess" Elizabeth Bathory, the most prolific female serial killer of all time, and I am being hunted by an ancient organization called the Scions of the Dispossessed, who have sworn to destroy her progeny. For four hundred years they have systematically murdered our kind in revenge for Bathory's purported atrocities against their peasant ancestors. They are peasants no more; today their secret society backs some of the most powerful offices in

Europe, with influence throughout the world.

But the Progeny—also called the Utod—are not without resources. We are gifted with a legacy passed through the female line. We can *persuade* others without words. We can appear to possess the characteristics that anyone looking at us wants to see. We have unnaturally strong charisma. We stand out in a crowd. Which is great if you want to be a rock star . . .

But terrible when you're trying to hide.

We can sense others like us. We thrive on adrenaline and have to burn it often—not a problem when you're running for your life. Most of us don't live to be thirty, the age at which our gifts begin to fade, making it all too easy for a hunter to take us down.

Hunters—the assassins of the Scions' lower ranks, each assigned a single Progeny mark—have their own unique powers. They can strip a Progeny's memory the moment the Progeny dies, making everything we know—our hiding places, our allegiances, and the identities of others like us—as vulnerable as an open vault.

Now anyone I discover from my past is in danger if I die. But everything I erased is what I need to stay alive.

Twelve days ago I fled to Croatia with the help of Luka, my former hunter turned lover. The Progeny underground has pockets called "courts" throughout the world, but nowhere as deep as within the borders of Bathory's former influence: the ancient Hungarian Empire. There, I reconnected with Ivan, Claudia, and her "sibling" protector, Piotrek—all Progeny, like me. Friends I once knew, strangers to me now. They don't know what Luka was, or that for helping me fake my death, he's now as hunted as I. To them, he's merely common, not one of us.

Hours after we met, Ivan turned up dead. Three more murders—monks, who helped protect our secrets—followed in his wake.

We went into hiding in Zagreb's underground, where Progeny rave until dawn, exorcising adrenaline in masked anonymity and safety. There, under the auspices of the Zagreb prince, Tibor, I met new friends Nino and Ana and found sanctuary with others like me: Progeny determined to pursue vibrant life on the edge of death.

Until the night Nikola, the high Budapest prince, arrived in Zagreb. In a private meeting, the traitorous "sibling" once sworn to protect my celebrated mother threatened the lives of Luka and the others unless I agreed to retrieve the thing he believed my mother and I both went to such lengths to conceal: Elizabeth Bathory's diary. A document Scions believe contains the account of her atrocities and justification for their existence . . . and Progeny believe to be the record of her innocence, which will end the murder of our

17

kind. An item so revered that either side will kill for it.

That night, Nino was captured. Now I'm wanted for his murder. Ana disappeared a day later.

We escaped with the others to Vienna, where, with the help of a Progeny hacker named Jester, I located an anonymous safety deposit box—a fail-safe from my former life in case all of this went sideways. In it: my journal, an incomplete chart of the Scions' genealogy and rise to power, my baby picture, a letter from my mother, a strange set of her notes . . .

And a wedding ring.

Mine. Given to me by Luka.

Separated from the others, Luka and I fled to Bratislava, where he was captured by the Scions of the Dispossessed. Their leader—a figure known only as the Historian, whom I now know to be in league with Nikola—has given me five days to find the diary as ransom for his life.

In the custody of Rolan, a heretical monk whose sect infiltrated Scion ranks generations ago, I have learned what I am: a descendant of Elizabeth Bathory's firstborn daughter, Anastasia. A line of Progeny hunted nearly to extinction that those like Rolan have pledged their lives to find and defend.

With only my deceased mother's cryptic notes to go by, my search has brought me to a monastery on the island-within-an-island of Punat in Croatia, where I've found no diary, but a cache of information damning to the Scions . . . and something far more devastating:

The thing I would have died to protect. A secret so powerful I hid it even from myself.

I thought I erased my memory to save my friends. I thought I did it to save Luka.

I was wrong.

I did it all for her.

1

There are moments that both shatter and restore your existence at once. That hollow you out as your entire life up to that instant—and your entire life from that instant on—collide inside you and leave you gasping for air.

Standing in the monastery's sunny courtyard, I watch the nun come toward me. I'm startled to recognize her. Clare. My caretaker after my memory procedure as I recovered in the north woods of Maine. I have never seen her in a habit. I didn't know she was a nun.

But it's the baby in her arms that has tilted the axis of my entire world.

Stormy eyes. Luka's eyes. I would know them anywhere.

And I know this is my child.

Mine, and Luka's.

Several facts click suddenly into place, like teeth through a zipper:

The ancient Glagolitic numbers tattooed in ultraviolet ink along my spine: 924615.

September 24. The date on our wedding certificate.

June 15, nearly nine months after that.

The way Luka paled the night we deciphered those symbols, which I used to retrieve my safety deposit box in Vienna.

"Audra," Clare says. It's the first time she's ever called me by my real name. "This is Eva. Your daughter."

I am shaking.

She hands the baby to me. I take her gingerly, stare at that little face—the tiny nose, the wisps of her lashes. She's beautiful.

"You gave her up to a foundling box at a hospital in Rome. One monitored by our order for the infants of Progeny who dare not keep their babies or even know their whereabouts in case their memories are harvested and the children discovered."

She has an accent. Croatian. She must have concealed it from me in Maine.

"A foundling box?" I ask, throat dry as the three other kids she's tending chase one another, laughing, into the colonnade.

"Yes. A small hatch on the side of a hospital for unwanted infants or babies a mother cannot raise. The Utod have left us their children for centuries, knowing they will be fostered in anonymity, undetected even by other Progeny, who cannot sense them until they come of age."

But she's wrong. The wave of hyperawareness I've felt on meeting other Progeny is nothing to the insistent pull of Eva's small figure. She has a gravity like the sun.

I hold the baby close and it's like I'm taking a missing piece of myself back—the single key to everything that makes sense out of the whole.

The lengths I went to hide her. The fail-safes I left myself.

My willingness to die.

I hold her close and inhale the scent of her downy head. My mind may not remember her, but at the mere smell of her, my heart races.

I take in her chubby cheeks, the curve of her tiny mouth, opened in a toothless smile. She blurs through my tears and I don't know what I'm crying for more—the fact that I don't recall the little face staring up at me, or the fact that I'm holding a piece of Luka, too. Maybe the only piece I will ever hold again.

Does he know? I wonder.

Someone else has come into the courtyard to stand beside me. Brother Daniel. The monk who received me and spent hours this morning laying out the contents of a subterranean archive chronicling the four-hundred-year rise of the Scions into a massive, unstoppable cabal. The guardian of their true history.

"And now you see," he says quietly.

"What have you done?" I whisper.

I came here in a blind bid to save Luka's life in exchange for the Bathory diary. But now . . . how can I possibly put myself in the way of any hunter, let alone go up against the Historian herself with the full knowledge of Eva's existence firmly rooted in my mind?

"Why would you bring her here?" I say.

"Show her to me? Knowing what's at stake—the danger you've just put her in? Everything I did. Everything I erased! You've just undone it all!"

Eva starts to cry and Clare reaches for her.

"No!" I back away from them both, desperately clasping my daughter against me. But even as I turn away, I know there's nowhere I can go. I can't take her with me. I can't protect her.

"I knew when you realized the full reach and influence of the Scions, that you would see it as hopeless," Father Daniel says. "A fight that cannot be won."

"It *is* a fight that cannot be won!"

"It must be won! For your sake. For hers. What do you think the Historian would do to her—or worse, with her? The child of a hunter and one of the last—possibly *the* last—remaining Progeny of Bathory's firstborn daughter? She will be nothing but a weapon to them! Nor will she find sanctuary at any underground court if your kind find out what she is. She will be ruled an abomination."

"Don't you dare call my daughter an abomination," I say dangerously, as I bounce Eva in my arms, trying to quiet her.

"Now you know what is at stake. What must be done. Abolish both sides of this war, Audra. Or your daughter will never be safe, consigned to living always in hiding—in isolation. Without a people of her own to help or shelter her. Would

24

you have her walled up? Living on an island as Ivan did? You've seen what the Scions are willing to do to our brothers! We can no longer protect you as we have. And you will likely not live to protect her, either."

That last statement sucks the air from my lungs. Not the prospect of death; that shadow has been hanging over my head since birth, bleaker by the day. No, it's the thought of not being there to protect her, teach her who she is, how to survive. Of leaving her scrambling for the scant written words of a dead mother somewhere in the path of the freight train called the Scions.

"And now you've exposed her!" I say angrily.

He reaches toward Eva. "We will take her away, and even you will not know where she has gone—"

"The hell you will!" I clutch her tighter.

"Audra," Clare says. "If you are captured or killed, they will never find her location. They cannot take a memory of what you, yourself, do not know. And on the day that this is ended . . . she will return to you. I swear it."

And then, I get it.

They never intended to give her back to me.

They only intended to trigger me. *She* is the reason I never accessed the cache of information in the vault below, but saved it for the inevitable day I would need it to protect her.

Though the rational side of my brain knows

taking her with me now would be tantamount to killing her, I feel brutally betrayed—by myself, most of all. Standing here with Eva in my arms . . . how am I supposed to let her go again?

"Please. Just . . . let me have a little time with her."

I could make him let me keep her. Could *persuade* him to give me another hour with her, which would still never be enough.

But even as I think this I know that time is running out. I glance up toward the sun, slanted far enough west to hide behind the roof of the courtyard. Luka had two days left to live when we arrived on this island, and the day is dwindling fast.

I turn away, cuddling Eva, memorizing her face. The little whorl of her ear. Her sparse hair—dark blond, like mine. The furrow of her feathered brow as she stares at me with Luka's blue eyes.

I cradle her head in my palm, kiss her chubby cheek. "Next time there'll be no good-bye," I whisper.

I pretend not to hear when another monk comes to say the boat is waiting. Or when Clare calls the children, saying it's time for them to go.

Too soon, Clare takes her from my arms. My breath leaves me all at once, like a sucker punch to the gut. Eva begins to fuss, and I try to make shushing sounds that come out as sobs instead.

She begins to wail, and even as my heart shatters I tell myself it's because she is like me. That her eyes recognize patterns, faces, and that she knows me. And I hope that I am right, and that she does—in case it has to be enough to last a lifetime.

2

The minute Clare, Eva, and the other children are gone from sight, Brother Daniel's hand is on my shoulder. He's talking, saying something, but my attention has vanished with my baby, and it's all I can do not to scratch and kick my way past him to chase after her. I can *feel* her leaving me.

"Where will they take her?" I demand.

"You know I cannot tell you that," he says, trying to steer me the opposite way. And for a moment I have the sense that this must be what it's like to be the ward of a mental institution.

"Are you sure she'll be safe? Will you be able to check on her?" Adrenaline is sizzling in my veins and I don't have the time or luxury to run or swim to exorcise it.

"Yes. I promise." Brother Daniel stops, turns toward me. "And one day, Audra, you will see her again. I believe it. I have prayed for it. As I have prayed for you since you were small."

I stagger after him, pressing the heels of my hands to my eyes. And though his words are meant to be reassuring, they're not. Because prayer's what you do when you have no options left.

Luka deserves to know—that we have a daughter, and that she's safe. But chances are he'll never live to meet her.

I feel sick.

"Is there a bathroom around here that I could use?" I ask, and Brother Daniel escorts me down a visitors' hallway.

I lock myself inside the restroom, slide down the chilly wall.

My breath comes in ragged wheezes, the result of a toxic cocktail of exhaustion and grief. At Luka's pending murder. At letting my daughter go—again. My mind may not remember her, but my body *knew*—perhaps in the same way that it knew Luka, and reached for him, even as I questioned whether I could trust him not to kill me.

My heart won't stop pounding in my ears. I squeeze my temples, eyes shut, and wonder if I'm having a panic attack.

Because I don't like the thoughts that are coming to me.

The first is that my odds of getting Luka back alive, assuming I could find the so-called diary, were slim to none to begin with. Even if the Historian were to release him, she could never afford to let me survive now that I've laid eyes on the information in Brother Daniel's vault.

The second is that no hunter can harvest my memory of Eva if my brain is too damaged or has been dead too long.

Third, I threatened to drop myself into the Danube just the other day if the Historian's lackeys laid one more hand on Luka. It was enough then to stop their brutality. And she could have killed me the night I met her in the Budapest underground, but she needed me to decipher my mother's notes. Which means there is something—*something*—she wants very badly in that cache of information.

And the minute she knows I've found it, I have no more leverage to keep Luka alive. I'm a dead woman again, either way.

And Eva is an orphan.

My last thought is this:

Screw them!

Because I will not let them take one more thing—one more *person*—I love from me while I'm still breathing and alive enough to do something about it. And I will not die a victim.

If the information in the vault truly is a weapon, then by God, I'm going to wield it.

I shove up from the floor, remembering the pings that exploded from my phone after I emerged from the vault with Brother Daniel earlier.

I pull out the phone, slide the screen to life, and note the time with alarm: 1:47. The longest I've spent in a single location, even to sleep, since leaving Budapest.

Claudia: Well??
Claudia: Anything?
Jester: Audra, what is happening?
Jester: We are worried.

30

Claudia: Piotrek is about to leave for Croatia if we don't hear from you and it's your fault.

The last one was just twenty-eight minutes ago. I tap out a quick reply:

Am fine. Hold tight.

A rap on the bathroom door.

"Audra? Are you all right?"

For a dead girl, I sure have a lot of people worried about me.

"Fine," I call, moving to the sink to splash water on my face. My eyes are red, grainy from lack of sleep. I squint at myself in the mirror. But all I can see is the masked face of my enemy, the Historian.

My name is Audra Ellison. I am twenty-one years old . . . and you have just poked the mother bear.

I emerge from the bathroom to a relieved-looking Brother Daniel, and move with him swiftly down the hall.

"You look like a new person," he says.

"No," I say. "Just more of the one I was before."

I follow Brother Daniel to the storeroom sealed with the biometric lock and the archive he has risked his life to curate. Seventy-nine Franciscan monks have died in its service through the centuries—three of those murders in the last two weeks alone.

"The true diary," Brother Daniel called the collection, gesturing to the piles of intercepted letters, testimonies, pictures, e-mails, and articles that he spent hours removing from their locked drawers this morning. Some of them crumbling from age. Some of them printed as recently as this year. My own mother contributed to this account before she died.

It's now after 2:00 P.M., and Rolan has been waiting at the jetty this whole time.

"The guy who brought me here," I say. "Can someone let him know I'm okay?" I ask.

I volunteer you.

"I'll take the message myself," he says.

I thank him and watch him go, already sensing the slight drop in my adrenaline from that tiny act of persuasion alone. Just enough to help me focus.

I wonder what Brother Daniel would think if he knew that Rolan is a heretic—a member of the secret, fanatical sect that left monastic life a century ago in order to infiltrate the Scions by essentially breeding themselves in. Which technically means he's a Scion hunter with the ability to harvest my memory. As far as the Historian knows, I'm in Rolan's custody.

But right now, he's the only non-Progeny I trust, other than Brother Daniel.

Alone in the vault, I work my way through the first pile, taking photo after photo with my phone. Not all the items are in English, but it isn't hard to make out the story of account ledgers, money transfers, news stories on deaths, accidents, and suicides. IMF rulings, a brief crash in the European market a couple years ago. Investors who profited from the crash. The rise of a media mogul. A large merger. Stock surges. A squelched investigation. All the makings of one of those conspiracy theory string boards, and just about as linear.

I move swiftly. For all I know, we might be hundreds of kilometers from Luka, and he has less than two days to live. Don't think about the fact that if a single one of these cases could be proven, it might take years and hundreds of thousands—perhaps millions—of dollars to convict. Or that I am not powerful or acquainted enough with foreign law to know where or how a person would even begin.

The adrenaline building in my veins makes me feel like screaming, but I pause when I get to the heavy book of Bathory's descendants. It is the only complete genealogy of its kind. How many of the victims in this book had children whose names were never recorded?

Eva's face floats before my eyes. Her baby smell clings like a gentle touch. I grab the front of my shirt and lift it to my face, inhale deeply.

There it is, just faintly. Proof that she is real.

I force the thought away and take pictures of several e-mails I can't make sense of until there's only a small stack of printouts and clippings left. There's a flash drive, too. I shove the items into one of the folders there, pocket the thumb drive, and let myself out, closing the vault behind me.

I jog down the corridor, willing my phone to regain a signal. The moment the first bar appears, I dial Claudia.

"What's taken you so long?" she snaps, her accent heavier when she's irked.

So much I could say. So much I don't dare. I settle for: "I've got it."

Silence. And then an audible exhale. "Oh my God."

"I need Jester."

"She found it," I hear Claudia whisper. Someone grabs the phone.

"Audra?" Jester says, strange incredulity in her French voice.

"It's not what you think."

"What do you mean?"

"I'm going to start uploading pictures."

"Pictures? No! It's not safe. You have to come here."

I've just let myself through the door at the end of the private corridor when Brother Daniel meets me in the outer hall.

He's visibly upset.

"I'll call you back," I say and abruptly hang up.

"I tried to send your driver away," Daniel says. "I told him you no longer need him . . ." And then he notices the folder in my hands. "What are you doing?"

"I'm leaving."

"You cannot leave—not now!"

"I'm sorry. I have to. I've already been here too long."

"We have a safe house waiting for you on the mainland. We will arrange your safe passage tonight, after dark. Please! Eva is young, many years away from coming into the legacy. There is time."

"No. There isn't."

I don't tell him about Luka. That I have just over a day to make a single effort to get him back.

Just then Rolan appears behind him.

"We need to go. Now."

"You cannot be here! This is a private wing!" Daniel says to Rolan. "Please," he says, turning to me. "There are things you do not know."

I hesitate. *What else could there be?*

"You cannot just leave like this. As you are."

I know what he means is having seen and learned all that I have. With the archive's location and contents in my memory. My getting killed by a hunter now would expose it all.

"Audra," Rolan says.

I don't know what's happened to put that urgency in his voice, but right now I'm not going to question it.

"Start the boat," I say. "I'm right behind you."

He disappears down the hall, and I turn to Brother Daniel.

"What things?" I ask.

"Your powers of persuasion, of charisma . . . We were the ones who helped those before you learn to exercise their gifts," he says, drawing me aside. "Let me help you, teach you!"

"I've already . . . exercised them."

He shakes his head. "Yours are not like the others'," he says, fingers biting into my arm. "They are stronger—more deadly. If you do not learn to control your powers, they will destroy you. You will lose *everything* you are fighting for!"

I feel those words like ice on the back of my neck.

But if I don't at least try to save Luka—now—with the hope that one day we'll see Eva again, there is nothing to fight for.

"Tell me now," I say, drawing him along with me toward the courtyard, and out.

"It is more than I can tell you here!"

"Talk fast," I say, pulling my hat from my pocket, tugging it down low over my head.

"The harder you try to impose your will, the worse it will be for you. The more you act out of desperation, the more it will cost you," he says, breathing harder but keeping up with my swift clip. "Your ancestor, Erzsebet, was given to seizures. The same could happen to you. There is a physical cost. No, this way," he says, taking me out through a side exit, toward the jetty.

This is not news to me. Incessant nosebleeds have become a way of life—most recently in Bratislava just before Luka was taken. But as far as I know I have never suffered any seizures or debilitating brain damage.

Well, that last might be debatable.

My phone pings. Jester.

Do NOT send photos. Unreliable.

Daniel keeps talking as we move. "There is a spiritual repercussion as well, Audra. The adrenaline you burn by using your gifts, by reacting out of fear, by holding to what you love too tightly—"

"You're telling me not to be afraid? Not to care?" Fear of losing what I love is the sole thing that has driven me since the day I erased my memory. Unafraid is the one thing I don't know how to be.

He stops on the edge of the jetty, where the last of a group of perhaps fifteen tourists is boarding a ferry bound for the larger island of Krk. The private boat Rolan and I arrived in is nowhere to be seen. Rolan stands, one foot on the gangway, waiting.

"I'm telling you that if you cannot control your mind, your gifts will destroy it. As they nearly destroyed your mother. I wish you would not go. I fear I will not see you again in this life."

In that moment, I feel for Daniel. I really do. And wish I could reassure him.

But right now I can practically feel the minutes ticking down.

"I'll come back. I promise," I whisper, rising up on my toes to embrace him. "Keep my daughter safe."

"She is safe. But as for you . . ."

"Eva's all that matters."

Daniel's brow furrows in dismay as I release him.

"There's one more thing I need you to do," I say. "Pack up the contents of that vault tonight. Send them somewhere I would never know to find them."

He nods as Rolan gestures impatiently from the gangway.

"Please do not make me regret the day I let you leave like this," he says.

"I'll do my best."

I hurry to the ferry and board, turn back toward the dock as we pull away.

Maybe he's right. Maybe the smartest thing I could do right now would be to flee to a safe house on my own.

But Eva is, for the moment, safe beyond even the reaches of my vulnerable memory. And Rolan is my sole hope of keeping Luka alive.

Brother Daniel clasps his hands, watching us go. I offer a wave, and to my surprise, Rolan does, too. No. Not a wave. He's making the sign of the cross, his tattoo visibly displayed on his wrist.

The double-barred heretic's cross.

Brother Daniel staggers on the dock, eyes wide, already shrinking in the distance.

3

"What happened to our boat?" I mutter to Rolan halfway across the turquoise bay.

"Better to leave in a group," he whispers, doing his best to sit forward, blocking me against the gunwale as I pull a wad of toilet paper from my pocket and feign seasickness.

Easy for him to say. He's not the one risking an aneurysm by having to *persuade* the others on the ferry they haven't seen my face on the news.

Just another tourist. One who might barf at any moment. Look away, folks.

But I'm grateful for the burn as it siphons off the adrenaline and my knee slows its jackhammer bounce against the wale. Five minutes ago, I was ready to jump out of the boat and swim my way to shore.

My nose is bleeding by the time we arrive in Punat on the larger island of Krk eight minutes later.

"We've got problems," Rolan says the minute we're back in the car. It smells like stale coffee and Turo Rudi chocolate bar wrappers.

"What now?" I ask. I don't know how many more revelations I can take today. Especially of the problem variety.

"They found Gregor's body."

"Whose?"

"The other hunter I killed the night we left Budapest."

This is how far I've come. That I can forget the fact that just three days ago we dumped the dead body of Rolan's Scion partner in Budapest's inner city.

"So they're onto you. That you're helping me."

"The body hasn't been identified."

"Yet."

"Yet. And there are Scions on the police force."

"Which means the Historian could find out any time."

With Luka still in custody.

"That's not all. I had to give them something. They're undoubtedly tracking this car. We were in one place so long, I had to tell them you were close—very close—to finding the diary. And so I took the liberty of telling them you now demand proof of life every six hours for the next twenty-four."

He pulls out his phone, thumbs through to a video. Today's proof of life, which came in just over an hour ago.

I exhale a sigh of relief.

Until I start the recording.

Luka, bound in the same metal truck trailer as before. He's gagged, but the blood has been cleaned from his face. His left cheek is purple, an eye swollen mostly shut. But I release a slow breath if only because he looks far more alive than he did two days ago.

The minute his eyes fasten on the screen, they widen in horror and he begins to thrash in his bonds. And then I realize: I wasn't there when the video came in. All Luka saw was Rolan, staring back at him from the other side of the camera where I was supposed to be.

"She's alive," I hear Rolan say. "I'll relay the message that you are, too."

Luka quiets, chest heaving.

The video ends and I click the phone off.

"Thank you."

Rolan nods.

"So if they're tracing this car, and we were on Košljun nearly four hours . . . They're going to think I found something."

He glances sidelong at me.

"I take it you found it."

"I guess this is the point where you're supposed to kill me and harvest my memory," I say slowly.

"Actually . . . I was supposed to kill you, take the diary, and *not* harvest your memory."

I blink.

"That doesn't make sense."

"It does if I'm not to know what's in the diary."

"It's not a diary," I say at last.

He looks at me but doesn't ask. And the fact that he doesn't somehow makes me feel unexpectedly alone.

I have a daughter. Her name is Eva. I saw her, and she's beautiful.

The knowledge wells up inside me. I want to blurt it out—to him, the world.

But as much as I trust him, Rolan is not the person I should be telling.

He accelerates down Highway 102, breaking the speed limit.

"What are you doing?"

His jaw tenses. "We need to get as far from Košljun as possible, go somewhere else. Somewhere south, out of the way. Sarajevo or Montenegro."

Though I see his logic—we've zigzagged all across Hungary, Slovakia, and Croatia already—we don't have time. Gregor's body could be identified any minute. The Historian might even now be receiving an urgent call about one of her hunters, exposing Rolan.

I can't think. The images from the vault are crashing together with the video of Luka, the map of Croatia I memorized with a single glance—the curse of a photographic memory and what I used to think was ADHD.

I chug the remainder of a cold cup of coffee, willing the caffeine so calming to the Progeny to take effect. But all I can see is Eva's tiny face. I squeeze my eyes shut, fighting for focus.

A minute later, I dial Jester.

"I don't trust any VPN outside of Sweden

for you to upload those pictures," she says.

"Can you exchange our car's GPS for that of another car heading south?"

"And the location on my phone," Rolan adds.

"Not in the time you have. Get a different car."

As soon as we've crossed the mile-long bridge from Krk to the mainland, we turn south to the small village of Smrika, ditch the car in the back of an apartment complex.

Coming around front, I *persuade* a woman just getting into a white Citroën SUV to give us her keys.

Fifteen minutes later, we're headed back north and then east on the A7.

"You realize you're going to be a fugitive," I say.

The sun is setting behind us, an extravagant display of reds and purples. And all I can think is that it looks too much like blood and bruises. Somewhere, presumably west of us, I imagine Eva being fed and bathed, prepared for bed.

My arms ache at the thought of her. And I'm probably doing the stupidest thing in the world by trying to get her father back. But I can't fathom trying to tell her ten, fifteen years from now that I could have tried, and didn't.

Assuming I live that long.

She's safe. She's safe. As long as I don't know where she is, she's safe.

Jester won't talk about the specifics of what

I found, insists that we meet them in Zagreb or Maribor tonight. When I hedge, Claudia and I end up in a heated argument about the selfishness of risking my life that ends with her yelling at me. But I know her well enough to know she's afraid.

"Rolan's about to be made," I say. "He can't go back. If anything happens, he'll get everything I've got to you." I don't have to say "including my memory."

It doesn't help.

"So there never was going to be an exchange," I say to Rolan, as the sun drops below the horizon.

"No."

Well, that puts a damper on things.

"Just me dead and you delivering the so-called diary to the Historian. And Luka presumably killed as soon as she knew I was dead."

Rolan is silent.

"How long until they identify the body?"

"A day, if we're lucky."

It's nearly seven. The offices are closed unless their forensic experts work in the evening, though that might just happen on American TV. By morning then, just to be safe.

"Where were you supposed to take the diary?" I ask.

"I was to be given a drop location."

"You don't even get the honor of giving it to the Historian face-to-face?"

"No one sees the Historian's face."

But I nearly did, five nights ago in Europe's largest underground gathering: the Budapest court. The same night she sent me on the mission for this cache in exchange for Luka's life. I don't know how many times I've cursed myself for not lunging for her mask—or better, her throat. Except for the problem of her holding a gun on me with one hand, and Luka's life in the other.

I've already quizzed Rolan about how all this Scion stuff works.

Who knows who the Historian is?

No one except her immediate circle.

How do they communicate with you?

Via the same voice you've heard.

Did you know it was the Historian herself, that night in Budapest?

It's the question that caused his hands to ball into fists. I've replayed the night in Budapest over and over. The way Rolan and the other hunter came in. Robed and masked as she was, even her own hunters didn't know it was her.

No. Had I known, she would be dead. But given all the guards there, most likely so would you. And there would be no one to stop the Historian's successor from assuming power.

I slide down in the passenger seat, mind racing.

"So once I retrieved the 'diary' you would have been given a drop. And then?"

"And then, I assume, I would have found a

sum of money in my bank account. Or a job offer with a large salary waiting for me."

"Sorry."

He shrugs. "When the members of our sect began to marry into Scion families, we put ourselves in the path of wealth. I was always embarrassed by it. Not because I was holy—definitely not that. But because I had parents who forgot what it was to live under Communism. I left when I was a teenager to attend military school. I already knew then what I was, had been taught by my grandfather, who considered my father too corrupt to carry our mission. But I . . . I abhor wealth. It is maybe the only one of our original vows I have ever honored."

"Well, this works out fine then. Because I can help you be poor."

He gives a slight smile.

"Rolan, where are the others like you?"

"Scattered across the continent. I just happened to find you first."

"So, how are we going to do this?"

"I don't suppose I can convince you to run and let Luka go."

"No, sorry."

He's quiet for a moment before he says: "Then you have to kill me."

4

The next proof of life comes promptly at 6:00 P.M.

Luka, looking more refreshed even than before but visibly tense, bound and tied to the same chair that is seemingly bolted to the floor of the truck-trailer. The cords on his neck instantly relax at first sight of me.

"I'm close to finding it, Luka," I say, trying to sound unrehearsed and hopeful at once within our darkened car. "The diary—it's real."

At those words, however, he tosses his head, trying to yell something behind the gag. And I know he's telling me to take it and run. To get away from Rolan. Because he doesn't know about him. The truck hits some kind of bump and the camera jolts in the hands of his captor, and then the feed abruptly shuts off.

"Good," Rolan says.

But I am far from good.

It was shorter than the others. Far too short.

I thumb through to the folder of feeds dating back the last four days, pull up the one that just recorded.

"Something happened at the end. Did you see that?"

"They're not going to give you any more than they have to," he says.

48

"No, something else." I play the feed again. The camera has never been perfectly steady, obviously held in human hands. But something about that jolt—

"There," I say, hitting pause and scrolling back.

"I don't see it."

I advance the recording a frame at a time. Just before the feed ends, the picture tilts, inadvertently incorporating the first other object I have ever seen in the truck interior. Something mostly yellow and linear that's normally beyond the angle of the camera.

"What is that?" I say.

Rolan frowns. "How did you even notice that?"

"It's a gift," I mutter.

I back up a frame, and then swipe forward. The object is in a total of three frames at the end.

"It looks like a—" He fumbles for the words in English. "The metal instrument for moving . . ."

"A pallet jack!"

"Yes. But so what? Any truck can have a . . . pallet jack."

I replay the frame.

"It has something on it. Looks like a company name." Though it's too fuzzy to read on the tiny screen.

I call Jester.

"I'm sending you something," I say, plugging the minidrive from my pocket into Rolan's phone.

"I told you not to—"

"It's the latest video of Luka. There's something there, at the end, with a name on it."

I download the file, transfer the drive to my phone. I don't trust Rolan's. A moment later, I'm uploading the video to Jester, full resolution.

"At the end, there's something in the truck."

"What is that?" Jester says, switching to video chat.

"A pallet jack. But I can't read the name on it."

"A what?"

"For moving things from a truck."

"Aha . . . ah, yes. All right. Let me see what I can find." She clicks off.

We drive in silence for an hour after that, head east for lack of a better direction. Luka was taken in Bratislava. I met the Historian in Budapest. Either one of them could be anywhere by now. I tell myself it doesn't matter—that I have the thing the Historian wants.

We've just pulled into the parking lot of a large hotel on the outskirts of Zagreb by the time Jester videos back.

"Audra, I think I have something for you," she says. Her dreads are tied high on her head with a purple scarf. Claudia and Piotrek peer at me from over her shoulders. I give them a little stupid wave. It's good—so good—to see their faces.

"If I render the image, this spray-paint lettering that seems black—but is really blue—spells out 'Vad . . .'"

" 'Vad'?"

"Which are the first three letters of the Vadasz Freight Company . . ." An image takes over the screen: a trucking fleet painted in yellow and blue.

"It is the largest freight carrier in Europe," Piotrek says. "Hello, Audra." He waves back.

"And . . . they are based out of Budapest," Jester says.

"Then he's in one of—what? A couple hundred trucks?"

"More like three thousand. It's a very large fleet."

My heart sinks.

"*But,* Vadasz has a very sophisticated IT network and logistics system," Jester says.

I pause. "So you can find him."

"I don't see 'hostage' listed as the cargo for any truck in the system," she says dryly. "But we know he was taken four days ago near Bratislava. Once you set a location for the exchange I can track any Vadasz truck as it arrives within a radius of that point."

I sit back and exhale.

"Okay," I say and glance at Rolan. "I know what to do."

5

Parked in the back of the hotel lot, my attempts to sleep are worthless.

I wonder where Eva is. What she looks like when she sleeps. I count back the forty weeks of my pregnancy, try to calculate the day of her conception—right around the time Luka and I got married. Wonder what our lives were like, realize I may never know.

Rolan snores softly from the driver's seat, the exhaustion of the last few days evident in the lines on his forehead. Meanwhile, my knee is bouncing against the console hard enough to bruise.

Just before midnight, I shake Rolan awake, grab his phone, and check to be sure there are no identifying landmarks in the view behind me.

The video feed comes a minute late, at 12:01.

Luka, sagging in the same chair. This time he does not thrash or try to talk through his gag, his eyes intently focused on the camera.

"Hey," I say. "You trying to get a little rest, too?" I don't have to fake the fatigue and hope it disguises the fact that I've rehearsed these lines a hundred times.

A muscle in his cheek twitches.

"I ran into a little roadblock," I say, glancing

down to hide my expression. "But I think I can find a way around it."

I glance up just in time for the video to end. And I don't like the last look I see on Luka's face.

It's far too serene.

The look of a man prepared to die.

I instantly search the recording for any hint of Luka's location, but there is nothing—not even a bobble. They're no longer moving.

Of course not. They're near the place they intend to dump his body.

"Call them now. We have to call now!"

Rolan takes the phone from me.

"Not yet," he says. "Calm down." But the buildup of angst and adrenaline inside me feels like a tsunami. I yank open the car door, get out, rest my hands on my knees. Try to force myself to breathe.

"I won't make it the next six hours," I rasp. A breeze rifles through my hair. I close my eyes and suck in a breath. Will my lungs to expand.

"You have to. Our plan won't work until then."

My phone blips from inside the car and I lunge for it. Jester.

"Audra . . ."

Jester, normally so composed, hesitates.

"What is it?" Somewhere in the last three days I've lost my ability to tolerate even split-second silences.

"They've identified the body."

My pulse drops out.

"Someone's been working around the clock, apparently. It just got logged in to the police system. As an Adran Horvat, who apparently disappeared months ago."

"That isn't right. His name's Gregor and he didn't die that long ago."

Adran Horvat. I've seen that name before. Can picture it, even, painstakingly penned at the top of a short biography . . .

On a page of the Progeny genealogy in Brother Daniel's vault.

"Adran Horvat was one of us," I say. Gregor definitely was not.

"Then they're covering Adran's death with the body of one of their own. Regardless, they know."

"Then we have to move. Are you sure you can do this?"

"Not alone," Jester says. "Luckily, I have some associates on standby."

"Who, the hacker group Anonymous?"

"Let's just say I have friends in the CCC."

I have no idea what she's talking about, but it doesn't matter now. I end the call and turn to Rolan.

"They know."

Rolan takes a deep breath. "Are you ready?"

The phone shakes in my hands. It rings four times before a male voice answers.

"*Da.*"

Russian?

No, Romanian.

"English," I say.

"Who is this?" the voice says evenly, far more alert at this hour than I expected. But the sound of it sends instant ice down my spine.

Because I remember that voice.

"You know who this is," I say unsteadily.

"Hallo, Audra."

They are the same words intoned in the exact oily drawl I heard on Ivan's phone, an hour after his death.

"Where is your keeper, Audra?" he asks.

"He's dead. Like his partner, Gregor."

A pause. "I don't believe you."

"Then you don't know me as well as you think you do." I pull the phone away from my cheek, thumb to a series of photos, and send one through the call.

It's a grisly image of Rolan taken earlier that evening. Grainy and dark, but it will have to do.

The phone audibly vibrates on the other end.

Again, a momentary silence.

"I want to talk to the Historian," I say.

"I am the acting voice of the Historian. You may relay your message through me."

"Happy sex change to you," I quip, neither knowing nor caring whether I just blew the

Historian's cover. In fact, I hope I did. "I want proof of life at six A.M., or I burn the diary."

"Very clever, Audra. And here I was told that you had yet to find it."

"Oh, I found it," I say, with a slight sneer. "And it looks *very* interesting. Not that I've read it. That wouldn't be smart, would it?"

An appreciative exhale on the other end, almost akin to a soft laugh.

"I'll contact you after I receive the next feed, during which I will ask Luka a question only he will know the answer to. If he does not or cannot answer, I will know you have fabricated the feed, and the diary disappears forever."

Rolan gestures sharply, and I hang up before the voice on the other end can reply. I remove |the SIM card immediately.

The minute I do, weird calm washes over me. There's a peaceful kind of crazy that comes with knowing you've got nothing left to lose.

6

I stare in the darkness after that, the words of Brother Daniel echoing in my head.

If you do not learn to control your powers, they will destroy you. You will lose everything you are fighting for.

Reacting out of fear . . . holding to what you love too tightly . . .

But I don't know how to do anything but hold to what I love too tightly.

"Rolan," I say in the darkness.

"*Da*—yes," he says, voice husky from lack of sleep.

"Was Gregor the first person you've killed?"

He's silent for a moment before he says, "I proved my loyalty ten years ago."

I hope he doesn't see my shudder.

"You said you volunteered to take out Luka after he turned traitor. What happened to 'one mark, one hunter'?"

He sighs. "A hunter has only five years to make a kill."

"I've heard." Luka and I had three years left once. It was the reason we fought; he was willing to settle for the time we had left. I wasn't.

"If he fails, a more seasoned hunter may be

brought in before that, depending on the value of the mark."

I didn't know that detail. I wonder if Luka does.

"I volunteered to prove myself of further service. It was my best chance of getting to you before anyone else could. You know my mission has always been about you. As far as I can tell, you're the last surviving Firstborn female. hich makes you the most powerful of your line."

But I'm not the last. Which is why I had to erase every trace of Eva to hide her from both the Scions and power-hungry Progeny like Nikola. Why I'll never be able to return for her as long as the Scions exist.

By 5:45 A.M., we've driven to the outskirts of Neunkirchen, Austria, and parked along a side road in a copse of trees. My calm of last night thins with each passing moment.

At 5:59, Rolan assembles the phone. The feed rings through ten seconds later.

Luka, appearing tense in the same chair. This time, however, he's not gagged. His eye, swollen shut for days, has opened. He stares at the camera, and I sense he's memorizing my face.

"The scar on my elbow. How'd I get it?" I say without preamble.

Silence.

"The scar on my elbow," I start again. When he makes no sound, the camera tilts, drifts across the floor. A thud against flesh. A stifled grimace.

The camera pans up, directly into his face at close range.

He won't answer. He's refusing.

He wants me to cut and run.

"I know what the numbers mean," I say suddenly. "The tattoo. I know what it is."

He blinks, inhales sharply.

"Run, Audra! They're going to kill you!" he shouts.

"I'll send instructions," I say and click off.

Rolan dismantles the phone.

My next call is made on a new burner phone picked up in Graz.

"I take it you are satisfied," the voice says by way of answer.

"You will transport Luka to Vienna by eight A.M."

"Impossible."

"Then the diary disappears. If Luka is not alive, the diary disappears. Vienna, eight A.M. I will call you with instructions."

I click off and pull apart the phone.

"Find us a hardware store," I say.

We stop along the E59 just outside Vienna. At 7:36, Jester pings.

There are 11 Vadasz trucks inside the city limits. 4 entered the city in the last half hour.

I pull up a map of Vienna, but I'm really only familiar with one area of the city.

That I remember, anyway.

At 8:00 A.M., I call from a second burner phone.

"Yes," the voice on the other end says. The syllable is clipped, the indolent drawl gone.

"The intersection of Auerspergstrasse and Josefsgasse, in fifteen minutes."

I hang up, count to sixty, and call Jester back.

"Anything?"

"A truck just pulled onto Donaufelder Strasse, across the river. It was the last one to enter the city."

"That's got to be the one."

We leave the car, and I persuade the next large vehicle we see—some kind of produce truck—to pull over.

Get out. You're the one millionth driver to pass this stretch of road.

The driver emerges from the truck, looking confused.

How do you like your new Citroën?

He takes the keys like he's just won a show-case showdown, grabs me, and hugs me while jumping up and down.

Sixty seconds later, we're speeding toward Vienna.

"Where's the truck?" I ask Jester, the minute we enter the city.

"Crossing the river. Arriving in twelve minutes. I've got them on street camera."

I glance at Rolan, pull my hat down lower on my head.

We pull off the highway, and I grab the hardware store bag from the back before giving him a quick hug.

"Thank you, Rolan. Sorry you're dead. I'll see you in a few."

"I hope," he says.

Positivity has never been one of his strong points.

I get out of the truck and start down a side street, head lowered, phone held to my cheek.

"I see you," Jester says, her end on speaker-phone.

"Just in case any of this goes sideways, I love you guys," I say.

"Don't say that." Claudia, in the background.

"I'm sorry for leaving you before, Claudia," I add.

"Shut up!" she says. "Don't you dare say 'good-bye.' "

I smile slightly, and jog toward a man in a business suit getting into a VW station wagon.

I need your keys.

Only when I get in the car do I realize it's a manual transmission.

The clutch grinds, and I chug toward Highway 1.

"What is that horrible *sound?*" Claudia says.

"You have to push the clutch at the same time that you shift," Piotrek says, voice ringing out from the phone on my passenger seat.

"No kidding."

"Vadasz truck, turning left onto Landegerichtstrasse," Jester says. I grimace in an effort to recall the map while shifting gears. Landegerichtstrasse turns into Auerspergstrasse in five blocks.

"Rolan is thirty seconds out. Audra, accelerate."

"I'm hitting a red light—"

"Run it."

A car narrowly misses me, careens into a vehicle to my right. I gun the engine, tachometer fluttering in the red, and hit greens for three blocks.

A phone buzzes in the background on the other end. I hear Jester pick up the call, her swift flurry of French.

"Audra," she says a few seconds later. "Turn around!"

"What?"

"Turn around! Get out!"

"I can't just turn around!"

"There are three gunmen on roofs at the intersection!"

"I'll take care of them."

"You can't even see them!"

"Just get me to the intersection!"

"Audra." Piotrek. "You cannot do this!"

"Watch me."

I upshift, weaving past two and then three more cars.

I throw the strongest persuasion I've got ahead of me, driving it forward like sound waves compacted in front of an ambulance.

A wild oath from Jester. Claudia, shouting in the background.

The cars in front of me drift lanes, and I accelerate.

I can see the Vadasz truck with its bright yellow cab fifty yards ahead, ambling toward the intersection of Josefsgasse. I speed past three more cars and close the gap, unable to get around a black SUV. I brake fifteen yards out behind the SUV—just as Rolan's produce truck barrels into the intersection, ramming into the side of the yellow Vadasz cab.

The trailer jackknifes into the next lane, crashing into two vehicles.

"Audra, get out of there!"

I kill the clutch. Grab the bolt cutters from the passenger seat. Dash from the car, shedding the hardware store bag as I go.

All around us traffic crashes or skids to a jammed halt. Pedestrians scatter from the sidewalk.

Ahead of me, the SUV's doors open. A man in a dark suit gets out on each side. Shades over their eyes, hair cropped close.

Run!

They do run—right toward me, guns raised.

Stop them.

Pffft! A shot whizzes from above. The first man's leg buckles beneath him. He goes down with a scream. The second man drops on the other side of the SUV. I run straight toward the first and swing the bolt cutters at his head. Kick the gun from his hand. It skitters into the curb.

Glass shatters from the direction of the Vadasz truck cab as I reach the back of the trailer. My hands are shaking so hard I can barely get a grip on the cutter handles, but somehow I manage to clamp down. I drop them the minute the lock gives away. Shove the first bolt up, pulse pounding in my ears.

For a minute, I think: *What if he's not here—if he's already dead, gone?*

I tug the right side open, and there he is, gagged and bound to the same metal chair, blinking against the light.

Luka.

My heart stops, and it's all I can do not to launch myself into the truck and run for him, wrap my arms around his neck.

But he isn't alone.

The pallet jack from the video comes flying toward me. I whirl away, back against the other door. The jack veers and crashes into it with a boom that reverberates through my spine.

I look wildly around, spot two guys running out

of the café twenty yards away—a server and a beefy-looking cook, apron still on.

You. Help me.

The next instant they're running straight for the back of the trailer, but I have another problem: a third suit emerging from the SUV.

Luka's captor comes charging out of the trailer. He's tall and grizzled with thick shoulders. The cook grabs him around the neck and hauls him to the concrete. A shot shatters the SUV's window.

I grab the cutters, leap into the trailer. Hurry to Luka, clip through the zip ties—three at each wrist, five at each ankle.

The instant Luka's free he shoves up and rips off his gag.

A metal hinge groans behind us. The light disappears.

In the darkness, I *feel* more than hear Luka rush past me. He throws himself at the trailer door. It shudders and swings back open, hitting the figure behind it.

I run after Luka as he leaps from the trailer, tackling the man below—the third suit from the SUV. They roll away. The suit lands a punch to Luka's jaw. Dirty hair flies from his face.

Luka grabs the man's head and drives it into his own with a sickening crack. The man falls away, and Luka drags himself up onto a knee. He lifts his head and grins. His teeth are red. I have never seen this Luka: feral and uncaged.

I stumble from the trailer. He starts to say something, but before I can make out the words, I scream as the man launches himself at Luka again. Together they crash into the curb. Fingers grapple for throats and eyes. Luka's legs scissor, and then he's on top of the man, fistfuls of the man's shirt in his hands, fabric cinched tight around his throat. The man flails, claws at Luka's hands, eyes bulging as his face turns purple.

"Luka!"

He looks up, murderous eyes glossed over as the form beneath him goes limp.

Recognition transforms his face. He lets go. Staggers to his feet. The form twitches beneath him—alive, if not by much.

"Audra." His voice is a rasp. In three strides, he's cupping my face. "You're bleeding." His thumb traces a wet smudge above my upper lip before he pulls me hard against him, breathing heavily.

My arms wind tightly around him, not believing he's here, with me. Alive.

"My God, I thought I'd never see you again," he murmurs against my hair before holding me away from him and shaking me by the shoulders. "What were you thinking? You should never have come!"

Sirens in the distance.

"Rolan," I hear myself say. "We have to get Rolan."

66

Luka stiffens. *"What?"*

I tear myself away, hurry to the produce truck buckled against the cab. There's a form slumped over the wheel. The door is open; two men have freed him from his safety belt. From their gestures I'm pretty sure they're saying something about not moving him.

Get him out.

The thought drives a spike between my eyes.

"Get him!" I yell, sagging against the cab. Luka shoots me a glance and then pushes past the bystanders. Seconds later, Luka and another man are holding a groaning Rolan between them.

And all I can think is, *Get to the car.*

I stagger after them as they help Rolan past the shot-out SUV. The two suits who took hits earlier are gone. Dropping into the driver's seat of the VW, I floor the clutch, fire the engine. Luka shoves Rolan into the back and slides in after him.

"Go!" he shouts, slamming the door.

I fumble us into reverse, back the length of a building, and then shift swiftly to neutral, yanking the steering wheel as far right as it'll go. The front of the car slides around, spinning the other direction. I jolt into gear, pull up onto the sidewalk, bystanders scattering around us as I accelerate up a side street.

"Audra!" Someone's shouting from the phone,

still live, on the floor. Luka climbs into the passenger seat and retrieves it as I take a sharp left, away from the onslaught of sirens.

"I've got him," I say, as my vision begins to blur.

7

"Three gunmen. An SUV full of armed men . . ." I can practically hear Piotrek running his hand over his hair. Jester, all this time, has been silent.

"You had no way of knowing those snipers weren't hunters!" Claudia says.

"I took a chance." I had banked on the Scions not having time to assemble a handpicked squad.

"A chance you couldn't afford! You can't *persuade* people you can't see!" Claudia shouts.

"But she did," Jester says strangely, at last.

"We're alive, aren't we? Just keep the police off of us."

I've forgotten how much I haven't told them.

"Audra," Luka says quietly after we've hung up. "You're bleeding again."

I'm more than bleeding. My vision isn't right. I have to close one eye to not see two roads, like a drunk trying to get home.

Rolan groans, says something in Romanian under his breath.

"What about him?" Luka murmurs.

"He's coming with us."

"No, he's not."

"He's half the reason you're alive!"

Luka stares at me for a long moment, outrage and questions in his eyes.

"Long story," I mutter.

"You should never have come for me," Luka says, shaking his head.

"You're welcome."

"I mean it, Audra!" he insists, though I sense there's much more he'd say if we were alone.

Jester chimes back in.

"Audra, turn around. There are blockades on every major roadway leaving the city and you're all over the news."

"Turn around and go where?"

"Find a place to hide until dark. It's your only chance."

"No. If we stay in the city now we'll never get out." Blood drips from my nose to my lips.

"Audra," Luka says. "You can't keep this up."

"I'm fine!" I say, spraying tiny droplets of red.

"You're not fine. You nearly blacked out back there!"

"He's right," Rolan says.

Luka holds the phone closer to his mouth. "Jester, do you know any Progeny in the city? Anyone who can hide her?"

I don't like the way he says *her* instead of *us*.

Jester's saying something, but I'm no longer paying attention. I spot a parking garage and swerve into the entrance, scraping the bumper.

I swing the VW into an empty spot and kill the engine. Movement, between two rows of cars—a man walking toward his car. I reach over to the glove compartment, retrieve the folder inside it, and get out.

Luka and Rolan spring out after me.

"No," Rolan says.

"What do you mean, 'no'? We can't stay in that," I say, flinging my arm toward the VW.

"*You* can't stay in that," Rolan says, coming around to gently take the keys from my hand.

It dawns on me, then, what he means to do. I hold the keys away.

"No. Absolutely not."

"He's right," Luka says.

I round on Luka. "He broke his cover to keep you alive! And you're going to just let him drive off into their hands?"

"Not for him," Rolan says. "For you. Because you would never have fled without him. Now you have to get out of the city. They saw. They know what you are, if they didn't before."

"What do you mean, 'what she is'?" Luka says, eyes narrowed.

"Get out of the city," Rolan says. "Hide. Now that the Historian suspects you found something, she won't stop until you're dead."

"Wait—'she'?" Luka says. And then his gaze drops to the folder in my hand. I clutch it tight to my chest. It's cold, like hugging a gun.

71

"Go," Rolan says.

"Not without you."

"I may have pledged my life to protect your bloodline, but, fortunately, I do not answer to you," he says.

"They know you helped me. They'll kill you!"

"They have to catch me first," Rolan says and opens the VW door.

"Wait." I hurry toward the businessman getting into his car. A moment later, I lead the man to the VW and hand Rolan his keys.

"At least take a different car," I say.

He nods, starts for the car. I go after him and wrap him in a tight hug.

"Thank you," I whisper.

"Stay alive," Rolan murmurs. A moment later, he's speeding out the exit.

I stand there and watch him drive away, followed by the man in our former VW.

And all I can think is: *What have I done?*

"Audra," Luka says, somewhere behind me. I turn to him, stupefied.

"I don't know what you found or what the story is between you two . . . But right now, we have to get out of here."

We exit the garage on foot via the crosswalk into an office building, take the stairwell to the ground floor. We walk at a fast clip, his hand under my arm. Twice, my knees nearly buckle; there are far more people in the lobby than I expected. And our faces are playing on the news station in reception.

Don't see us.

I look up once in time to see a woman stare blankly past me. Her shoulder brushes mine, and she glances back, startled as if she had run into a ghost.

We exit the building, turn down the street. Luka guides me to the first alley we come to, where I collapse against the wall, clutching my head. The migraine that had subsided to flashing lights behind my eyes is back with the vengeance of an aneurysm.

"Audra!" Luka says, shielding me from the street.

"Do you know how to drive a motorcycle?" I grate out.

"Yeah, why?"

A moment later a motorcyclist pulls into the alley, gets out his spare helmet, hands over his keys.

As we double back toward the river, the ride is a blur of twilight consciousness beneath the late-morning sun, the hum of the motorbike far too steady for my racing Progeny heart. I tighten my arms around Luka's waist, fingers splayed against his chest. Lay a helmeted cheek against his back as one of his hands covers my own.

Just across the river Danube, Luka pulls over

under a bridge to call Jester. I look out at the graffiti-covered wall lining the pedestrian walk along the river, follow those muddied waters south. Somewhere, miles from here, they flow past the shores of Csepel Island in Budapest, where my mother's body was found. I have never been able to look at them without thinking of her, and of death—the one constant in any Progeny's so-called life.

I watch a river cruise ship inch its way upriver, as tall as a two-story building. Wonder what it must be like to be a tourist on those grisly waters—to have so few cares that one could drink, photograph, and journal a week of life away.

Luka paces back, clicks off the phone.

"Traffic is backed up for a mile at every exit from the city," he says. "They're searching cars."

"Then we can't leave by road," I say, sitting straighter with effort. The adrenaline is back, just a tiny tendril itching at the back of my spine.

"What'd you have in mind?" he says, getting back on the bike.

I point south to the light rail bridge with its tram wires down the middle, pedestrian walk on either side.

At the bridge, we abandon the bike and Luka grabs my hand. We're still wearing our helmets. Even so, heads turn in our direction as though alerted by an inaudible siren, set off by the Progeny *charisma* in my veins.

Twenty yards in we lean out over the handrail, as though contemplating the river below. The ship is approaching.

"You're crazy, you know that?" Luka breathes. I want to tell him this is the kind of thing Nino and Ana would have done into their old age for fun had they survived so long.

The thought of them sends a pain through my chest so hot that the minute the prow of the cruise ship passes beneath us, it's all I can do to climb onto the rail as fast as I can and jump, if only to escape it.

We drop onto the roof of the ship's observation lounge. Slide down onto the railed walkway of the upper deck. Gasps, a scream from above. I glance back toward the bridge drifting slowly downriver in our wake, the pedestrians glued to the rail.

You didn't see that.

My head is swimming. Luka half-carries me below, where he raps on the door of the first stateroom he comes to.

A middle-aged man answers the door, brows lifted in surprise at the sight of our helmeted heads.

"Frank?" a woman says from behind him. I look up.

We're here to clean. Go up to the lounge and

stay there. The couple glance at one another. A moment later, the woman retrieves her purse, asks for extra towels, and hands Luka two euros as they leave.

Luka catches the door before it closes, helps me inside. He's barely bolted the lock behind us when I collapse on the rumpled bed.

8

By the time I wake, the sky has darkened to a rusty sunset. I stare out the window, transfixed by the string of lights along the shore, the silhouette of a church in the distance. Somewhere in that riverside city people are sitting down to dinner, tucking in children, worrying about lovers or jobs. Somewhere out there, other twenty-one-year-olds are studying in dorms, going on dates, or meeting friends at cute outdoor cafés. As the sky burns down to embers, I wonder how many Progeny walk those streets . . . and how many hunters follow.

Luka pulls me gently toward him, curling me close in sleep. Warm breath against my hair. A thing so simple, I barely believe it's real. I never thought I'd feel that again.

If I close my eyes, I can almost pretend we're safe. Can imagine lolling in bed for hours, just watching the world pass by.

A few minutes later, Luka raises his head and the illusion shatters. His eye is swollen, a fresh cut drying beneath his brow—a restless edginess in his good eye. His hair is damp, freshly washed, tucked behind an ear. He's shaved, causing the black bruises on his face to stand out more starkly than ever. It hurts to look at him.

Because somehow, I'm positive this is my fault.

He touches a kiss to my temple and then props his head in his hand.

"Are you all right?" he says, studying me closely, something like fear in his eyes.

I tilt my head back to squint at the ceiling and nod. And though the roar in my brain has subsided to a dull throb, my entire body feels like lead.

I roll away, push up from the bed. Slide my feet to the floor . . . and then stare.

All around us, loose pages are laid across the dresser and sofa, spread out in lines on the floor. No fewer than ten are tucked into the frame of the mirror.

The contents of the folder.

At the mere sight of them, my heart begins to race. I bolt up, ignore the immediate prickling of my vision, and start blindly grabbing them off the dresser.

"What are you doing?" I shout, gathering them together before scrambling for the lineup on the floor.

"Audra. I didn't do this. You did."

I freeze on my hands and knees, shove away from the pile on the floor as though it were a snake.

"You were sleeping so hard, I actually checked to make sure you were still breathing," he says. "You were like that when I went to shower. When

I came out . . ." He gets down and crouches beside me, gathers up several pages like I'm some mental patient who has just lost all her marbles.

Apparently my sleepwalking ways are back.

I see the questions in his eyes. But I'm not ready to answer. I take down the rest of the pages—articles and hard copies of e-mails—and catch sight of myself in the stateroom mirror. I don't recognize the girl I see there: blood crusted on her chin and upper lip, down the front of a grimy shirt. Hair hanging in greasy strands past the hollows of her cheeks. Circles beneath her eyes. A shell of the woman who met me in the mirror back in Maine. At least the scrubby patch above my ear has grown out enough to resemble a botched haircut.

I shove the contents back into the folder and excuse myself to the bathroom, lock myself in. I undress and take refuge in the spray of the cabin's tiny shower, use up an entire little bottle of shampoo. By the time I turn off the water, my headache is almost gone. Loitering as I finger-comb my hair, I realize this is the first time I've bathed in nearly a week.

Now that I have, I should be out there with Luka, celebrating that we're alive. Making up for lost time. Making love.

But a lot has happened in five days. And it's hard to make love when you've closed yourself away with your secrets.

79

I wipe the steam from the mirror. Slowly open the towel tucked around me.

I turn sideways, lay my hand over the curve of my belly. Think back to the night Claudia dressed me in a pair of velvet pants as we prepared to enter court our first night in Zagreb. They were mine, from before—and so snug I nearly caught my skin in the zipper.

"Audra?" a soft rap on the door. "Are you all right?"

No. "Yeah."

I wrap myself back in the towel, strangely self-conscious. Emerge from the bathroom and steal to one of the drawers in the closet. Pull on a turtleneck, a pair of khaki pants—both a size too big. Despite the fact that I would pretty much kill for a clean pair of underwear, I draw the line at bogarting another woman's practical cotton briefs. Commando it is.

It occurs to me that I'm unabashedly stealing, but given that I had three men shot yesterday and have been branded a terrorist, it seems like the least of my sins.

Luka's got the television on, is surfing through the channels. He stops on one, turns up the volume though I'm not sure why; it's in German.

"Audra."

I walk over . . . and then sink down onto the bed, staring at it. My picture is plastered across the screen.

I don't need to speak German to understand the word pasted like a banner beneath it:

Terrorist.

Luka comes to sit beside me.

I try to think of something clever to say about being upgraded from "murderer," painfully aware that in all this time since I got him back we haven't spoken. Not really.

He reaches over, covers my hand with his own, twines his fingers with mine. His knuckles are scraped, cuts across his wrists from the zip ties.

The hand of my husband.

Of my daughter's father.

Those cuts are because of us.

He picks up the remote, mutes the TV. Silence and expectation fill the room like dread.

For five days I've dreamed of nothing but what it would be like—might be like, since assuming I'd succeed was nothing but a pipe dream—to have Luka back. To be back in his arms. To tell him everything . . .

But I hadn't counted on the everything I'd have to tell him. And right now, I have no idea how he'll react to what I'm about to say.

I pull free and get up. Try to choose my words. But it's hard to pick and choose when there are only four words that say what he needs to hear.

"We have a daughter." I turn back to find him staring at his empty hand.

In that moment, I hate myself. For not running

81

to him and gushing about our baby. For not begging his forgiveness for not having told him. For not shaking him and saying that of course I went back for him, that there was no way I would ever let him die—not while there was breath in my body and how dare he ever doubt it.

That he was never alone.

But instead I stand there frozen, not knowing how to have this conversation. Hating the Audra of before for making me feel like the interloper. For doing this to Luka. To us both.

"Eva," he whispers and looks up at me.

I fall back a step, dumbstruck. "You . . . *knew about her?*"

Relief, betrayal, anger wash over me in such quick succession I don't know which one to grab on to.

"It was my mother's name," he says quietly, looking down at his hands. "We named her Eva Amerie."

I sit down hard on the corner of the bed.

"Luka, I need to know . . ."

He nods. "The night you came back to me and said you still wanted me even though you knew what I was, I asked you right then and there to marry me," he says softly. "You called me an idiot. And then you said yes. We got married the next day. It didn't make sense. *We* didn't make sense. But I didn't care. I wanted as much life as we could get out of this existence . . . I told you about that."

My mind reels back to the conversation that day in Graz on our way to Zagreb's underground court. Was it just two weeks ago?

"You said we fought," I stutter. "That I became obsessed with finding a way out."

"We did. But I didn't tell you the whole story. You had found something of your mother's by then. A stash of her notes."

I have to work to suppress a shudder. To tamp down the adrenaline jittering along my arms.

"You started talking about bringing an end to the Scions—something I said was impossible. It was dangerous to talk about. Dangerous to even think about. But you were obsessed. You began meeting secretly with Ivan and others. You barely slept. Went nearly every night to court, and came back in the morning with this *fire* in your eyes. I was jealous. I felt like I was losing you. Especially when the courts in Budapest and Zagreb began to swell. I could sense that they were as fixated on you—on what you represented to them—as you were on the idea of bringing the Scions down for good."

"Then why didn't I?" But I already know the answer.

"When you found out you were pregnant, it changed everything. I had never seen you terrified before. You weren't afraid to become a mother—in the morning light, I swore you looked like the Madonna of paintings. But those moments were always followed by dark thoughts about what kind of future any Progeny child could have. You became quiet and withdrawn. You went less and less to the underground, and began to scour your mother's letters as though something new would show up in them that you hadn't seen before. Something you had missed. Twice you disappeared for two days at a time. I was frantic, convinced you had left me for good, though you swore each time you returned you never would . . ."

His eyes, when he looks at me, are haunted, and I know what he's thinking: that I did leave him, irrevocably, the day I erased him from my memory.

He rakes back his hair. "One day in March, you said we had to go. We were in Zagreb. You had gone to court the night before and came back the next morning in a panic, saying your work had been exposed."

Ivan's words the last time I saw him, come back to me:

It was March. We were in Zagreb. One night, you simply vanished . . .

"Exposed how?"

"You wouldn't say more than that. But I knew it had to do with your mother's letters. Suddenly, you didn't trust anyone. All your plans to destroy the Scions . . . for the first time I heard you say it couldn't be done. We knew we didn't have three years left. Not anymore. That the day might

84

come when they'd take one of us, or try to use me against you . . ." His voice turns hollow.

"What did they do to you?" I whisper. I had refused to let myself think of how they might interrogate or torture him, knowing the mere thought would reduce me to a catatonic huddle, kill any chance I had of finding the only leverage that would matter—and Luka, in the process.

"Nothing that could ever make me give you or Eva up," he says, gaze hard. And there it is, in his eyes—the killer. The hunter who nearly strangled a man to death earlier today. I wonder if the Audra of before would have stopped him.

"Eva was born June fifteenth. We had gone into hiding in Spain and then in Italy. You *persuaded* a local midwife to deliver her in secret. The next day we took her to a foundling box in Rome known to Progeny circles." His voice breaks. "You had begged me to find a place for her, somewhere safe. But I was already connected to you. Any child I would have tried to give up under my name or arranged an adoption for would have been immediately known for what—whose—it was . . ."

Like that, the killer is gone. And somehow, the sag of his shoulders is far more frightening.

"I saw her, Luka."

He's on his feet in an instant.

"Where?"

"Krk. A monastery—on an island in the bay."

85

"Where is she now?" His eyes are wild. I can practically hear him calculating the distance from here to there, the number of hours and minutes.

"I don't know. Safe. They couldn't tell me where."

He sinks back down as though struck.

"Is she beautiful?" he says hoarsely.

My expression crumples and my voice comes out with all my heart in a tight whisper. "She's perfect."

He heaves a ragged breath and leans forward, hands over his face. And then he's sobbing.

I cover him with my arms, my body. "I'm sorry," I say again and again, clasping him tightly, my tears against his neck.

If I ever looked down on a couple for giving up a child—and I don't know if I ever did—I take it back. If I was ever less than compassionate toward the parents of a lost child, I repent. My heart breaks, is breaking—over and over. For the baby. For myself. But most of all, for him. Because I have mercifully forgotten. But Luka . . . Luka remembers it all.

And I wonder how he can look at me at all for the tragedy I've brought to his life in repayment for his love.

We hold each other as the shoreline drifts by, silent and stealthy as a life, escaping a mile at a time.

This is not the reunion I imagined. The need and skin and heat of my imagination have given way to broken bereavement.

Jester texts to say she's located the ship's itinerary and will send us an address before we dock in Regensburg. We've switched TV channels to the ship's closed-caption station, where a miniature vessel on the digital map wends a blue path north, toward Germany, so slowly as to appear static.

For as quiet as I am, for as still and tight as my arm is around him, my mind is racing. Cannot help but pick at the pieces of a past I don't remember like the scab of a wound.

"Luka."

He murmurs and turns his head, and I realize he's been sleeping.

"What happened . . . after?" Right now I can't bear to say Eva's name any more than I think he can bear to hear it.

He rubs his face. "You went into depression. We both did, but yours . . . was dark. I wanted to talk about everything about her—from the way she was born to the moment she opened her eyes, to the sounds she made when she slept . . . I needed to keep her memory alive, for myself. But you couldn't stand to talk about it. You were focused completely on what you had to do to keep her safe. You talked about dying. About how losing your memory felt like a form of dying. I hated hearing you talk like that." He pinches his forehead, as though engaged in a simultaneous, louder conversation in his mind. "After a while I came to realize that it was your way of paying some price. As though you felt you had to die to have the hope of having her back again."

In a way I guess I had.

"When did I get the tattoo on my back?"

"Probably when you went to the States to begin the trial at the Center. You went ahead of me, so that when I came in a few days later, it would look like I had followed you."

"To kill me."

He nods, the faint lines around his mouth deeper than I remember.

"After your second appointment at the Center, you came back in the best spirits I had seen you in for months. 'We'll get her back, Luka,' you said. And I was surprised to hear you say that, because that had always been our plan—getting her back. But I remember you said it that day several times, as though you finally believed it."

"How were we going to get her back?"

"I was supposed to take you to the monastery on Cres Island on what would have been Eva's tenth birthday."

"Ten years?"

"I think—you didn't say, but I think . . . you were waiting for someone to die."

Nikola.

It has to be. Nikola, who once drafted a Progeny census in an effort to locate other direct descendants of Anastasia like me and destroy them. Nikola, easily in his mid-thirties when few Progeny survived to thirty.

Nikola, who openly confessed to killing my mother.

Last week wasn't the first time he's betrayed me.

"You were supposed to take me to Cres to do what?" I say.

"Meet with someone you had prearranged. Resume what you started before Eva could come into her gifts or expose herself in a search for her birth parents."

So I hadn't gone into hiding, rolled over, and given up. I had planned—been planning—to finish this once she was safely removed from my memory.

I had not abandoned my child, or the Progeny cause.

As though reading my mind, Luka says, "Audra, everything we've done—everything you did—you did to protect *her*. The night we deciphered the tattoo on your back, I was afraid you had realized what the numbers meant. Thought you might ask me straight out, see through any lie I threw at you . . . I couldn't tell you about her! Not while there was any chance another hunter could get to you first. Knowing they could take your memory . . ."

"I'm sorry," I say, again and again, cupping his face, smoothing back his hair. Because I am. Sorry I left him alone in this. Sorry I left him to grieve in silence. And I'm angry, too—at Nikola, at the Historian, at the cruelty of an entire war that left Luka and me no more options than to tear off pieces of ourselves until there's nothing left.

Most of all, I'm angry at myself. For all of my bitterness toward my mother for not being here for me, for giving me up even to keep me safe. Because I've done the same to Eva. She isn't just any Progeny kid. As a direct descendant of Anastasia and the child of a hunter, she'll be the most hunted of the hunted. And now that I know she exists, her life is in danger every minute I breathe.

Staying alive will never be enough.

I end the Scions or die.

9

I order room service to be left outside our door: burgers, fries, and coffee. Bottles of apple juice and extra sandwiches. And ice cream—chocolate.

"What are you doing?" Luka said when I picked up the room phone and dialed the restaurant.

"It's called living."

The minute the food arrives and the hallway is clear, we pull the tray inside, wolf down the burgers. It's been days since either of us has eaten a real meal.

"So what was all that stuff?" he says, gesturing around the room at my phantom crime board.

"It's what the Historian was prepared to kill you to get."

I tell Luka what happened the night I left him in Bratislava. About the note from Nikola. How I went to Budapest to bargain for his life, not knowing he'd already been taken.

"Do me a favor," he says. "Quit trying to protect me."

I drag a fry through a puddle of melted ice cream.

"I mean it, Audra. You're the one we have to worry about now."

He doesn't have to finish his thought: now that I know about Eva.

I tell him about Rolan's heretic sect. My mother's notes. The church in Nyirbator. How the minute we got to the monastery in Košljun, I knew the diary was there.

"So . . . the diary . . . is our *child?*" he says strangely.

"No. The diary is a cache of incriminating information on the Scions that has been collected for centuries. The minute I started looking through it all . . ." But how do you explain what it's like to see the future, all at once, in a single instant? Luka dead. Me, lost to the murky waters of the Danube. Rolan on the run with my memory, as much a fugitive as the rest of us. Lives, flashing by, in the space of a moment?

I retrieve the folder, spread out its contents on the bed. As his gaze slides from item to item, his face falls—along with his hopes of ever seeing Eva again.

I grab his wrist. "But then, a couple hours later, she was there. Eva. With Clare. Whose name I'm pretty sure isn't really Clare. That's what they call Franciscan nuns—Poor Clares."

"They exposed her to convince you to fight," he says, anger written in the tight line of his jaw.

"Well it worked," I say.

He flips an article across the bed. "You can't fight this! You saw what they did with the media!"

Throughout the evening the story of my "terrorism" has gained new developments—including barrels of explosives discovered in the back of Rolan's truck and a botched plan to bomb the Austrian Parliament.

At least Rolan—whose photo was added to mine several hours ago, along with Luka's—hasn't been taken into custody. I take a small bit of comfort in that.

"We have to fight it." I reach over and retrieve the article—about an IMF chief acquitted of fraud after awarding a tycoon hundreds of millions of euros in some legal dispute against a conveniently defunct state-owned bank. "There are names in here, Luka."

He digs his hands into his hair. "The only ones with enough power to go after these people—if they're even Scions—are other Scions!"

"Maybe. All I know is that there's something in here the Historian wanted badly enough to send me after it. To let me live long enough to find it knowing I was the only one who could. And now that I've seen it . . ."

Luka's eyes meet mine. And I know he's just realized he's looking into the eyes of a dead woman.

"Audra—" He slides to the edge of the bed in

93

front of me. "I'm begging you. Don't pursue this. I can't lose you and Eva both. Not again. Not for good. We'll find a place. Somewhere farther away. Eva's safe. We'll hide, hole up on an island like you always wanted. We'll get a shack in Fiji. We'll wait. Give the world time to forget us . . ."

"Don't you get it?" I say. "The world may forget us, but the Historian *never* will. And what about Claudia, Piotrek, Jester? How safe do you think they'll be after helping me? There's nowhere safe for them, either. And I won't spend the rest of my life as a walking time bomb!"

"You can't protect everyone!"

I grab his hands. "You're right. I can't. Which is why I need to know why the Historian wanted this so badly. Nikola called it a weapon. It's time for us to use it."

He's quiet for a long moment before he gets up and paces away to stare out the window.

"Luka."

He doesn't move.

"Piotrek said you *persuaded* three gunmen you couldn't see," he says at last.

He turns his head, his perfect profile silhouetted by the lights along the river.

"Is that true?"

I don't answer.

"You're right," he says quietly. "The Historian

will never stop hunting you. Not just for what you found but because of what you *are*. Like Rolan said: They've seen it now, if they didn't know before."

He curses softly, under his breath.

"Did you know?" I ask.

He turns and leans back against the sill, shakes his head.

"That you're Firstborn? No. I considered the possibility while I was being held captive, but told myself it was impossible."

"Firstborn. Is that what they call it?" I say dully.

"It's what the Scions call it, or so I've heard. You're a myth, Audra. Jester was right that day in the car: Anastasia's line disappeared a hundred years ago. Killed off, supposedly, before it could get stronger."

"What do you mean 'stronger'?"

"That's what happens with each successive generation—it gets stronger. At least according to legend, which might just be Scion hate-mongering. That day you practically broadcast your persuasions ahead of you in Vienna, and when you did it again at the airport in Bratislava . . . I chalked it up to some freak thing you did. When Rolan said what he did about being sworn to your bloodline, I thought he meant the Progeny as a whole. Which didn't make sense to me. None of it did until he said the thing about the Scions having seen what you are for themselves. I figured you had recruited a small army of Progeny to pull my rescue off. That they were in the crowd of bystanders. When I realized you and Rolan acted alone . . ."

"Jester and her hacker friends helped," I point out.

"Audra, you *persuaded* a bridge full of people to forget that they just saw us jump onto a cruise ship!"

"If it's any consolation, I didn't know either until you were captured," I say bitterly.

"Hopefully that means no one else did until yesterday. Whatever your mother did, she must have never let on what she was. Not even to Ivan. Or the Historian would never have let you leave her sight alive. And Nikola would have killed you himself."

I flash back to my conversation with Rolan the day we left Budapest.

Anastasia's line has been hunted by a faction of princes for generations in an effort to keep you out of the Scions' hands.

Pretty bad when you can't even trust your own kind not to turn on you.

He blows out a long sigh. "How much do you trust Claudia, Jester, and the others?"

"With my life," I say.

"I hope that isn't misplaced. Because if we stay, you'll never be safe in another underground court again. Not while Nikola's alive. And they can *never* know about Eva. A Firstborn female with a Progeny's ability to sense other Progeny and a hunter's ability to strip a Progeny's memory, and who can pass an even more powerful legacy to her own heirs . . . Do you know what the princes would do to her? Never mind the Scions! Do you see why I want to run?"

I feel the color drain from my face.

The image of Eva's eyes—Luka's eyes—so large in her three-and-a-half-month-old face breaks something inside me.

I cross to the window. "You have to go to her. Find out where she is. Go away with her, Luka. Stay with her. Protect her." I clasp him by the shoulders, and realize that I'm pleading with him.

Because he's the only one of us who can.

He shakes his head. "If you're going to do this, you have to stay alive. Not just for your sake, but for hers. Which means I stay with you. I told you weeks ago I made you a promise. You just didn't know it was a marriage vow." He pulls me close, and I hold on to him for dear life as he rests his chin on the top of my head. "No more secrets. We find a way to finish this, together."

Together.

The words of the letter I wrote to myself before float before my eyes:

He'll kill for you. Don't let him. Kill for him, instead, if you have to. One of you has to live.

The phone on the dresser chirps with Jester's ring, and I let go of Luka, steeling myself for the long good-bye.

"Yeah," I answer, clearing my throat.

Jester's voice is frantic. "Audra, someone got video of you and Luka jumping onto the ship—"

"That's impossible."

"No, it's not. Someone you *persuaded* found the video on their phone. It hit social media thirty minutes ago. We hacked several accounts, but it's too late. It's blowing up. The police are moving along the river, closing in at Passau."

"What are you saying?"

"You won't make it to Regensburg. You have to get off the ship!"

10

I grab a TSA-approved Ziploc bag from the toiletry kit in the bathroom, drop SIM cards, the flash drive, my current phone inside. Fold up the contents of the folder, shove them in, and seal it.

"Audra," Luka says, from the window.

I drop the Ziploc into a plastic shopping bag. Cinch it up tight, slide the loops over my wrist.

Luka crosses the room, unbolts the door.

"Time to go."

We run down the corridor toward the back of the ship as the PA system comes on to announce an emergency stop in Passau, first in German, then in English and French.

"Here!" Luka says, pulling me toward an open-air stairwell. We hurry down to the lower level, peer over the rail. Sounds of music and shocked conversations drift back from the restaurant on the top deck . . . along with the *thwap thwap thwap* of an approaching helicopter. Below us, the reflected lights on either side of the river stretch like a ghostly watercolor painted across the surface.

Luka climbs over, reaches to steady me as I join him, back against the rail. Hair blowing in his eyes, he takes my hand.

"I love you, Audra," he says.

I love you more.

We leap together.

The frigid water slices fatigue from my limbs, seizes up my lungs. I surface with a ragged gasp, every nerve beneath my skin stabbed to icy life. A shout—Luka, ten feet upriver. A beam of light rushes toward me. I dive below the surface, death grip on the plastic bag knotted around my wrist, and angle toward the bank.

The next time I surface, the helicopter is directly above the cruise ship, following it to the dock. Police lights flash from the road. I search for Luka, unable to help the morbid thought that the Danube that claimed my mother might claim another one I love. He resurfaces a few feet from me, points farther downriver.

By now my teeth are chattering, but I am more alive than I've been in days. I strike out with the current, will warm blood into my limbs . . . Swim for an eternity, carried away. I can no longer keep my jaw still. Twice, I gulp water instead of air, my lips too cold to know the difference.

A hand grabs my shoulder.

"There," Luka says, the word a stifled breath. I swim woodenly toward the cobbled bank. Scrape my knee against the stones, though I don't feel the pain. Crawl from the water into the chill September air.

Luka hauls himself from the river behind me,

breathing heavily. My legs feel like tree stumps, thick and numb. We stagger toward the road. I broadcast a desperate persuasion. A minute later, a car stops and unlocks the doors.

We crawl into the back as the man in the driver's seat—a guy in his twenties with unruly short hair—notches up the heat.

"Side streets," Luka says, and I nod, shivering too hard to answer. A moment later, we're headed through a wooded area, north.

Luka strips off his shirt and then mine and pulls me against him, and I can't tell whose skin is clammier. It takes a full fifteen minutes before my fingers are warm enough to unknot the plastic bag, pry open the Ziploc, and retrieve my phone. I call Jester.

"You made it," she says with an audible exhale. And then, to the others, "They made it."

I rub my hand over my face. It's got to be nearly eighty degrees in the car, and the tip of my nose is still so cold I can barely feel it.

"Audra, get out of the area as fast as you can. It's small, not like Vienna, and they're locking it down. If you don't get out now you'll be trapped."

"Where are you?" I say.

"Heading your direction. But we're an hour away. Can you get out?"

I don't know. "Yes."

"Head west, if you can. They'll expect you

101

to get out of the country, to run for the Czech Republic. Stay off major highways. Get to Munich. And, Audra . . ." She hesitates.

"Yeah?"

"Be careful. They saw what you can do and know what you are. There's been more than one report of known hunters leaving their marks since this morning."

"What do you mean 'leaving their marks'?"

"A handful of Progeny know or at least have an idea who their hunters are. I created a secure message board a couple years ago to collect as much information as we could. To learn more and create our own database."

"You're *crowdsourcing* the Progeny?"

"Why not?" Her voice takes on an angry edge. "They've done it to us for years with genealogy sites and DNA testing!" She takes a breath. "What I'm trying to say is that several suspected hunters have recently disappeared."

"That's good, then . . ."

"For the Progeny they're hunting, yes. But I think they've all been pulled to pursue a single target. You."

I flash back to my conversation with Rolan— an experienced hunter officially assigned to Luka and me both. I glance at Luka. He mouths, *What?*

But I don't dare tell him. I have two options and two options only when it comes to the Scions. And hiding isn't one of them.

"Okay," I say, trying to sound normal. Whatever that is. "We'll call when we're out."

I click off, and Luka looks at me.

"What did she say?"

"She said get out. They're setting up a perimeter."

The line of his mouth is grim. I don't need to tell him that next time the shooters won't be common.

I sink down low in the seat, pull up a map, point wordlessly to Munich. Luka nods, understanding.

I guide us toward the town of Tiefenbach, angling northwest, away from the river. Our driver's got a gym bag in the backseat, and I rifle through it, hand Luka a rugby shirt, pull on a crewneck two sizes too large for me.

And then we wait as the pavement rolls by beneath us. I force myself to look away from the map on the phone, to count minutes instead. Every one that passes without our getting shot at or stopped is a minute more that we have to think, to plan, to escape.

To live.

We've just emerged on the other side of Tiefenbach after a painfully slow meander through town and gone a couple miles, maybe three, when our driver slows and then comes to a stop.

"What are you doing?" I say in English, sitting up. And then I see it: a line of cars ahead of us, inching its way forward. Blue lights in the distance. A blockade of police vans.

Luka reaches for the door.

"Wait," I say.

I turn in the seat, take in our options. A field of some kind to the right. Wooded area to the left. An SUV ambling toward us fifty yards back. I turn my attention to its driver.

You.

Three seconds later the SUV accelerates toward us. At the last instant, the driver swerves onto the grassy shoulder and barrels past us along the line. Shouts from the direction of the barricade.

I swing my gaze forward in time to watch the SUV crash into the side of a police van.

"Now."

We slide out the driver's side, not bothering to shut the door. Run for the trees, crouched low.

From the edge of the wood, I look back just long enough to see passengers emerging from their cars, some of them capturing video of the accident.

We run, fast and blind in the darkness. I trip, stumble to my knees. Luka yanks me to my feet and pulls me on—running until my lungs burn.

I slow near a break in the trees, lean over to haul in a coughing breath. Luka stumbles to a stop just ahead of me, breathing hard.

"You know what?" he says, hands on his knees. "You scare me."

I give a mirthless laugh.

We emerge on the edge of a shorn field. Luka points at something ahead: a barn, illuminated by wan light from within. We start out at a jog, but then Luka is shouting at me to run. I glance back, catch sight of blinking red rising up over the trees in the distance.

Police drone.

I will my legs to churn—faster, faster. Until I trip and go sprawling, a row of dry stubble stabbing me across the chest, scraping my chin.

A dog sounds a frantic alarm ahead. A few seconds later the door on the adjacent house opens, throwing a sliver of light across the deck, silhouetting the man in its frame.

Luka grabs me under my shoulders, drags me upright. Pain shoots through my ankle, which refuses to support me. He wraps an arm around my waist.

"Come on!" he says, and I hobble alongside him like some three-legged racer.

"Was machen Sie denn hier?" the man shouts.

Go back to bed.

We hurl ourselves the last ten feet to the barn. Luka slides the bolt, shoves open the door. When I look back, the form on the porch has vanished though the dog has not; it lies down, peering beneath the rail at us. But it is silent.

I drop to the floor inside. Hay, manure, and a million microallergens assault my nostrils. Somewhere beyond us, a horse nickers.

Luka squats down beside me. "Which one is it?"

I point, and he gently rubs my ankle. Though my skin is cold, I'm sweating down the inside of my T-shirt. My pants, still damp, feel itchy over legs pumped full of blood.

Is this what my life has become—what it will be? Run, escape—just to run again . . . until I can run no more? A few hours' rest on a good night . . . capture and death on a bad one? Did I have any clue how oblivious I was to reality those short, frenzied nights at court in Zagreb?

No. None.

Even those five nightmarish days in pursuit of the diary, not knowing if Luka lived, were a luxury compared to this.

Because this time, he could die in front of me.

One of you has to survive.

I have one purpose now, and that is to do the most damage to the Scions I can while staying beyond their reach. On the day they catch up to me, or that I can do no more . . .

"I don't think it's broken," Luka says.

"It's fine," I say. I get onto my good foot, shift my weight, and grimace. He catches me by the arm. "It's fine!" I say angrily, pulling away. Because angry is far better than afraid.

"You can't *persuade* it to heal," he snaps and then mutters: "At least I don't think you can."

Much as I hate to admit it, I don't think I can, either.

He swipes his forearm across his face, holds out his hand. "Let me see that map."

I hand him the phone. Wonder if this is karma for the damage I caused back there. No, can't be; I've left plenty of others far worse in my wake these last twelve hours alone. Still, I wonder if the driver of that SUV is all right.

I always thought of myself as some kind of conscientious objector. Funny how that changes the minute someone's out to kill someone you love.

Luka's frowning, eyes ghastly in the light of the phone's screen.

"That blockade was here." He points. "Which means there's probably another here, here, and here," he says, indicating the closest roadways. "If we keep to the woods, I think we can get around them." He glances at me with a frown. "Can you ride?"

"Ride what?"

He goes to one of the stalls, and I exhale a laugh because I think he's kidding. Until I realize he's not.

"What? No!"

"You told me once you could," he says lightly.

"Well if I did I don't remember!"

He opens the stall door, slips inside. A metal light flickers on. Clink of metal bits. He emerges a minute later leading the horse by the bridle toward a bale of hay.

My mouth falls open.

"What? My grandfather had a farm. Come on." He steps up, grabs a handful of mane, and swings onto the horse's back.

"Luka, there's no saddle—"

"There's no time!" He reaches toward me. I limp up onto the bale, hook my arm through his.

Seconds later we break from the barn in an all-out gallop.

I close my eyes, arms clasped tight around him. The ground rocks the breath from my lungs with every stride.

We dash for the tree line, Luka low over the horse's neck, with me glued to his back. I squeeze my eyes shut against visions of us being thrown to the ground and paralyzed. I don't care what he says I told him; nothing in me is at home on a horse.

The minute we enter the woods, the air changes. Colder, tinged with earth. We slow, picking our way over rocks and bramble, and I swear I can smell the sap in the pinecones. The spruce needles, broken underfoot. Hear the wind rifle through beech boughs overhead.

Luka turns, looks around us, his hair against my cheek. I tighten my arms, breasts pressed against the heat radiating from his back. I wonder if he can feel my heart pounding against his spine, as I can feel his, beating beneath my palms.

He stops to check the map. I note the little blue

dot that is us and feel a laugh well up inside me at the ridiculousness of our bareback GPS system. At how stupid we must look in our rugby and oversized shirts.

But also because we're alive. Stupid shirts or not, I am acutely aware of him—from the scent of his nape in my nostrils to his hips between my thighs.

We made life together once, in the face of pending death.

"I love you," I whisper fiercely. He turns his head and his arm tightens over mine, pulling me firmly against him.

He guides the horse up a small ridge, and we emerge near a road.

"Audra," Luka says, nodding toward a bank of blue lights in the distance. The last roadblock is a half mile back. Luka glances toward the overcast sky. Not even a bird.

We pick our way along the edge of the wood past the next bend, and stop. I slide down awkwardly, my legs trembling from the exertion of hugging that barrel-chested horse. Luka dismounts more gracefully, and the horse turns toward home.

There's a sweet-looking Mercedes coupe coming at us from the east. I glance at Luka.

A moment later we're nestled in leather bucket seats, waving to the driver on the side of the road.

Headed west, toward Munich.

11

Munich is flooded with people, tents, and parties. A city in the full swing of Oktoberfest.

We ditch the car on the outskirts of town, climb onto a party bus packed full of college kids, where I manage to acquire a blond braid wig and green felt hat off some drunk chick.

Club Anarchy, just off Ottostrasse, is not the kind of place I imagined for this reunion. Music pounds out the crowded entrance onto the street, where a line goes all the way down the block. I check the address again, look at Luka, who shrugs.

A group of girls in matching purple wigs yells at us as we skip past a line that is two parts Goth cirque, one part Burning Man. Several more heckle the bouncers as I *persuade* them to lift the rope and let us in.

"It's the *underground* German underground," Jester said on the phone.

"How do you get more underground than the underground?" I said weirdly.

"You go to an aboveground court with no prince. Run by a commoner named Arrick Drexel, who is in love with Progeny culture."

"What do you mean a commoner in love with Progeny culture?"

"Rumor has it he had a Progeny lover, who told him everything before she died in a car accident before her memory could be taken."

Car accidents can be faked. I ought to know. I have to wonder if this Arrick's lover is actually dead, or walking around protecting a kid somewhere in secret.

"Look for Arrick. We'll find you."

"How will I know which one is Arrick?"

"You'll know."

The moment I limp inside on Luka's arm, I stare. The ceilings are rough and rounded like caverns. A strobe flashes overhead, not unlike the one in Zagreb's underground court. But whereas Tibor's bank of televisions was housed in a separate room, screens here are everywhere, openly surveilling the costumed crowd.

The entire place smells like smoke machine and perfume.

I pull my hat lower, help myself to the cape of some gilded disco queen sporting a hot pink afro. A tattoo artist works in the corner, but unlike Progeny courts, bars line every wall. A DJ plays on a stage at the far end of the main room, lit up in so much red the walls seem to drip with it. Overhead a purple-haired mermaid lounges on a daybed suspended on steel cables, tossing glitter on partygoers below.

I glance at Luka, who looks like he just ate something weird, and look out across a crimson crowd tinged purple from the LED glow. Past psychedelic pirates and leather Cinderellas, sinister clowns and living dolls with oversize eyes. Half of them are painted with fluorescent neon designs—stars and hearts and wannabe tribal tattoos.

My eye lights on a tuxedoed witch doctor. But it's not his feathered top hat or the skull on his lapel or the black Joker-like mouth that catches my attention. It's the neon dragon painted around his eye. The dragon, biting its tail.

It's a cheap, juvenile imitation, like plastic knight armor on Halloween night. But so is this entire place—from the "blood" on the walls to the revelers dancing not from the sheer exultation of being alive, or even to chase life's frenetic energy, but in booze-deadened states, falsely animated by the liquor thinning their blood.

He's listening to something some masked tiger woman is whispering in his ear, laughing intermittently, but the minute I start for him, his eyes fasten on me. His gaze flicks once to Luka and back as he says something to the tigress, which she accepts with a visible moue. And then he's crossing the floor to meet us.

"Come," he says, taking each of us by an arm, leading us the other direction. Back, toward the corner, to a door he quickly unlocks. Luka frowns and I hesitate, but the witch doctor leans in and shouts near my ear over the din.

"I am a commoner. Do you actually think I would try to keep you in? Come. Quickly."

His accent is heavily German, but his English is as precise as the trim on his sideburns.

We step onto the landing of a metal staircase lit by fluorescent lights. The minute he closes the heavy door behind us, the drone of industrial music dies to a smothered hum . . . replaced by unmistakable energy of another kind from somewhere beyond.

"Who's here?" I demand, turning on him.

He's not a short man, and now that he's standing a foot away, I can tell that he's also not as old as I first took him to be behind the white makeup that has carefully concealed a neatly trimmed goatee.

He smiles broadly. "If you pass the test, you will see."

Luka grabs him by the front of his tux and shoves him against the stair rail. "She's not here to pass tests."

Arrick, pinned in place, exhales a high-pitched laugh. "All the better," he says. And now I know something with him isn't right. He's *enjoying* this.

I turn toward the Progeny presence and descend several steps, leaning heavily on the handrail. For all I know it could be Nikola waiting below to kill me.

"You're injured," Arrick says soberly. "I can send someone to you."

113

I glance back at Luka. "Bring him with us."

"Trust me," Arrick says, hands lifted. "I have nothing but your interest at heart. Hers, that is," he says as Luka lets him go. "I have an eye for her kind."

"He's one of us," I say, indicating Luka. "And you can't tell by looking."

Arrick tugs down his jacket with a vehement shake of his head. "Oh, but he's not. As attractive as he may be." He looks Luka over and then stares intently at me with near-scary fascination. "You're easy to pick out in a crowd for anyone who knows how to do it. To look for the shimmering coin out of a riverbed of stones. He did not catch my eye—not like you. Not at all, in fact."

The way he looks at me makes my skin crawl.

"Walk," Luka says, following behind him.

I hobble to the lower level, try the handle of the metal door at the bottom of the stair. Finding it unlocked, I shoot Arrick a warning glance, and pull.

The space before me opens into an elaborate sunken sitting room a story and a half tall. A giant glass lantern hangs from the ceiling, throwing tiny panes of color along the curtained walls. Iron balconies on both sides overlook the low, sprawling sofa, the oversize ottoman, carpets, ornately carved tables. Staircases line the front and back walls, ascending in opposite directions.

Silk curtains gather in the corners to pool along the floor. And across the entire far wall a painted lattice "window" looks out at a subterranean garden of candlelit palms as though we were not beneath the street in downtown Munich but in a Kasbah somewhere in Morocco.

"You like it?" Arrick says.

"It's very . . . uh . . ." The words "hookah lounge chic" come to mind.

"Welcome to my home. It is yours," Arrick says and then raises a finger, points above us to the twin balconies, where I see now that there are three curtained doorways on each side. "If . . . you can tell me which door the Progeny prize is behind." His brows lift.

"I don't like games," I say.

"Indulge me," he says and smiles.

Go away.

He gives a shallow gasp, eyes wide as he backs to the door.

"I am your servant," he squeaks, barely getting the words out before he exits.

The minute the door shuts, Luka checks to be certain we aren't locked in and I limp toward the far staircase. Luka comes to help me, and I point to the middle arch above.

He moves up ahead of me, reaches past the curtain to the door, and shoves it open.

I arrive on the balcony, but do not find the friends I expected. In fact, it takes me several seconds to identify the tall form seated in front of the small fireplace in the grungy black jacket, sleek ponytail gathered at his nape.

But I know the extreme arch of those brows as they regard me. The lips turned up in a mirthless smile.

"Audra," he says, all pretense of his former madness gone.

Tibor. The Zagreb Prince.

12

"Isn't today just full of surprises," I say.

I move toward the nearest seat. Can practically feel Tibor take in the stupid green hat, blond braids, disco cape, musty pants—and equally musty-smelling me. The myriad scrapes and cuts across my arms and chin.

"You look . . . well," he says, nearly as droll as I. He slides a gaze to Luka, who comes to stand beside me. "Though you could use some new accessories."

"What are you doing here, Tibor?" I say, dragging the hat and wig off my head.

"Is that any way to greet an old friend? You didn't miss poor Tibor?" he says, with a touch of the old lunatic swagger.

I tilt my head, waiting, in answer.

"I've come to talk. But not in front of him."

"He stays."

"There's nothing I don't know," Luka says.

"Well then, you and Arrick should get along famously," Tibor says, eyes wide.

I practically feel Luka glower at him in response.

Tibor looks down, brushes imaginary lint off the knee of his charcoal gray pants. "When Nikola first told me what he thought you were,

I didn't believe him. Even when you sensed him. I should have known. Nikola probably knew it all along. He knows many things he has not shared, I fear." He raises his eyes. I remember them as hard and glittering, but at the moment they seem far too human, fragile without their sinister eyeliner, the red-and-black samurai mask I last saw him in. The only time I ever saw him—at least as far as I know.

"What do you want, Tibor?"

"So flip! So disrespectful of your prince!"

"You're not my prince!"

He sits back as though wounded. "Don't forget I sent Jester to you," he says, but the anger in his eyes is already gone.

"Thank you. For that."

He crosses his arms around himself.

"I've come to tell you: do not return to Zagreb. It isn't safe," he says. "Court broke a few days ago when Nikola had me declared outcast."

I had seen Nikola threaten to do this very thing to Tibor just weeks ago—the same night Nikola threatened to kill Luka if I wouldn't find what I had discovered before I erased my memory. Days later, I discovered why: Nikola's been working for the Historian all this time.

"I didn't know."

He shrugs as though it were nothing. But then he looks at me, his gaze more earnest than I have ever seen it, at least in recent memory.

118

"I know you don't trust me. But you should. I loved Ivan. Ivan loved you. Not like *he* loves you"—he waves a hand at Luka and rolls his eyes—"but as the sibling, the brother you never had. He idolized your mother, you know. As Nikola did, once. As he does, still."

"Nikola didn't idolize my mother. He killed her!"

"So he said. That claim never set well with me. There was only one hand strong enough to kill Amerie—hers. But Nikola was insanely jealous of her. As he is of you."

I turn away, trying to shake the image of her body floating in the Danube, snared in the bracken of the shore.

"Jester said you declared war against him," Luka says.

Tibor shrugs again. It's practically a tic with him. "I never wanted to be prince anyway."

I blink. "Then why were you?"

"Because Jester and those that matter—your mother, Ivan, even you—needed a safe place once in a while. And resources."

"What do you mean, 'resources'?"

"Do you think you can *persuade* money into accounts?" he snarls.

My turn to shrug. "Yeah."

"Pffft! Not the kind it takes for Jester's pursuits. Servers in Switzerland. Payments to colleagues . . . bribes." His words drift, but he's staring at me. His voice drops. "She said you found it. That there's an end in sight to this rat's existence."

At that moment, he reminds me of Claudia the night her makeup was running down her face. Looking like a crackhead, saying this life wasn't living.

When I don't answer, he gets up, paces away.

"You won't tell me. Of course you won't. I don't care!" He stares into the fireplace, hands on his hips. He's thin—thinner than I remember him.

"Ivan believed in you," he says hollowly. "More even, I think, than he believed that God was good." He looks back at me. "It's very hard to believe that God is good when you spend your life on the verge of extinction. But Ivan, my big brother, believed it. Somehow. He believed in a messiah for his every sin. And for us. The last time we spoke, I called him an idiot and worse." He reaches back to scratch his neck. "I was about to throw my lot in with Nikola, who had been pestering me by then for months. Did you know that?"

I shake my head.

He comes toward me, and Luka moves closer.

"There was a way, he said, to rise above this pile and live—truly *live*—without fear. For once. With some surety for the future. A concept so foreign I couldn't imagine it. Had to have him practically paint me a picture," he says, spreading his hands in the air. "And he did. A picture of life in the upper world. Without looking over shoulders. Without wondering if I would make it to the age of thirty. Filled with *beautiful* superficial worries! Money. Losing weight. A job. Staying beautiful the older I got. A family . . ."

My skin prickles and I look fixedly at the fire. Will my face to stoniness, worried it'll give something away. That the mere thought of Eva will betray her existence. But Tibor is no longer looking at me.

"A life so mundane that we would search for meaning. Imagine! A life so secure, that we have to *search* for meaning because staying alive is such a given that we don't even know what it is for." He turns to me and laughs. But I don't.

"A life of true power, when ours is gone. Because when you're Progeny, those moments of *persuasion*—of power *over another*—are the only power you ever *feel*. Because you never feel powerful yourself. Not really. There is only power *over*. It's the loveliest deception, the easiest form of abuse, thinking you're powerful because you can make someone else do something. The sign of the truly weak," he says, lips curling back from his teeth. "Never mind that it costs you in the end. Maybe that's why Ivan used his gifts so seldom. He was wiser than all of us. In all my life, I saw him use them only a handful of times. To save me once. To save your mother. To save you."

I glance up at him, startled.

"You don't know what I'm talking about, do you? It doesn't matter. You don't trust me. So what. I don't care about my life. I'm not interested in that kind of illusion." He gets down in front of me, clasps the arms of my chair, peers intently into my face, so close that I can see the crooked row of his lower teeth.

"But you need to know. Nikola has gathered his court around him. 'The one true court,' he calls it. He's grasping, which means he's desperate. Desperate enough to hold on to a rat's life because it's the only one he knows. Because the minute this ends—if it even can end—who is he then?" He leans forward and whispers: "*Nobody*. He's already lost his gifts. He only knows one thing—how to survive. Not up there!" He points to the floor between us. "Down here. With the *rats*." He scrunches up his mouth into a series of disgusting rodent smacks against his teeth before pushing away.

"Which is why he's brokered his deal with the Historian. He wants to *save* the Utod—or at least that group loyal only to him—by keeping the Scions in power."

"How do you know all this?" Luka says.

"How do you think?" Tibor snaps. "I've played both sides of this game as well. I catered to

Nikola for far too long in the name of survival myself."

"Please don't tell me you're sharing this to ease your *conscience*," I say.

"It's called pragmatism. I have never been"— he gestures in the air—"a gambling man. Sometimes the only way to survive is to hedge your bets . . . play a little on either side."

"Is that what you're doing here?" I say.

"No. I came to tell you there's a split in the Scion ranks. It is the great irony of all of this, that what happens with the Scions or Progeny is mirrored in the other side. Now ask yourself: Why hasn't the Historian cracked Nikola's head open like an egg to find the goodies inside?"

"I have no idea."

"Because he was the way to *you*."

"Why are you telling me this—why come here to tell me in person, and not Jester?"

He leans forward, lifts his brows. "I came to speak, one prince to another."

"I'm no prince!"

"Aren't you? Whom do you think every disowned child of Zagreb is waiting for to draw him or her home? We're ruled by popularity. Which is why no princes in power are actually the leaders they should be—much like your American presidents," he says dryly. "I'm here because Jester, in all her brilliance, is no use to the Scions."

123

"Neither am I."

"Don't be naïve. It doesn't suit you. Nikola isn't the one the Historian truly wants, and he knows it. He would have killed you long before this except that you were the key to something his master wants. So he delivered you because his survival depends on keeping that master appeased. But now what's to stop him from eliminating you as he did your mother—to keep you from Scion hands and retain his place with them?"

Tibor produces a scrap of paper from his pocket, unfolds it, smooths it out on the table.

"What's that?" I say, not moving to touch it.

"The name of a Scion who wants to take down the Historian nearly as much as you do. What is the saying? 'The enemy of my enemy is my friend'?"

"And you want me to do what? *Help* him?"

"So high and mighty! So proud! Don't you see it? The Scions are afraid of you!"

I actually laugh.

"Think about it," he says, somberly.

"You know what I think? What you're suggesting would make me no better than Nikola."

"Stupid girl! There are no clear sides in this. No one is purely anything." He lifts his eyes. "Not even you."

Our gazes lock.

"You have more opportunity than you know. With or without the diary. Not because of what you found but because of what you *are*. But not if you continue to think in black and white. The world doesn't work that way! I didn't come thinking you'd tell me anything," he snarls. "I won't even ask Jester about it. But you should know there are Progeny on the streets of Zagreb, leaking into Hungary singing your name with no place to go. Our people. My former so-called subjects who have no more ties to me, whom I feel responsible for just because they danced in my hall! They will be cut down in Budapest for their belief in you, because Nikola has seen to it that your name has become a curse there. And they will *die*—if not by Scion hands, then by Nikola's. Utod turned on Utod. And then what do we have? Not even each other."

I'm stunned. By his bluntness. By the swift change in the underground in the course of a week. And for a moment I don't know what to say. He gathers up something from the chair on which he was sitting—a gold comedy mask—and I realize he's about to leave.

"Tibor," I say impulsively. "Thank you for what you did for my mother. For me."

He gives a small laugh. "Don't thank me. I was always a coward. Ivan's the one who should have lived. Now you only have me.

Lucky you. And what am I?" He smiles and bows low, arms out. *"Nothing."*

"I don't believe that," I say. "The Croatian court respects you. Needs you."

"No," he says, straightening. "They need you. Maybe you can't end this. But one thing I know: If you can't, we're already as good as dead. Most days, I'm fine with that. I'll be twenty-nine next month. But there are Utod roaming the streets who don't know what they are . . ." His jaw twitches. "Progeny, fifteen, sixteen years old. Who want to live, far more than you or I."

I look away. I don't want to hear that. This is a vendetta. It's personal. The last thing I need is the lives of faceless others riding on my actions—as well as my conscience.

I've had plenty of that already.

"But what do they know at that age anyway?" His laugh is slightly manic. Perhaps his insanity hasn't been a complete act after all. But then his expression instantly changes, as though the laughter was a mask he's just thrown off. "You know I dreamed, once, of being Firstborn? When I first heard the legends. Of having that kind of power, whatever it was, however it looked. But now . . ." He shakes his head, looks me up and down. "I don't envy you. It's hard enough, staying alive, when you're one of us. The day you stop fighting, you're already dead."

He looks down at the mask and then lifts it slowly to his face, fastens the strap behind his head.

"You can trust Arrick," he says, words muffled. "And Jester." He turns to Luka. "But are you sure you can trust the others?"

We stare at him, stunned, as he sprints for the door.

"Where will you go?" I shout after him.

Luka takes off and returns a moment later.

"He's gone. There's a back exit," he says.

He walks over to the table, picks up the scrap of paper, and then shows it to me. It contains a single name: Serge Deniel.

I snatch it from him and fling it into the fire.

"You know," Luka says. "Maybe there's something to what he said."

"You're kidding, right?" When he just looks at me, I exhale an incredulous laugh. "Work with a Scion?"

"Is it the strangest thing you've ever heard? Really, Audra?"

But I don't get a chance to respond as I sense the arrival of others. A moment later the door to the living room opens below.

13

It's not the reunion I expected.

"Audra." Jester and Claudia kiss me in swift turns as Piotrek claps Luka on the shoulder, says something about the state of Luka's face. The three of them look like they just came from some casual-chic photo shoot, Jester in her usual purple.

"I'll get your bag," Claudia says, and I open my mouth to say I don't have one before I realize she's speaking to Jester.

I glance among the three of them: Claudia and Jester, unpacking the laptop, the awkward way Piotrek shoves his hands in his jacket pockets. The cautious distance they've all moved back, as though I might detonate.

"So," Piotrek finally says, glancing around us. "This is a very strange place, yes?"

"Pretty much," I say, walking gingerly toward the sofa. "Happy, uh, Oktoberfest."

"What is this?" Jester says, tying back her dreads and glancing at me as though I were the one with the prosthetic leg. "You are walking like me now."

"There was a field, and don't even get me started about the horse." I give an uneasy laugh.

"She twisted her ankle," Luka says.

"I wondered what that smell was," Claudia says, not looking up.

Jester glances between us and, after a beat of silence, says, "Well, let's see what you found."

But right now I don't want to think about it. I want to reconnect with the only family I know. A family who apparently doesn't know how to act toward me anymore. I actually open my mouth to speak in an attempt to break this strange ice, to say I'm the same person I was before.

But that would be a lie.

I'm married—to my own hunter. I have a daughter, who is part Scion and will grow up to be more gifted than I, assuming she lives so long. I have secrets I can never tell them. That I, myself, should not know.

And I've just met privately with Tibor, who fled rather than run into them. What would Claudia say, to know the prince she once feared came here to chat—*"Prince to prince"*? What would Jester say, knowing Tibor was here and didn't stay?

"Anyone know where we can get some clothes?" I say instead.

Claudia offers to find some, excuses herself without looking at me. Like chicks do when they're upset.

"What'd I do to her?" I murmur.

"Nothing," Jester says. "Now that you're safe, we have a lot to do."

Nice to see you, too.

Jester sets up, and I pull the baggie from the waist of my pants, dump the chips from my progression of phones on the table. "It's one of these," I say. "The rest of it's here. I didn't have time to photograph them all." I hand her the flash drive and unfold the last of the cache, lay it out on the sofa.

Piotrek comes to examine the pages with a frown, as though they were some random garbage I picked up along the way. "This is no diary."

"There is no diary," I say. "There never was."

"There has to be!" he says, seeming baffled and offended at once by my statement.

Impatience wells up like anger inside me. Even if there was, it wouldn't make any difference! Even if Bathory's innocent—who cares? I'll tell you who doesn't. The Historian."

He blinks at my outburst, and I instantly regret it, though a part of me has far more lashing out to do. Not at Piotrek—not him personally. At any Progeny naïve enough to think some holy grail is going to actually end this. At the medieval idea that some magic talisman is going to save us all. How many Progeny have died holding out for that hope—raving in their dungeons by night, getting killed by day?

Piotrek looks from me to Luka, and back to the pages Jester has spread out around us as though we had brought back a bunch of used hamburger wrappers. "Then what is this?"

Only what Luka and I both just risked our lives for.

"A crime wall," I say, thinking back to the collage I created, sans string, on the ship. "Which I guess is a kind of diary," I concede. "Of corruption. Conspiracy to commit murder. No, just murder."

Jester picks up one page and then another, quickly scanning them.

"This isn't anything we didn't know," Piotrek said.

"Yes, but now we have *names*. Transactions that can be traced. Confidential letters—for hundreds of years," I say, gesturing to the stack. A conspiracy theorist's wet dream.

"You can't convict the past!" Piotrek says, frustrated.

"Maybe not," I say more calmly. "But you can convict the present. Look. This is dated last year," I say, lifting out a copy of an e-mail.

"*Oh, mon Dieu,*" Jester breathes, and Piotrek leans in to look more closely. "This is the president of the Curia—the Hungarian Supreme Court."

"How'd you know that?" I say.

She shrugs. "You remember faces and images. I remember names. And this woman"—she taps a name at the top of a page—"is one of the most influential people in Europe. And this

131

is a confidential European Commission e-mail address. If we so much as breathe a word of this to the wrong person—"

I know the look on her face. It was the same one I had just two days ago.

"Forget all that. We have to find the story, catalog names and relationships between these people or the groups they're affiliated with. Their circles of influence, who their family members are. Follow the money and the favors. There's something here the Historian either wants to know or doesn't want anyone to find. Whatever it is, we need it."

"The Historian already has to know all of this," Jester says.

"Maybe. But I think there's something here that can be used against her."

"*Her?*" Piotrek and Jester say in unison, looking up at me in shock.

"Yeah."

Piotrek exhales an incredulous laugh, and Jester says something in French under her breath.

"And there's twenty times this much on the chip," I say.

Jester is shaking her head, sorting the rest of the actual pages I brought with me around her into chronological order, when the name on one—some large stock purchase nineteen years ago—catches my eye.

Serge Deniel.

"Who's that?" I say.

She squints at it, clearly flustered. "I don't know. I'd have to research." She exhales heavily, plugs one of my SIM chips into a reader. "If there's as much as you say, this is going to take time. You might as well get some rest."

But the last thing I feel capable of is rest, especially with the tense dynamic going on with the others right now. Jester, escaping into the analytical ether. Piotrek, stealing glances at me as though I might morph into something else before his eyes. His sibling, Claudia, conspicuously absent. With Tibor's proposed Scion collaboration and Luka's saying I should consider it still echoing in my mind. With Serge's name on a purchase record right in front of me. The things they won't say. The things we—Luka and I—can't.

"Think there's a chance we can get some food down here?" Luka interjects into the silence.

"A very good chance," Jester murmurs, beginning to download the chip's contents.

"What's up with Arrick, anyway?" I say.

"He's . . . I don't know how you say it. A groupie?"

"Sounds about right," I mutter.

"In love with Progeny life."

"So what does he get out of this?"

"Persuaded," she says.

"What?"

"He only asks one thing from those of us who come here. *Persuade* him. To do anything. To think of something pleasant, hopefully. Let him forget for a while. He was very in love with Analise. We all were."

"Okay," I say. "That's kind of creepy."

"Is it?" Jester says, looking up at me. "Wanting to forget?"

I step back as though slapped. Her attention returns to her computer.

In the last twenty hours, I've been hunted by the police—twice—jumped onto a ship, into a river, on a horse, on a bus, and made my way here only to be confronted by a manic Tibor bent on taking out the Scions from the inside and given de facto leadership of a flock that knows my name but whose faces I've never seen. And I've just returned with the best chance we've ever had against the Historian and right now I'm so over all of this.

"You know what? I'm gonna get some rest," I say, and head upstairs. Probably with the same look Claudia had a few minutes ago, which just makes it worse. And without the dignity of a regular gait, which just makes it lame. Luka comes to help me, but I brush him off.

I feel angry, betrayed to some degree or another by all of them. Including him.

"Does nobody care that we have this?" I say

upstairs, not bothering to whisper. "That you and I both nearly *died* trying to get it here?"

He closes the door. "They're weirded out, Audra."

A series of bronze lamps illuminates the room in a mellow glow. The long daybed against the far wall is piled with colorful pillows. What does Arrick do in his free time anyway— moonlight as a professional lounger?

"And I'm not?" I say, dropping onto the cushions.

"What do you expect? You're not the person they thought you were."

"They should be happy! I can do more!"

"You know, you won't remember this, but at one time I wanted to be a footballer. A soccer player," he says, falling onto the pillows beside me. He rubs his brows as though they hurt. Bruised as he is, his whole face must. "My best friend, Bertrand, and I were on the same team for years, growing up. The year we turned sixteen, I was approached by a professional recruiter. I was ecstatic. Couldn't wait to tell Bertrand all about it. I thought he'd be happy for me."

"I take it he wasn't."

"He could barely look at me. It didn't help that he had always practiced harder than me. Started younger. We were friends after, but it was never the same."

"Your story sucks."

"Claudia has always known whose daughter you were. It's hard being the friend of someone who makes you feel invisible. The only thing she's ever had over you is that she knew more about this life and how to live it than you . . ."

"And she always will."

"Yes, but now you turn out to be this *thing* that everyone is in awe of. Including her."

"Well I don't want her to be!"

"Neither does she. But she is. And now she's wondering what that makes her."

"My friend," I say. "The only true, *surviving* friend I have from before, after you."

"Not in her mind," he says. "Audra, you're gifted. You're smart. You're strong. You're beautiful."

I groan.

"Those things alone make you a very hard person to be close to."

"Then why are you with me?" I say bitterly.

He rolls his eyes, and I know I'm such an ass.

"I'm just saying when something about who you are changes, it makes anyone close to you wonder how that also changes them."

I lean onto an elbow, study him in the low light. "You know," I finally say. "You're going to make a great dad."

The smile he gives me is sad. And I hate it, because it's like he's already accepted that he'll never really be that. In the same way that I can't think of myself as a mother. Because I'm not. Not really. A mom is someone who raises you, is there for you. Not just protecting you with her absence.

"So what am I supposed to do?"

He shrugs. "Be you."

"Easy for you to say."

"What else can you do? You can't *persuade* her to feel a certain way."

The door abruptly opens, and there's Claudia. For a moment, I panic, not knowing how long she's been standing there, what she might have heard.

"I found these in one of the other rooms," she says curtly, several items of clothing in her arms.

She holds a short stack toward Luka, who takes them and thanks her, and another for me.

I get up and move toward her. But instead of taking the clothes, I throw my arms around her.

She stands, stiff and unmoving, clearly caught off guard.

"I missed you," I say, leaning my head against hers.

"Me, too," she says at last.

"I was scared," I say. "Really scared."

Her arm closes slowly around me, the bundle of clothes clasped between us.

"So was I," she whispers.

Luka slips out to change, and Claudia lets me go. Taking a step back, she looks me up and down—much the way Tibor did less than an hour ago.

"Well, you certainly don't look Firstborn."

"So I hear."

She shakes out a pair of black jeans and a sweater and holds them toward me. And I'm only too glad to shed the dirty T-shirt and moldy, damp pants, to toss them onto the floor.

"What does it feel like?" she says as I pull the sweater over my head.

"Ahh," I sigh. "Amazing. I feel like I've been cold for a year—"

"No. I mean . . ."

"Oh." I pull on the jeans, which are snug, but it's not like I'm complaining. They're dry. "It hurts."

Her brow wrinkles. Clearly not the answer she expected.

"It's like the worst migraine in the world, until you nearly black out. With nosebleeds . . . and pain. Did I mention that it hurts? But not as much as dying, probably."

Most of the time, I forget how young she is. But standing there now, so pale, arms crossed around herself, the too-long sleeves of her sweater obscuring her hands, she actually looks eighteen.

And I realize this has been hard on them, too. Holed up and having to wait, not knowing in the silence between our calls whether I'm still alive. Knowing that the minute I die at Scion hands, everything I know about them will be exposed. It's the reason I haven't asked or been told any of their locations this last week. I guess in some ways it's easier being the one on the run.

"Finally I understand Ivan's strange devotion to you always," she says. "I thought it was because of your mother, though as far as I could tell, you were nothing like her. I—I didn't know."

"Me either." I shrug.

I give her a small smile, but she's looking at me much the same way Luka did earlier tonight on the cruise ship: concerned. No, afraid. Not for herself, but for me.

I glance down between us and understand her distance for what it is: self-protection. No one wants to get close to a dead woman. And Claudia's lost so many already.

"I'm keeping a secret for you," she says suddenly.

"What?"

"Your notes, of course. Your things from the safety deposit box."

"Thank you," I say, feeling guilty. I shouldn't have left them with her at all; should have asked her to burn them, if only for her own safety. But despite my photographic memory, I couldn't bring myself to destroy the only thing I ever received from my mother.

"But now that I've done this for you, you have to do something for me."

"Anything."

"Stop pushing us away."

I blink at her. "What do you mean?" I say, taken aback. "I'm pretty sure I haven't been the one doing the pushing since you got here."

"Really? Since I saw you last you've sent us to Switzerland, where you were supposed to join us but went to Budapest instead—"

"I had to, to keep Luka safe! But you knew that."

"And did it work? No. And so you went on that crazy five-day search for the diary . . ."

"I didn't have a choice! They were going to kill him!"

"And then to Vienna—again—for him, when you could have gotten killed with the diary *in your head*. Which means *they* would have it all!"

Is she seriously schooling me right now?

"What did you expect me to do, Claudia? Just let Luka die? We couldn't save Nino. We couldn't save Ana. But I could save Luka. And quit talking to me like I'm fifteen. You have no idea what this week has been like for me. And then to come here and get this from you—"

"Have you even considered since all of this began the lengths you have gone to protect him? How many times you have nearly died for him? I know you love him. But we"—she taps her chest—"are your *family*." Indignation has given way to injury in her eyes.

"Just because he's common doesn't make Luka's life any less valuable! It's because of him that I'm still alive!"

"Really? He's the one who took you in in Zagreb? He's the one who taught you to survive—*before?*"

I close my mouth. I've said too much already. If she knew what he was, I'd have far less of an argument for saving him.

"This has never been just about you, Audra. And it's not even about Luka. Every time you go out there"—she gestures to the world above us—"you put more than your life at risk. It's about all of us. Now, more than ever!"

"I did what I had to."

"And we kept you safe. Without our help you would be dead! And the diary—whatever it is—would have vanished with you. Would even now be in the Historian's hands."

"Well guess what? They didn't take me or the diary. Jester's downloading it now. And Luka's alive. Sorry if that upsets you," I say.

"I'm not upset. I like him. Piotrek does, too. We are glad to see him alive. And anyone can see he loves you. He'd die for you, I believe it. But the day may come when choosing him might mean *not* choosing everyone else who needs you."

I stare at her, knowing she might be right. Hoping to God she's not.

"Do you know they are calling you the newest Progeny prince?"

"Oh please . . ." But the skin has prickled on my arms.

"It's true. Tibor's been exiled. Everyone is saying your name. How it makes sense that Amerie the beloved zealot was Firstborn. Acting in secret all this time, hiding you away. And you, back from the dead like some Jesus Christ."

I roll my eyes.

"What do you want from me, Claudia? I'm here. The so-called diary is here. And it doesn't matter what they call me because the Scions are still out there. Which is—oh yes—*also why we need the diary*. Did I mention that I brought it? So I saved Luka along the way. What's it to you?" I brush past her toward the door.

"Do you know what they call Piotrek and me, whose fathers are not of the legacy?" she says from behind me.

I sigh. "What?"

"Half-blood. As though we only count half as much as a full-blooded Progeny. Even though we are as gifted—and as hunted—as any of the others waiting for you to save them. You, who might be dead right now without our help. While everyone else is hiding, we are the ones here with you. *With you*. So stop treating this as some personal crusade or cross you have to bear that no one else can understand. Because it *is* personal. To all of us!"

I turn around and consider her. And in that moment, I wish I could tell her. I wish I could show her a picture of Eva, tell her whose—and what—she is. But even then, it wouldn't do anything to convince her of Luka's worth. Luka, hunted in his own right for turning traitor to the Scions.

And maybe, with her not knowing any of that, it does look like I'm on some personal crusade. Because I am.

But that crusade also includes her.

I go to her and take her hands. "I swear, Claudia. I'm not doing this just for me. And I promise not to ditch you again. As for Luka . . . please, just trust me."

She sighs, looks away.

"Please?" I say again, earnestly. "I can't be at war with the Historian and Nikola and you, too."

She finally nods, grudgingly.

"Thank you," I say and pull her into a hug. She begins to shake in my arms, and I realize that she's crying. And with that, every sharp edge in my heart softens.

"Hey." I take her by the shoulders to look at her. She turns her head, swipes at her cheek. Without her spidery false purple lashes and elaborate makeup and wigs, she could be any number of girls plucked from the senior hall of any high school. Except, of course, for the haunted fatigue in her eyes.

That is solely a Progeny trait.

Somehow I sense that telling her I love her will only make it worse—cause her to brace for some inevitable shoe to drop. Nor will it help to say I won't die. Because I'm positive that would make me a liar.

"Come on. Let's check this crazy place out."

"Your ankle—"

"It's feeling better." Which is mostly true.

I take her by the hand and lead her to the exit. And suddenly we're just two girls hurrying up the back stairs. The hard drum of European trance music assaults us as we bypass the main floor of the club to the rafters of a precarious catwalk over the stage.

For as much as I've ridiculed Arrick's club as a childish sham, my pulse spikes and begins to hammer to the electric beat. I point across the walk to where the stairs continue to the roof, having wondered since I saw him how and where Tibor made his rapid escape.

Claudia steps onto the catwalk, and then next thing I know, she's running along its metal grate. Midway across, she leaps out over the dance floor. My arms fly out and I scream, sound swallowed by the roar of the music. But she doesn't fall— she's caught an aerial performer's abandoned silk to swing wide over the simmering mob.

I grab her the minute she's within reach, heart drumming the familiar staccato of adrenaline and alarm. But for the first time since we left Croatia, she is laughing.

I let her go. And a second later I've launched myself off my good foot at a second silk swath.

I grasp it in midair, sail out over the crimson crowd. I twine my ankle around the silk and let go to dangle upside down.

I fly wide, weightless. Snag a plastic cup from a raised, clueless hand. One of the drunken crew below finally spies us and points with a shout as Claudia kicks off one shoe and then the other into the throbbing melee. They dive for them like beads at Mardi Gras.

"It's a good day to be alive, Audra!" she shouts above the music, whipping her legs around until she twirls.

I have to work to get back to the catwalk, pumping arms and legs to climb to its metal edge. I grab for Claudia, who misses my hand the first time and then teeters when I catch her on the second, off-balance for a prolonged moment until I grit my teeth and tug her up beside me. She lands, catlike as a circus performer, as though the danger of falling just a second ago was all an act.

"You're insane," I say.

"Life is insane," she says, as we take off for the far stairs and ascend above the music.

There's a door up there, and we let ourselves out, leaving my soggy sneaker to prop the door open so it won't lock us out.

Below us, Munich is in the full throes of festival. We go to the edge of the roof, gaze out toward the grounds with their scores of crowded tents, carnival rides, and giant Ferris wheel lit up against the sky. Even from here we can hear the music of the carnival, laughter, and distant singing.

"I wonder what it's like"—Claudia sighs—"to spend a weekend playing like that. A life. Never looking over your shoulder. To meet new people and never be afraid they have come just to track and kill you. To be able to say, 'Let's do this again next year.' To make plans so far ahead."

Somewhere in my past, I have the faint memory of an amusement park with a looping roller coaster. Of milling from one ride to the next eating funnel cakes and ice cream, flirting with a group of boys. But Claudia has never experienced something like that. The thrills she seeks don't come with safety harnesses or cords, no mats to catch her if she falls.

The streets are congested, filled with foot traffic spilling from the festival to the clubs. Directly below us, the freak parade waiting to get into Club Anarchy stretches around the corner.

"Watch," I say.

I lean out far enough to see the end of the line. A few seconds later, the line starts to coil in on itself, like a snake. Claudia lets out a sharp exhale of a laugh. A few seconds later, the end uncoils . . . and then takes off running around the corner.

"Where have they gone?" Claudia says. We run to the other side of the roof, catch sight of them tearing down the block—follow them from wall to wall as they return from the opposite direction to regroup in front of the befuddled bouncers. A moment later they break apart, arms flailing in unison.

"What are they doing?" Claudia says, as a foursome of costumed guys breaks away from the line, and I swear one of them is dressed as a cowboy.

"Dancing!" I say. "Y . . . M . . . C . . . A . . ." I mimic, singing along to the unheard melody. Claudia laughs, watching with appalled fascination.

"You're making them do that?"

I nod, wondering vaguely how long I can keep this up. Delighted shrieks issue from the swing chair ride in the distance as I speed up the frenetic pace below. They signal the letters faster and faster while I wait for the pain to start behind my eyes.

But it doesn't come.

14

"Does it hurt?" Claudia asks.

"Not yet," I say and swipe at my nose, but my fingers come away clean.

I don't understand it. There have to be more than seventy people in that line.

"Maybe you've gotten stronger."

"Maybe." But even the simplest persuasion comes with a cost. And though I haven't felt any pain, the adrenaline burn leaves my limbs heavy.

"So . . . has anyone seen Tibor?" I ask with levity I do not feel.

She hops up to sit on the edge of the roof, back to the sidewalk below. A breeze rifles through her hair. She looks like a model in front of a wind machine on a fashion shoot.

"No. No one knows where he has gone. His court has scattered to the streets, though we hear some of them have defected to Budapest, where Nikola has offered protection."

"Protection from Tibor?" I say strangely.

"No, stupid. From you. Nikola has declared you outlaw. Saying that you're in league with the Historian."

"*What?*"

Pot, meet kettle.

"It's the most frightening thing he could say—a Firstborn ally of the Historian. They don't know what your powers are. No one has documented what a Firstborn can do for generations. There are rumors that you can start fires from a distance. Move objects. Kill on sight."

My brows lift.

"Well, they're going to be disappointed," I murmur.

"Obviously."

We stay there long enough to take in the night air. To steal a few last glances of the festival.

We should go down there, I think. Take a night and pretend that we are no one. I think of the way Tibor said the same about himself: What am I? *Nothing.* And I wonder if he's down there even now, on one of those spinning rides.

Luka finds us on the rooftop. Even with his bruises, he's so good-looking that I wonder what he saw in me—once he got past wanting to kill me. If I glamoured him or something with a supercharisma I didn't know I had. And I'm well aware that between the emotional revelation of Eva's existence and our quick escape from the cruise ship, we haven't had much of a reunion.

He comes over and slides his arms around me. After the last week, I want him close. Want to imagine what it will be like when we go back into our room downstairs, alone. I just need one moment of normalcy between us. All of us. Even

149

if it's just to look longingly out at the rest of the world. Luka might be my husband, but Claudia, Piotrek, and Jester are my family.

He smiles, but fatigue and tension have deepened the bruises below his eyes.

"Jester's got the photos downloaded."

By the time we return, Jester's not only got the photos loaded but has the first one projected onto the wall.

I perch on the edge of the sofa in front of a carafe of coffee, several liters of water, a platter of olives, cheese, dry ham, bread, and a plate of small cakes. I gesture at the platter and glance at Piotrek, brow raised.

"Arrick," Piotrek says around a mouthful.

"Is the door locked?" I ask, not sure I trust our host, no matter what Tibor says.

"Checked it myself," Luka says.

I pour myself a cup of coffee, gulp half of it down, still wondering about the missing migraine.

"I've put these more or less in chronological order, tried to group related items together. Run them through translation software for the American," Jester says with a wry smile, beginning the slideshow. Image after image in rapid succession.

"They're going too fast," Claudia says. "I can't read them."

"This run-through is for Audra. If there are patterns to be found, she has the best chance of finding them first."

I take each of them in, eyes scanning the image, and then the translation. Crumbling documents hundreds of years old. Journal entries. Purchase receipts. The translations aren't perfect, but they're clear enough to crack the meaning on images already in memory but not understood. To watch the story unfold . . .

Twelve families. Peasants. Meager purchases: an animal here or there, a small shop. One of the men awarded a piece of land for saving a minor noble in a war against the Turks. Humble inroads into the merchant class by the mid-1600s—a generation after the death of Elizabeth Bathory, shortly after the time her exiled children return from Poland to Hungary.

I stare at the slow march of history as the descendants of those families convert to Catholicism, become landowners—not only in Hungary but in Moravia and Vienna. One of them finds work in an aristocratic print shop. Several more are recognized for their service under the Habsburg king in driving the Ottomans from Hungary. Two of them become squires. Several more serve under the Turks in Wallachia. Scions, flourishing on both sides of the conflict in a fraternity that transcends political and religious borders. I can't help but think back to

151

Tibor's words about hedging bets, playing both sides.

Scions, fighting against the Protestant Reformation and later in the drive for Hungarian independence, winning power and affluence. A progression of stealth operations behind the scenes of Europe's great events. The increasing ability to pick mostly winning sides in conflicts—and be rewarded.

Travel to France on a diplomatic mission that coincides with the marriage of Marie Antoinette . . .

Service rewarded under Napoleon Bonaparte . . .

An early 1800s obituary for a Prussian man who went mad and took his life. A Polish woman who leapt into a river. Victims, no doubt, of the Scions, who are by now avid merchants, a few of them landed lower nobles and courtiers.

Claudia curses, leaning back hard into the sofa as image after image drifts by. You don't have to look for long to get the general idea.

I sit forward as we reach the 1900s, my eyes drawn to the names, the growing industrial wealth. The wire transfers. The stock and corporate purchases. The political careers, the bank takeovers. The first Scion elected to the European Parliament, in 2004. The deaths of several models, rising rock stars, a young comedian, a chef, a mission worker, an international student.

I shudder. That could have been—was, once—

me. Their deaths are ruled suicides, overdoses, self-inflicted gunshot wounds. Accidents.

Government bribes by construction company giants. Tax fraud. Environmental crimes. Money trails. Securities fraud. Kickbacks. World sporting event bidding corruption. And an entire trail of evidence and witnesses for each—not to mention a few would-be whistle-blowers . . . several of whom died convenient, tragic deaths, their accounts never brought to light.

We have names. We can trace families. Novak, Luka's surname, among them. Though it's common enough, I felt the imperceptible tension in his shoulders as it flashed onto the screen—once, twice, earlier. They are the same names as those on the Scion map I discovered in the bank vault in Vienna along with my mother's notes. The document might very well have been made from this cache—an early shorthand attempt at the genealogy of the original families involved. But here, now, is the evidence behind their rise.

All the while, something nags at the back of my mind.

"What I'm not seeing is what the Historian wanted from this pile," I say at last. "Is anybody seeing it?"

"We're not seeing anything this fast," Piotrek mutters.

"What we don't have is the name of the Historian herself," Luka says.

"Herself?" Claudia says, eyes wide, looking to me for confirmation. *"Kuja!"* she spits, before falling into rapid conversation with Piotrek in what I assume to be his native Polish.

"Jester, are the names Otto Errickson, Attila Bertalan, or Cristian Alexandrescu on any of these documents?"

"Just a moment," she says, searching as Claudia, Piotrek, and Luka turn quizzical glances to me.

"No," she says a moment later. "None of them. Why?"

"They were all Historians. Somewhere between seventy-five and two hundred years ago."

"How can you know the names of three Historians?" Claudia says.

"They were on the Scion map I recovered from my mother's notes in Austria—the ones you hid for me."

Piotrek leans back into the sofa with a low whistle.

"But the Historian's office had its own line down the side," I say. "Like it was a progression of its own."

"Chosen not by family or birth," Jester says. "But then by who? The Historians before them?"

"I assume. The three people recorded there—all men—didn't have the same surnames."

"A Scion not known to other Scions," Piotrek says.

"Which means no Scion actually knows who the Historian is either," I say and have to catch myself from looking to Luka for confirmation. Instead, I point to the wall.

"A secret office," Luka says slowly, as though working it out in his mind, though I know he's really just telling the truth. "That the Scions give allegiance to because it appoints hunters from their families . . . and then helps raise them up through the favors of other Scions at the Historian's bidding."

"All of them living posh lives in the open. All of them former killers," Claudia says with disgust as the parade of images continues.

"But these Scions are all trading favors," Jester says. "Which means that none of these people in here—these power players—can actually be her."

"We're talking about a puppet master," I say. "Who came into power sometime in the last year."

"The last year?" Piotrek says. "How do you know this?"

"Because the date was on the Scion map. She's new, whoever she is. And apparently radical."

"So that's why the killings have been different."

"You said Nikola's aligned with her," Claudia says. "Could *he* know who she is?"

I glance at Jester, who has been obsessed with

155

Nikola on Tibor's behalf for some time. But she only shrugs. "You're the one who saw them together," she says.

I frown, thinking back to the night I met her—alone in a cavern with them both. Nikola could have ripped off her mask at any time and known her face.

Of course, she also could have had him instantly killed by any one of the guards outside. So I guess there's that.

"Someone has to know who she is," Jester says. "Someone who takes her orders. Someone who sends her commands out. Who was corresponding with you in your negotiations for Luka's proof of life?"

"A voice. On the number you tried to trace," I say dully.

"It's an anonymous, chipless phone out of Asia. What about Rolan's contact?"

"Same guy. I got him from Rolan."

"If the last Historian knew who his successor was going to be," Piotrek says, "this one knows who hers will be. There has to be someone who finds the document with her appointment when she dies."

"A legal proxy of some kind," Luka says.

"Yes."

The page with Serge Deniel's stock purchase appears on the wall.

"Stop," I say and point. "I want to know who

he is. Can you find out?" Jester drags the document out of the queue.

I watch till the end. Perhaps twenty minutes in all. Until the images, imprinted in my brain, have begun to blend together. One on top of the other.

I lie back on the sofa, close my eyes as Jester starts from the beginning again for the others. The images fly apart, a maelstrom behind the dark lids of my eyes that makes me feel vaguely motion sick, like a bad case of the bed spins.

I discard the first three hundred and fifty years of the story; they're no use to us now. Lay the rest on a mental canvas, begin to shift them around. Toss out those more than fifty years old. No, thirty. Connect money transfers with corporate takeovers, conglomerates with political offices. Legal awards to planned bank failures. Fraud with corporate rises. Wealth with power.

Until the images blur. Until the names run together.

It's barely 1:00 A.M. when I haul myself upstairs, leaving the others to their grim cinema. I am weary in a way I didn't know was possible, the sleep of yesterday having been only enough of a teaser to make me more tired.

Luka appears in the doorway, rubbing his forehead, and closes the curtain in front of the door.

"You look terrible," he says. His slight, lopsided grin only accentuates the black circles beneath his eyes, the bruises healing to a greenish tint on his cheek.

"Speak for yourself," I say, falling back onto the daybed. I stare up at the ceiling. I've never known how to give in willingly to sleep. For the last week it's come as a tidal wave after I've pushed myself to the brink of persuasion-induced stroke, and nights spent at court before that.

He lies down beside me. A moment later, he finds my hand, lifts it to his lips. I turn and lay my head on his shoulder, slide a knee over his thigh.

"They're going to find out," he says quietly against my fingers. "About me."

They are the words I've been dreading.

When Luka was taken, I obscured the portion of the Scion map with his name before I delivered it to the Historian—who promptly burned it. And though I haven't thought about this moment since rescuing Luka, I think I've known in the back of my mind that it was only a matter of time.

I close my eyes, will him not to speak. But Scions cannot be persuaded.

"I'll have to go," he says. "Maybe not tonight, but tomorrow or the next day."

He turns onto his side. "Say you'll come with me," he says, eyes intense.

It would be so easy to say yes.

"We belong together," he says. "Come with me."

"This isn't finished. And until it is, Eva—" I catch myself, aware of the fact that the door isn't closed, and then whisper, barely above a breath: "*She* is not safe."

He doesn't answer. After a beat of silence, he looks away.

"Luka . . ."

"This will never be finished," he says. "So what then? I walk away from you? Don't you see? I don't know how to let you go!" He clasps me in his arms, eyes locked on mine.

He's home and heat and comfort. Above all that, he's mine. I know it in my soul. He'd die for me—for Eva.

And that's the problem.

"You seemed fine enough letting me go when the Scions had you," I say.

"What I wasn't fine with was you getting killed trying to save me. I was trying to protect you. *Both of you!*"

"How is you dying not leaving us?"

"It's not the same."

"Isn't it? What about the rest of your family? Aren't you worried about your parents?"

He falls back to stare at the ceiling, shakes his head with an exasperated sigh. "Of course I am. I even called my father's house once, from a burner phone. No one answered. And I couldn't have said anything if he did. As far as he knows, I've disappeared."

"He lives alone?"

"My mother left him a few years ago. I haven't talked to her since my nineteenth birthday."

"Wow. I'm . . . so sorry," I say. "I didn't know."

"You did," he says dully. "You just don't remember. When we named Eva, it was like you were trying to give a part of her back to me, I think." He rubs his eyes. "It doesn't matter. My grandfather was the Scion. They don't know anything about it."

"Of course it matters. You could tell your dad you're in trouble. He could help hide you until it's safe . . ."

"No."

"No parent could turn their back on their own son—"

"I can't, Audra!"

"Why not?"

"Because I'm more of a danger *with* either of them than if I stay far, far away. You of all people should understand that!"

His words cut. I shove angrily away, but he grabs my arm and pulls me back.

"I made my choice!" he hisses, something desperate in his eyes. "Don't you get it? I left that life forever! For a new one—with you."

I'm breathing hard. Furious and horrified. At him, for what he just said. For his stubborn love.

For his willingness to leave me. To not leave completely. At myself, most of all.

"We both did," he says more quietly.

But I have no recollection of that choice. There is only this: the shards of the life I woke up to . . . just in time to watch it crumble to pieces.

Someone downstairs calls my name. Alarmed, no doubt, by the ruckus.

"We're fine," I call.

"Audra!" Jester shouts, more loudly.

I get up from the bed, and this time Luka lets me go. I wipe my eyes on my sleeve, push through the curtain to lean over the rail of the balcony, find the others still gathered on the sofa. "Sorry. Everything's okay." Except that it's not.

"I think you'd better see this."

"I've seen all of them already." But even from here I can see she has paled. Claudia is staring across the room at the wall.

"Not this."

"What?" I say irritably as I head downstairs.

"I must have downloaded this from one of your SIM chips," Jester says and points to the image projected on the wall.

It's a text message:

You did not deliver as promised. But I know where you've been.

Beneath it is a photo of the monastery in Košljun.

161

15

There are moments that shatter your existence.

I stare at the monastery and in that single glance feel Eva fall away from me.

"Luka!" I shout. "Luka!" He appears on the balcony, takes one look at me, and then hurries down the stairs.

"That's him, isn't it?" Jester says.

"The one working for the Historian," I say, words tumbling over one another. But my tongue won't work fast enough to keep up with my racing mind. "The—the same one who answered Ivan's phone the night he died."

"What is it?" Luka asks, obviously alarmed, and then follows our gazes to the wall.

"The monastery where she found the cache," Jester says. It takes him a moment to comprehend; he's never been to Košljun. The instant it clicks into place he turns to me, face white.

Jester's trying to say that it doesn't matter if the Historian's lackey knows where I found the cache; I asked the monk to hide or destroy it—didn't I?

"Audra?" she says. But I am barely holding it together.

"When did this come in?" Luka demands.

"Around noon . . ."

I scavenge for my current phone on the table, cannot bring it to life, the battery dead. "Your phone!" I say to Jester. "You called the monastery before I arrived with Rolan, right? Find the number."

"Audra, calm down. You already have the cache and the originals are safe. What's left for them to take?" Claudia says, as Jester pulls the phone from her bag.

"Just dial it!"

I have known what it is to be so amped that I'm ready to leap from my skin. To have to run, swim, jump onto the nearest moving vehicle or off the edge of a building just to feel normal again.

That's nothing compared to this.

Jester's flustered, scrolling through numbers down the screen, trying to locate it. The minute she does, I rip the phone from her hand.

I dial and hold it to my ear. It rings and rings.

I pace away, hang up, dial again. Luka tears at his hair.

And I know they're watching us. Baffled by our reaction. But I can't tell them that the guardian of the cache in our possession keeps something far more precious to us both: the location of our daughter.

The line rings and rings. A tiny logical voice reminds me that it's the middle of the night. That the monks are asleep or in prayer.

"You drove here, right?" Luka asks Piotrek.

"Yes, but—"

"Give us your keys."

Claudia grabs my arm. "Audra, you can't go back there. There's no reason!" I shake her off as Piotrek hands me the key fob.

"Where is it?" Luka says.

"The black Skoda," he stammers, clearly perplexed. "Across the street."

"I'm sorry." I'm running toward the door as I say it, sending ahead for Arrick to unlock the one at the top. He wants to be persuaded? He's getting it.

We take the stairs two at a time. I no longer feel the pain of each step. The top door unlocks just as we reach it, and there's Arrick, looking ecstatic, eyes wide and not a little glazed over.

Move.

But I don't mean just him. The knot ahead of us parts into an aisle leading all the way to the door. A strange, manic squeal issues from Arrick as we brush past him, and I don't even want to see the look on his face.

We burst out onto the sidewalk. I click the fob, scanning the street.

"There," Luka says, pointing to the lights flashing against the opposite curb.

We run to the car, and I throw Luka the keys, get in. Find Jester's phone still in my hand.

I hit redial as we head west out of Munich.

164

The streets are a mass of congestion; I clear the lane in front of us all the way to the edge of the city. Wipe the blood from my nose. My head begins to pound until I'm practically seeing double.

"You can't keep this up," Luka says, veering into the next lane.

"I am so tired of people telling me what I can and can't do!"

"You know this is probably a trap."

No. I hadn't considered it until now.

"You think it's possible they know?" he says.

"How could they? I mean, yes—maybe. I don't know."

Trap or not, neither one of us says a thing about turning back.

I map the way to Košljun, have to retype it three times. The shortest route is six hours long. "We have to get to an airport," I say.

Luka's face is tense, his fingers curled around the steering wheel. "There won't be any flights this time of night. And by the time we get there you'll be wasted."

"Then drive faster."

Jester calls from Claudia's phone as we escape the city.

"Audra, there's no point in going."

"I have to. I'm sorry."

"If the cache was still there, they've already gotten to it. But even if they did, they don't have

165

it all. We can work with the part you brought back. And, if we work fast enough, we can do some damage before they can cover their tracks."

"It isn't just the cache," I say.

"If they've gone after the guardian, you're already too late."

I'm on the cusp of asking her to alert the local police. But there are no police we can trust. "I have to try."

"Audra, I know what you're thinking."

"I don't think you do."

"Claudia told me what happened at the monastery on Cres. I don't mean to sound heartless, but this Brother Daniel . . . he knew the risk. They all did, and took it of their own free will. He wouldn't be the first monk to die."

I don't answer.

"Listen to me. They have no more leverage on you. They're trying to lure you out with the only thing they have—and you're letting them," she says urgently. "There's nothing there for you, but I promise, they'll have eyes looking for you just in case."

"I have to."

"Audra, what's this really about?"

"I can't tell you. And you wouldn't want me to. But, Jester . . ." I think of what Claudia said back at Arrick's. "It's important. Not just to me—or Luka. For others like us." I don't dare say more.

A hissed string of French. "You should know you're scaring us."

"You're safe. Stay there—"

"Not for us, for you!"

"I'm fine."

"No, you're not."

"Just keep working on the photos. They're far more important than I am."

We hang up, and I press my fingers against my eyes.

"Is there anything at the monastery?" Luka asks. "Anything that can tie Brother Daniel to—"

"I don't know."

I find an extra shirt I recognize as Piotrek's on top of one of Claudia's wigs in the backseat, bunch it up, hold it to my nose. Try to will the bleeding to stop.

I dial the monastery again. Call, over and over, hating the ambling ring of the phone. Every minute is the longest of my life.

"I'm sorry," I whisper. Though I don't know whom I'm saying it to.

I see her again, there, in the courtyard. Huge eyes, baby-fine lashes. The tiny fingernails so neatly clipped.

"Her hair's the color of honey," I say a moment later.

He rubs his face, doesn't answer, and accelerates around a car.

We drive through the night. Speak little, except for Luka's intermittent questions.

"Did he know where Clare took her?"

"I think so."

"Daniel's not Progeny, is he?"

"No."

Luka actually seems to breathe a little easier at that. Because it means Daniel's memory can't be harvested.

I haven't heard a word from Rolan since the day we parted at the parking garage in Vienna. I wonder if he's closer to Krk than we are.

And then I wonder if he's even still alive.

I send a text to his old number, not even knowing if it's still in use.

Are you there?

No answer.

Twice I consider calling the number. The one that leads to the creepy oil slick of a voice.

Hallo, Audra.

But calling now would only alert him to the fact that he's rattled me.

"I should never have given her up," I say after a long silence. "This is my fault. If she were with us, we would know where she was. Whether she was safe. We should have gone and gotten her like you said."

I feel guilty then because there are other lives

168

at stake here: Brother Daniel, and those in the monastery itself. As far as our friends know, the brothers are the ones I'm worried about. But all I can focus on is Eva. Is this what it means to be a mother—to fixate so much on one living soul that the world shrinks to the ground she's on, and whether she's safe?

"We had no choice," Luka says finally.

"Of course we did. You probably wanted to keep her. And now here we are, in the same situation we were months ago, except this time I spend as much time trying to figure out what I knew as I do trying to keep us all alive! How did I ever think going into hiding was a good idea?"

"I didn't," he says faintly.

"What?"

"I didn't want to keep her." He rubs his eyes and refocuses on the road. "I didn't see how we could be a family. How I could be the thing I had seen other fathers be. Not like this. Not with . . . what we were. Are."

I sit in silence for a long moment before I say: "Did you ever wonder . . . did you ever think that maybe, given everything, we were never meant to be together?"

It's the kind of thing you should never ask. But I can't help it. What were we thinking, fighting these kinds of odds and four centuries of history?

"Of course I thought that," he whispers. "We both did. But I couldn't leave."

He doesn't have to say the obvious: that I did.

My phone beeps. It's Jester.

"Audra. I searched that name."

"Name . . . ?" I have no clue what she's talking about.

"Serge Deniel."

"Oh, yeah."

"He's a French billionaire with a major defense contract. He supplies most of the satellite surveillance systems in western Europe."

"That explains how they're tracking us."

"Now listen to this: It turns out that stock purchase was for the majority share of GenameBase—the DNA testing company behind three of the largest for-profit genealogy companies in the world. Each of which offers direct-to-consumer DNA testing online. All of which test mitochondrial DNA. Audra, are you hearing me?"

"Yeah."

"Do you know what that means? Do you know what mitochondrial DNA is?"

"Maybe? Just tell me," I say, impatient to get off the phone.

"It allows people to locate ancestors along a direct maternal line. It means GenameBase can trace the legacy through our mitochondrial DNA—through the female line. The DNA is passed to a son, but not to his children. The same way our gifts are. Audra, this guy has to be feeding information on lost Progeny directly to the Historian!"

My head snaps around, attention snared at last. It's the thing Rolan and Nikola both preached about. The End of Days as far as the Progeny are concerned. The reason we'll never survive another generation.

"If we can disable him, we'll cut off the Historian's access to new or orphaned Progeny," she says.

And that, at least, is something.

"How do we do that?"

"I'm not sure yet. I'll keep digging."

"Let me know." I pause. "And, Jester . . . thanks." I hang up.

We have to stop for gas. I'm about to *persuade* the guy just finishing filling up in front of us to loan us his credit card, and then I take note of his car.

We hit the road thirty seconds later in the white Lotus Elise and rocket down the highway.

Jester calls again a short time later. Her voice is strange.

"We got into the database. Audra . . . there are certain families flagged in there. Some of them—Progeny bloodlines—with one notation. Some of the names I found in the cache of photos you gave me . . . they have another. Audra, he's not just supplying Progeny names to the Historian. He's been flagging potential hunters—future Scions—from several family lines for years."

I glance at Luka.

"Hello?"

"Sorry. I—I was just thinking about the Scion map I found in the vault in Vienna," I lie. "Progeny have been trying to do the same thing for hundreds of years."

"Yes. But now . . . it's all here. We know who they are," she says with slow gravity. "Audra . . ."

For a moment, neither one of us speaks. And I know in the silence she's asking me a question. And by refusing to ask "What?" I'm telling her the answer.

"I'll check in with you later," I say and click off the call.

"What'd you find out?" Luka asks, staring straight ahead.

"She knows about you."

16

Just before 5:00 A.M. I stare out the window, Jester's phone held to my ear, the monotonous old-fashioned ring on the other end like blips of white noise. On and on, forever.

I wonder what the others will do now that they know what Luka is. A hunter. A member of the same Scion class that has killed every loved one lost to them—except for Andre, who took his life rather than let his memory be harvested.

I wonder what Claudia must think of me. If they hate me for having brought a Scion hunter into their company, home, hiding places. And not just theirs; I brought a hunter to court in Zagreb. Will Jester even answer the next time I call? For all I know, she's already broadcast my betrayal via her Progeny Dark Web. Nikola knew and could have betrayed me to his court and Tibor's both. I wonder why he never did.

It takes a moment for the interruption on the other end of the line to register.

"*Da, molim?*"

I blink, sit up, heart pounding.

"Hello? English?" I stutter, glancing at Luka, who looks at me sharply.

"Hello?"

"Hi—is Brother Daniel there? This is a friend of his. It's urgent."

"Brother Daniel—he is gone. Yesterday."

I let out a breath. "Where did he go?"

"I am not allowed—"

"Please, it's an emergency. Life and death. This is Audra Ellison. I was there with him two days ago. Do you remember me? I need to know how to reach him."

A pause.

"Hello?" I say, voice shrill.

"Audra," he says, audibly troubled. "I can only say this to you. He left in such hurry. He has gone to the monastery in Pristava. You may find him there, but he will leave again tomorrow."

"For where?" I say, my initial relief giving way to alarm.

"He did not say."

I click off, breathe my first true breath in hours. He's on the move—a good sign.

Luka glances at me.

"He's in Pristava," I say. I open a map on the phone, having no idea where Pristava is, and locate the small suburb of Nova Gorica, in Slovenia. Less than an hour away.

Luka sits back, shoulders visibly relaxing. "I want to meet him," he says. "I need . . . to see him." And I know what he means is that he needs to see Eva, and that the monk is the closest he may ever get.

We speed along the A2, and I breathe deeply again.

"He left," I say, repeating it again in my mind like a mantra, willing my heart to slow. And miraculously, it does.

I text Jester our change in course, more out of curiosity about whether she'll even respond.

And then I have a strange thought: Does it matter? She has the cache. She and her hacker friends can do more damage with that information than I ever could. I told Luka in Munich I couldn't leave—but why? I sit back, stunned. Because really, what use am I now? I've done the thing everyone wanted. I delivered. I'm a liability at this point. Why not just disappear?

I glance at Luka, and then at the relatively quiet highway before us, seeing with new eyes.

We could keep going . . . just drive. To Greece, take a boat to a quiet white cliff house somewhere on Santorini, where we can swim in the Aegean. Or as far east as Istanbul. There, to wander the Grand Bazaar and drink coffee until the day that it's safe to travel north again, to Eva. When we can become the family we were meant to be. And discover who we really are. Individually. Together. Without all of this.

But of course, it can never be that easy.

Pristava, which is called a suburb but looks more like a village, sits along the highway. The town is so small it doesn't warrant a real exit—you just spin off at the roundabout.

It's nearly dawn by the time we wind our way along a tree-lined drive toward the monastery on the hill dividing Pristava from the town of Nova Gorica, and the sky seems charged with invisible light. We're so close to the Italian border that I'm uncertain whether we've inadvertently crossed over, especially when a row of cypress trees comes into view.

The monastery is far larger than I imagined: A sprawling, white-walled complex big enough to accommodate hundreds, with a single bell tower over the chapel at one end.

We pull up to the outer entrance—a frescoed arch supported by two squat turrets, on either side of the drive. An iron gate in the complex itself stands twenty feet beyond it, still closed for the night. I can't make out the image on the arch—only the life-size crucifix that hangs before it. And I'm struck again by the morbidity of the faith that buries its luminaries beneath church floors—when they don't just leave the sarcophagi to adorn a back chapel, as the Bathory family did in the church at Nyirbator—observing death in the name of life.

I think I understand something about that now.

Luka cuts the engine ten feet from the arch and looks at me. Even in the darkness I can see that he's nervous. I take his hand.

"Ready to wake the place up?" I ask, though we both know I'll be the one doing the waking. He takes a breath and nods, as though he were going to meet Eva herself. Because if Brother Daniel is here, there is at least a chance that she is, too.

He gets out and comes around to my side of the car. I've already opened the door, but he holds it wide, as though we were on a first date. He offers his hand, and the car is so low he practically has to pull me out. As we move toward the monastery, he doesn't let go.

Five feet. They're all the difference in the world. One minute, your life is untethered, crazy, and uncertain. You could be on your way to Greece by day's end for all you know, leap into the Aegean by nightfall.

The next, you realize how wrong you are about everything.

A floodlight bursts from our right as though triggered by our motion.

Another lights up from the left.

But they're not turned on us. Their twin beams meet on the arch above us, and illuminate a horrific sight.

What I thought was a crucifix is a flesh-and-blood man, arms outstretched by ropes. Blood is dripping from his feet.

I scream, drowning out Luka's startled cry. Because I know that face contorted in death, the mouth a black rictus of pain.

"Is that him?" Luka says, in the most terrible voice I've ever heard.

I stagger back, fall to my knees, hands over my mouth, smothering the hysterics flying from it, dark things from Pandora's box. Because in that moment, it isn't just Brother Daniel on that makeshift cross, but every hope we've had—the reason I've done this, the promise of a future—hanging there dead, staining the gravel below.

Flicker of movement in the darkness. Shadows, rushing from the gate. Luka shouts, drags me to my feet and toward the car. A gunshot punches the hood.

Tires on gravel from the corner of the chapel. Headlights, blocking the drive.

Black SUVs speeding toward us.

I get the door open, fall into the seat. A shot cracks the air, shatters the passenger-side window. Luka jerks back, stumbles against the door. Crimson explodes down his sleeve. I scream and grab him by the shirt, haul him in against me.

"Luka!"

"Drive," he says roughly, rolling toward the dash.

I crawl across to the driver's seat. Start the car, throw it into gear. Gun forward zero to thirty, plowing one of the forms up onto the hood. Shift into reverse, gears grinding, spin back with a spray of gravel. The form tumbles off as Luka's open door swings wide.

I hurl hard persuasion toward the dark convoy. No dice; our back window splinters into a fantastic web of glass.

I shove us into drive. An instant later, we're tearing across the grass. Luka's door slams shut as I weave between the cypress trees I admired just moments ago, each one a killer now.

"Are you all right?" It's an idiot question. Luka's been shot. There's blood all over. What I'm really asking is: *Will you live?*

"I'm fine," he says tightly. "Try not to kill us."

There's a vineyard just south of the complex; we hurtle down an unpaved lane between the gnarled vines. Headlights leap into the rearview mirror as we reach the end of the row. I veer down the side of the hill past a large estate, cut toward the main road.

We hit the pavement with a scrape, turn hard left.

Behind us, the dark convoy appears around the hill, speeding toward us from the monastery drive. My silent command sends a spike through my brain as the lone car between us skids across the road. Not enough to cut them off, but maybe enough to slow them down.

The SUV that pursued us through the vineyard bounces onto the pavement—and then accelerates, closing the gap between us.

My last-second turn in to a residential maze

of streets throws Luka into the console. The SUV is on us.

"What are you doing?" he grits out. But the map by which I navigated the way to the monastery is pixel clear in my mind.

I broadcast a desperate plea. Four blocks later, a car pulls out of a driveway in our wake. The SUV veers into a yard and swings back, still in pursuit.

Another car backs into the street behind us. And another and another. The SUV clips the first and rams into the second, shoving it into the third.

I head for the next major intersection, where a car waits as though for an invisible light that will never change.

I stop, get out, and run to the other side for Luka, whose left shoulder is soaked in blood. I drape his good arm behind my neck, and we hurry toward the other vehicle, already exited by its driver.

Ten seconds later, we're speeding toward the main roundabout and taking the second spoke—east on a dimly lit road, trying to outrun the dawn.

17

We pull over just long enough for me to find and shred a rag from the trunk, do my best to bandage Luka's shoulder through my blurring vision. He's pale but alert, and the shot is clean—a deep graze. Or as clean, at least, as a gunshot wound can be, which seems like an oxymoron to me.

"You need a doctor," I say.

"We need to get farther away. I'll live."

My vision is blurring badly. Luka can sense it and insists on driving.

"No, you're hurt."

"And you're about to black out."

I pull over. We switch seats.

We head east, south, east again, directly into the first glow of morning. Not trusting that we are safe enough to speak about what happened. Unable to even if we wanted.

I have lost track of where we are. On the map. In life. I bend low until my forehead rests against the glove box, face hidden from the world. A world I no longer want to be a part of.

Luka doesn't try to comfort me. He has no comfort to give. Twice I hear him pound the steering wheel. Exclaim something in Croatian, followed each time with a surge of violent speed.

My nose won't stop bleeding. My head pounds.

181

I claw at the neck of my sweater, convinced it's choking me. I can't breathe.

I can't not see him. Brother Daniel, hanging from that arch. His bulging eyes. His contorted mouth, as though his life had been ripped from it. His hands, purple and swollen.

I'd say a prayer for him if I knew how. If I thought God heard the words of sinners.

No, not sinners. The cursed.

And I don't know what I'm mourning more— that Brother Daniel's selfless commitment was so violently repaid . . . or the state of my soul. Because despite my horror, all I can think about is our daughter.

"Do you think . . ." Luka begins at last. He swipes at his forehead, glossy with sweat. "Do you think he told them anything?"

"The blood was still dripping from his toes," I whisper. I don't say the rest: That the threat in that text was twelve hours old by the time Jester found it.

But Brother Daniel died more recently than that.

"They tortured him," he says.

Silence, heavy between us. I press my palms to my eyes. "We'll never find Eva. Oh my God . . . we've lost her."

"No. There has to be a way. We'll find Clare!"

"How?" I demand. "Without a picture? Without knowing her real name?"

"How many Franciscan nuns can there be?"

"For all I know, she isn't even really a nun!"

No one in this mess is who they seem to be. Everyone is wearing a face not their own—deceiving someone, if only themselves. Luka, with his eyes wide shut, believing if he stays far enough from his family, they'll be safe from retribution. Claudia, that blood equals loyalty. Piotrek, that her relationship with him is any-thing more than survival. Jester, that she could trust me, if only because of whom they all wanted me to be.

That I would somehow save them.

We drive aimlessly for miles. I don't know where we're going, nor do I care. The sun is up, blithe and indifferent, shining more brightly than it has in a week.

"Even if he told them about her, it doesn't mean they found her," Luka says at last.

I nod, for his sake.

If fate is merciful, Eva is still safe, wherever she is. Is being moved, even now. Or already in a place that even Brother Daniel himself didn't know. Having guarded the interests of Progeny so long, he must have known some-thing about their methods of keeping secrets—even from themselves.

"Now what?" Luka says.

But I don't have any answers. All I know is that there is no going to Greece or Turkey for us. Without surety of Eva's safety, we are tied, once again, to a land haunted by every soul associated with Elizabeth Bathory. Prisoners as surely as if we had been walled up within its borders.

18

We stop, midmorning, at a clinic outside Ljubljana. With dwindling reserves, I *persuade* a young doctor to meet us at the back door, gloves already on. I refuse to let her brush me away as she treats Luka, giving him a shot of something for the pain, a bottle of pills for later. After which she leaves town on an impromptu holiday. My suggestion.

We find a small inn. Take a room under an American name.

Jones. Because why not.

Nothing matters now.

I sit dully in a faded orange chair that smells faintly of cigarette smoke facing a TV that isn't on.

"I can't keep doing this," I say.

Luka gazes with half-lidded eyes at me from the bed. He doesn't answer. He doesn't need to. Because neither can he.

I resolved two days ago to fight. But in the hours like lifetimes since then, I've been running just as much as—more than—before.

At some point, Luka sleeps. I do, too, though my dreams are filled with tortured monks and dying messiahs, dark mouths agape. The archive cache flies past me in a windstorm and I try to catch as many pages as I can before they blow away.

The last paper I grab is not a page from the collection at all. Just a headline in my hand:

KILL LIST.

I jolt awake in the orange chair, heart racing.

Because it's true: The cache is a veritable kill list of the most powerful Scions in the world. What's a Historian with no more Scions to command?

I get up, go to the bathroom to splash water on my face. Scrub away the blood crusted beneath my nose. Stare at the person in the mirror, water dripping from her chin.

Is that the face of a mother? A savant, a savior . . .

. . . a monster?

Because I may not be what anyone thought, but I'm not ready to roll over and die. As long as there's a chance Eva's still alive, I will fight to find her, to hold that small hand in mine.

But I am no monster. Even if it's in my blood.

I turn and lean back against the tiled bathroom counter, racking my brain, the pickax pounding in my head having faded to a dull thud.

If I could find the Historian, I would gladly rest my moral stance long enough to kill her. I could do that if it meant saving Eva, and Luka. But my only link to her is the voice on the phone Jester tried and failed to trace.

There's Nikola. But if what Tibor said was

true—that he's not the one the Historian truly wants—I have no doubt he'd kill me in an instant.

Shunned by my friends, who do I have left? Tibor, cut off from the underground in exile—presumably without a hunter on him now that they've all turned their attention to me.

But Tibor did give me something in return: a Scion powerful enough to be at odds with the Historian. A surveillance contractor with the means to help me find Eva.

There are no clear sides in this, Tibor had said.

I fish the phone from my pocket and click it on.

Three missed calls appear on the screen.

Jester.

The calls came in, minutes apart, around the time we arrived at the monastery. No wonder I didn't hear them. Their quick succession worries me, and I instinctively dial back.

She answers on the second ring.

"Audra? Are you all right?"

"We're fine."

A moment of silence, and then: "I just saw the police report from Pristava."

I'm sure. Another heinous act to add to my public litany of sins.

"He was dead when we got there," I say. I don't go into details. On the other end, I can hear traffic, a truck passing them by. They must have left Munich.

"Where are you now?" she says.

"Ljubljana. Luka's hurt."

"Can you get to Graz?"

"Probably." I hesitate. "Why?"

"We'll meet you there."

I shake my head. "I can't leave Luka. I won't."

"Bring him."

This is so not the disowning I expected, and though I don't say it, I'm wary of her motives.

My suspicion translates in my silence.

"I won't lie, we all felt betrayed," she says.

I feel awkward knowing she's cooped up in a car where Claudia and Piotrek can hear what she's saying, if not our entire conversation.

"I'm really sorry."

"We talked for a very long time this morning. I was angry. We all were. But you should know that Claudia defended you."

Claudia, my staunchest critic? I wonder if we're talking about the same person.

"She told me what Ivan said about you," Jester says. "That you never did anything without reason and many things contrary to it. I don't know what you're doing in the company of a hunter, let alone how you ever became his lover, knowing what he is. But I saw the proof of life recordings when I downloaded your SIM chips. How he told you to leave him and run. The way he refused to respond in an effort to save you, and tried to say good-bye . . ."

I'm silent.

"We also know he must have faked your death so you could disappear. I don't understand your relationship, and I have to say I don't approve. But it's obvious what he's done for you."

"He has nowhere to go," I say. Just like me. Just like Rolan, wherever he is, if he's even alive.

"Well, maybe one day soon none of this will matter. Audra, we have enough on one of the names—the Curia president, Lazlo Becskei—to leak it."

"What? Where?" I ask. "You can't go to the police or the media or Interpol—"

"To several whistle-blower and international open journalistic sites that publish information from anonymous sources."

"You're sending it to *WikiLeaks*?"

She clicks her tongue. "No. To *newer* organizations committed to government and corporate truth telling. Founded, in part, by yours truly."

"Is there anything you *don't* do online?"

"A few things," she says, sounding vaguely amused.

"How could you possibly know the day would come that you'd have any hard proof to expose?"

"You told me."

I blink in the fluorescent light of the bathroom.

"Why didn't you say anything?"

"Apparently there are a few things we have not told one another," she says wryly. "Anyway, I'm uploading the information on the first one to our servers in Switzerland now. With any luck, it'll be on the radar of media companies, conspiracy theorists, and watchdog groups by tomorrow morning."

"So fast . . ." I breathe.

"We will release information on one high-ranking Scion every day—or as close to that as possible—for as long as we can . . . or until there is nothing left to release."

"That's— Wow. That's great."

But even as I say it, I know that while the leaks may piss off the Historian, they also won't shut her down. Not completely.

I point this last part out to Jester.

"You're right. But it *will* create a breach in her support network of high-ranking and powerful members. Members the others will be forced to cut ties to. More than that, it will scare them. Don't you see, Audra? *This* is what she wanted to avoid—the reason she wanted the cache. Without them, she cannot function!"

"It won't stop the killing."

"No. If anything, it may accelerate it," she says grimly. "The hunters who have yet to be initiated into the Scions' corporate ranks—those who haven't completed their kills—are zealous about their calling."

"I've heard," I say.

"Which is why I am so surprised someone like Luka could abandon it."

"It wasn't easy for him." The way Luka describes it, it was more like torture. A moral quandary of abandoning what he had been raised to believe was the highest good in order to love what he had been taught to be the worst evil . . . that nearly ended in his suicide.

"Yes, the Historian may strike back, and you are the top trophy. Which is why you have to get somewhere safe. Meet us in Graz. Besides, we need your help."

I recognize the olive branch for what it is. But she and I both know there's nothing I can do to help. That my being there will only put them in more danger.

Something else is bothering me, though.

"We know who the hunters are . . . We have their names."

"But not their targets. Only the Historian has that. Believe me, I have searched."

"You could release them."

"To what end? Until they kill we have nothing on them beyond a crazy four-hundred-year-old conspiracy theory."

I dig my fingers into my hair. "We have the names of the killers *before they kill* and we can't even stop them!"

"This is not *Minority Report*. But, Audra, this is the first blow any Progeny has ever struck against the Scions. It is something."

"I know," I say.

I also know it's not enough.

"Don't go to Graz," I say abruptly. "Go somewhere else, don't tell me where."

"Why—what will you do?"

"I'll be in touch. But do me a favor . . . Hold off on releasing any information on Serge Deniel."

I can almost hear her frown. "All right," she says at last. To her credit, she doesn't ask why. She doesn't need to; by asking her not to talk about it, I've told her enough.

"There's something else you should know," she says, before we hang up. "Another text came for you."

I don't want to know.

"I'll forward it."

The phone chimes seconds after we hang up. I stare fixedly at the piece of cheap art on the wall above the toilet until I think my heart will beat out of my chest. And then I look at the screen.

A pity about Brother Daniel. He had such interesting stories to tell.

I lean over, haul in a ragged breath. But this time, it isn't just fear constricting my lungs. My fingers begin to shake as I send a message of my own.

I'm coming for you.

I pull up a browser, search out the parent company of GenameBase.

The next call I make is to Serge Deniel.

19

It takes no fewer than three transfers to reach his personal secretary, who, of course, does not let me through.

"I'm afraid he cannot be reached. If you care to leave a message . . ."

"Tell him it's Audra Ellison. Give him this number," I say.

"Is he expecting your call?"

"Oh, he'll want to talk to me."

I hang up and lean against the cracked bathroom wall. Stare up at the ceiling, and then roll my head toward the door and Luka, resting on the other side of it.

The phone buzzes in my hand.

I glance at it. No number I recognize. Same area code I just dialed.

Click on.

"Hello."

"Audra?" A male voice.

"Speaking."

"This is Serge Deniel." His accent is French but far less pronounced than Jester's. "Our mutual friend said you would contact me. What can I do for you?"

Oh, did he? I imagine Tibor's smug expression.

"Do you know who I am?"

Muffled sound of traffic, distant horns. He's in a car, but not distracted enough to be driving.

"As a matter of fact, I do."

"Then I think the question is what I can do for you."

"We should meet. Where are you?"

"Ljubljana."

"And yet the news reports social media sightings of you in Italy."

I lift my brows. Jester.

"Yeah, well, I get around."

"I am in Zürich. I can be there in two hours."

"How will you guarantee my safety?"

"I will phone you when I land. You can name your meeting place then."

"I want you to know that I have passed sensitive information about your crimes to several of my . . . associates. Damning evidence similar to what's going public on one of your fraternal brothers tonight. They have explicit instructions to release your information immediately if anything should happen to me."

"It seems you have my testicles on the chopping block," he says tightly.

"I'm glad we understand one another. Have a safe flight."

I click off and open a browser, search for images of Serge Deniel. Forties, dark, short hair. Prominent widow's peak. Slightly crooked nose. Blue eyes.

I go out to wake Luka. Sit down beside him, shake his good shoulder gently.

He turns his head toward me, reaches up and pulls me toward him.

"Luka . . ."

His eyes don't open. His head tilts up.

His lips are soft. In all this time, we haven't kissed. We haven't made love. Not since . . . I don't remember what day it was. Not even the day of his rescue. Just pain, worry, and flight, ever since. Because a piece of us is missing. My expression crumples, and his arm folds around my shoulders.

"We'll find her," he whispers. And I don't know if he's awake or still in his drug-induced sleep. But I kiss him, wanting to make it true.

I miss the way things were before. Before I nearly lost him. Before I knew about Eva. I feel guilty admitting that even to myself. I wrote in my journal I wanted to give myself the chance to fall in love with him twice. And I suppose I did—though I'm pretty sure this isn't how I imagined it happening. Or Luka, either. I saw the way he looked at me when I woke up on the cruise ship. And again, in the too-short moments we thought everything was all right in Munich. And what did I do? I started an argument.

"I need you to wake up," I whisper. "Jester called. They haven't excommunicated us." I give him a small smile.

"That's . . . surprising," he murmurs, voice husky.

"But I need to leave."

"Where?"

I press my lips together, wonder if I can lie straight to his face.

His eyes open, pupils large in the light falling on the bed from the bathroom. "Stop protecting me."

"I'm not."

I am.

He rolls toward his good shoulder with a grimace. "Where are we going?"

"I contacted Serge."

He's wide awake in an instant.

"What?"

"Isn't that what you wanted?"

"I said it was worth considering—not that you should do it!" he says. He turns his head with a soft curse, not looking at me.

"It's the only option left."

He sits up slowly on the floral coverlet (why do cheap hotels always have floral bedspreads?) and glances at his shoulder. The bandage is crusted with blood. But at least none of it's fresh.

"Where are we meeting him?"

I frown. "He's coming to Ljubljana."

"What time?"

"Luka . . ."

"I said what time?"

"He's calling in less than two hours."

He nods and slides his feet to the floor, glances at me.

"Thank you. For not slipping out and leaving me a note or something."

" 'Course."

But I thought about it.

My phone rings at 2:07 P.M. Ten minutes early.

"I've just touched down in Ljubljana," Serge says.

"The corner of Slovenska and Rimska in thirty minutes," I say. "A car will pick you up—and only you."

He hesitates. I can practically hear the pull of his sleeve as he checks his watch. "Done." He hangs up.

We gather our few things—phones, car keys, a couple jackets brought by housekeeping from the lost and found, which is also where I managed to snag a clean top and hat—and leave the room.

The minute we step outside, I know we have made a horrendous mistake.

Across the parking lot, right where we left it, is the beaten-up Lotus.

In the horror and aftermath of losing Brother Daniel, we never changed cars.

Luka spins away with a curse.

"Oh my God," I whisper, mouth dry, panic rising in my chest. Luka grabs me by the arm, pulls me back under the eaves.

There's a beer garden in front of the inn's hokey little restaurant, sectioned off by a wooden fence. We hurry down the side of the building, through the entrance, and under the canopy of green outdoor umbrellas, past tables of cigarette smokers sitting around their afternoon drinks. I lower my head, will us to pass unseen until we emerge through the restaurant and out the back door.

The inn butts up against several buildings just off a highway, and we skirt between them toward the road.

A minute later a car pulls up just long enough for me to persuade the driver to take a long walk.

"What were we thinking?" Luka explodes behind the wheel.

But in our shock and grief, we weren't. Luka squints at the rearview mirror. I glance behind us and then crane my neck to peer at the sky. Crack the window, even, to listen to the traffic around us. But it's clear. Not a siren, not a blue light. Is it possible fate actually dealt us a break? God knows we're due.

"Call him," Luka says. "We can't meet him here."

Something like desperation rises up from my panic. "We've been ditching cars for days," I say. "They wouldn't expect us to have it. For all they know, someone else drove the Lotus here. Besides, according to social media sightings, we're in Italy."

"Yeah? And how long ago was that?"

"It was . . ." I glance at the clock.

Hours ago.

"We'll meet him. Just not here. Tell him to get to Karlovac."

I expel a slow breath and pull out my phone. It rings in my hand.

Serge.

"Audra, we have a problem. My source tells me they are looking for you inside the city."

"Are you sure?" I glance around us again, holding the phone away from my ear so that Luka can hear.

"Quite. Where are you?"

I don't respond.

"The airport is twenty-six kilometers north. Can you get there? The plane will be ready."

I glance at Luka.

"We're coming."

"You have someone with you." It's not really a question and he doesn't seem surprised. "I would normally recommend you stay off the highway, but . . ."

"I know." Get out of the city fast. Story of my life.

"What are you driving?" he says.

I hesitate. Glance around us again.

"Audra, I know you don't trust me. But I didn't come here just to lose you to the Historian. I can help you. Let me."

"See you at the airport." I end the call.

We speed west, weave into the passing lane as the traffic around us veers right.

We enter the exchange, and cars scatter from us like oil separating from water. I grab the wad of cheap tissue I shoved in my pocket back at the inn, hold it beneath my nose as my head begins to pound.

We enter the expressway. Traffic is thicker here than I would have guessed for a city the size of Ljubljana. I send four and then five cars—I can't tell how many because right now I'm seeing two of each of them—out the next exit.

As vehicles enter the on-ramp to our right, it takes more effort to keep the left lane clear. I gasp out loud at the sharp shard of pain behind my eye. For a moment, the cars crowd closer.

"There's a construction zone slowing traffic just before the bridge," Luka says.

"I see it."

"You have to clear it."

"I said I got it."

Luka's mouth tightens as he speeds up. The bridge is a hundred yards ahead, the construction zone camped just ten before it.

My hands go to my head, which feels like it might explode at any minute as my vision flutters like a monitor on the fritz. I squeeze my eyes shut and reopen them, force them to focus, but I'm losing it: In the side-view mirror a truck and several vehicles break away from the right lane in our wake and speed forward.

Thirty yards ahead of us, a truck abruptly pulls from the construction zone and lumbers onto the bridge. And I can't tell if that's just me, losing my grip, or—

"It's a trap!" Luka says as the truck pulls to a stop at an angle across both lanes.

Traffic closes behind us. There's nowhere to go. Four men have exited the truck in black tactical gear, armed.

Luka points ahead of us, to a smaller SUV. "I need that, right now."

For a hellacious instant, it doesn't move.

"AUDRA!"

Eva.

The SUV swerves from line. Accelerates onto the bridge.

Luka floors the gas.

"What are you doing—" The last word flies from my mouth with my breath as Luka closes the distance in seconds and then pulls into the right lane, even with the SUV's back tire.

At the last instant he turns directly into the SUV. I scream, the sound cut short by the impact. The SUV swings around, goes rolling into the air.

I watch it career for an eternity as we slide forward after it, each split second like a thousand frozen images captured in the flash of a strobe.

The SUV smashes into the truck and those standing before it with a deafening crash.

We skid to a halt yards away, panting and breathless.

Luka glances at me. "Are you all right?"

I nod, ears still ringing.

He shifts the car into reverse, hits the gas, and glances in the rearview mirror. His eyes widen. A horn blares just before a truck rams us into the wreckage, sends us spinning, bouncing into the guardrail. I scream, grab for the dash, the door, trying to brace myself.

The world upends, sickeningly weightless. Glimpse of wreckage, glimpse of sky. Green trees . . . the river below.

There is nothing soft about water. The impact crushes, and I am dazed. Vaguely aware of us traveling, carried away. Hearing everything—nothing—at once as the world is a roar, more muffled by the instant. Except for Luka, shouting my name.

It's cold. Shocking my limbs to reflexive life. Rushing around my legs to my waist, seizing up my lungs. I need to close the window, or open it the rest of the way—I'm not sure which. But I can't move. Am vaguely aware of Luka struggling, saying something. Grappling over me. Working desperately at the window, the cold rising to my neck.

At some point, he cradles my chin and lifts it

above the water. No longer shouting. His words soft and shuddering. He kisses me, his lips wet but warm around his whispers until the river swallows them whole.

I need to tell him something. To live. That I love him. And something else—to not let them take my memory. To take it for himself. Because I know now what this is stealing my voice, making it bubble up before my eyes with my breath. But no air comes back. Sends me jerking against the door, bashing my head against the window when I try.

I always knew that the fight of my life might cost me my life. That's why they call it that, isn't it? Because even if it isn't a lifetime long, it has consumed just that, in full.

Weightless. All is quiet. Except for Luka, still struggling over me as the sound fades from my ears.

For the first time I can remember, I am not afraid.

20

I can't spot the little midge floating on the water. An arm stretches out past my shoulder.

"Look right there, in front of that rock."

I squint and follow the line of that finger toward a tiny white thing like the tuft of a dandelion, riding its way downstream.

"I see it!"

A quick snatch and it disappears. The figure behind me straightens and sets the hook with a whoop. Begins to reel him in.

"Got him, Audra!"

"We got him!" I shout and clap my hands, glance up at him with a grin. The sun is behind his head, and his eyes crinkle at me. He bends down and sets the rod in my hands, his larger ones over mine as we tug and reel.

It is the first fish I've ever caught myself. I'm five, and that night when we get back to our summer cabin, my mom takes a picture of me proudly holding it next to my father. His name is Jesse and hers is Amy. She has laugh lines and freckles from too many days in the sun and long, curly hair that is nothing like mine.

My best friends Hannah, Bryn, Blake, and I lounge across the bed of my parents' RV in shorts damp from our swimsuit bottoms, watching the eleventh Doctor defeat Prisoner Zero and then escape the Weeping Angels.

We've spent the entire day slathering sunscreen on ourselves and floating in a giant inner tube on Lake Okoboji, and the evening eating burgers and s'mores until mosquitoes drove us inside. Never mind that I've been forced into hours of strategic planning about how Blake's going to get Josh Hoffman to ask her to Homecoming this year. At least it keeps them from asking about whether I've talked to Aiden, whether I want to, or have thought about it (the answer is no). Bad enough I have to see him at swim practice.

Meanwhile, Hannah's bemoaning the fact that she's the only one close to flunking chemistry ever since the day I managed to memorize the periodic table during a single study hall.

"How'd you do that, anyway?" she says.

I say something about my mom being on a ginkgo biloba kick, not wanting to talk about my new meds.

We make plans about Iowa State, where we're all going to room together. Figure out how much money it'd take to backpack across Europe after freshman year.

It is the best sweet sixteen ever.

Two days later, my parents tell me I'm adopted.

• • •

Josh just asked me to Homecoming. I don't even hang out with him or his friends! I said no, but I should never have confided in Hannah. Now Blake's refusing to talk to me.

My parents finally agree to let me transfer schools a week after I quit the swim team. Now that we've gone a third humiliating round with the principal and Bryn's and Blake's parents over the fake account that showed up online— complete with a series of slutty confessions and pictures of me changing into my swimsuit— they're finally letting me disappear from Sioux City High forever.

The night they tell me, I cry. They think it's relief, and it is. But I'm angry. Angry they waited so long. At my former friends for what they did. At everyone who looked at the page and even shared it. And at myself, for feeling so ashamed.

Emily is squeezing my hand so hard it hurts. Her eyes shine when she gets excited like that— like a weird cross between a girl and a puppy. When they call my name instead of hers, I brace for the worst—which turns out not to be a good thing because she literally screams and grabs me and jumps up and down so that I have to hold on to the side of my dress before I have a major malfunction.

Going up for that tiara is the most mortifying moment of my life.

"Congratulations!" Emily squeals at me when the whole thing is over and the royal couple has been announced, before snapping a series of selfies that I mostly endure. But I am grateful—so grateful because of the kind of friend she is. Because I know she wanted this and I know I did not. Had to be convinced even to come tonight with a group of our friends in a dress my mom picked up on sale just yesterday from the mall and a pair of Emily's shoes.

The whole year's been weird that way, from three guys asking me to prom to girls like Emily wanting to be my friend—a bizarre turn halfway through my new school's first semester that actually made me wonder if I was being set up.

She laughs and teases me about being the first chess team prom princess in the history of high school as I wonder how long I have to keep this thing on my head.

"We're celebrating with giant burgers at Harlow's!" she says to the others.

I say I need to check in at home, tell the group of friends I came with to go on without me, I'll get a ride and meet them. It's a lie. The truth is, I'm having a case of postsocial anxiety, weird energy jittering in my veins, pulse pounding in my head. As soon as I leave the gym, I take off Emily's shoes and jog barefoot down the street.

It makes me feel better. At home I change into jeans and sneakers, tell my parents my friends are waiting outside . . . and then run the two miles to Harlow's.

But Emily never makes it. She dies in a car accident with her boyfriend on the way to the restaurant.

I mope after graduation. Take a job at the bingo hall if only because no one my age would ever be caught dead there. Buy some weed from the renowned stoner down the street and smoke it in the backyard after work—until the night my dad catches me and takes away the car for a month.

I don't care; I've become selectively agoraphobic, careful not to go anywhere I might run into anyone from my old school . . . unwilling to see anyone I know from my new one. I make excuses when friends text or call—or I just don't respond—and after a while, they stop. That's all it takes to lose new friends: a few weeks.

I beg off on spending Fourth of July at the lake, say I have to work (a lie), that I'll catch some barbecue beforehand at Aunt Cherie's.

Which is why I'm at home when the police show up.

It rains the day of their funeral. Standing there with my umbrella, all I can think is, *I'm an orphan. Again.* Which is stupid, because I'm eighteen and practically an adult, which means I'm too old to be an orphan.

At my aunt's house I excuse myself to the all-season room to pace in front of the screened windows. Because I will scream if one more person says they're sorry or asks if there's anything I need.

I need my parents back, you moron. I need them to never have gone to the lake. To not have gone boating.

Or at least to have taken me with them.

I stare out at the rain soaking Cherie's potted geraniums. Right now the kids I grew up with are working summer jobs, hooking up at parties, and getting DUIs. And I'm preparing to box up my parents' possessions and store them in Cherie's garage. She's already hired a lawyer to put the house I grew up in on the market. In which case, I want nothing more to do with Iowa.

Only problem is, I turned down University of Chicago for Grinnell before all of this went down.

The next day I load up my car and take off for Illinois. Show up at the admissions office. Plead with them to give me a hearing . . . convince them to extend my invitation.

And come away, miraculously, with an acceptance and a scholarship.

The minute I arrive in Budapest a month ahead of my junior year abroad, I am awestruck. By the architecture on the corners of buildings. The millennia of history beneath my feet. The Parisian feel of the cafés I pass by on my way from Erzsebet Square to Andrassy Avenue— the Hungarian Champs-Elysees. By the hilly Buda and the urban Pest. The Gothic dignity of Parliament on the bank of the stately Danube. Especially at night.

I feel small and intimidated and try not to look like a gape-mouthed tourist as I walk the last few blocks to my hostel. But I also feel free. Free from the strange, sidewise glances of students on campus that make me imagine they've found some digital ghost of my fake online past. Of the therapy I know was important in the wake of everything that happened in high school and after—but that caused me to relive it twice a month for years. Of the obligatory trips back for holidays and summers that once took place at the lake I can no longer stand to visit. And of Bryson Wells, who had a religious crisis of conscience shortly after we started sleeping together that caused him to propose as though it were an edict handed straight down from God.

Free from the Audra Ellison I was. Finally able to start fresh, scorched earth left behind.

I have twenty-seven days before I officially arrive at Eotvos Lorand University, and I will need every one of them.

I have come to Budapest to find my birth mother.

I've been to fourteen offices, and visited three leads to a woman that the DNA genealogy site I used before leaving the States said was my closest match. Some kind of cousin or something, last name Szabo.

But I can't find this cousin, because when I visit the three addresses associated with her, no one has heard of her.

In rudimentary Hungarian (those "fluent in three months" learning programs lie!), I leave my mobile number and where I'm staying just in case they remember anything later. But I'm discouraged.

I had convinced myself if I came here I might find not only the Barbara Bocz of my adoption papers but some missing piece of myself. I had allowed myself the furtive fantasy of seeing her face, of her even hugging and crying over me, the daughter she gave up because of some teenage pregnancy or broken relationship. Had even imagined the possibility that by the time I started classes at the university's art program, we'd have begun meeting for weekly coffee, or lunch. That she would tell me stories about where she grew up and I could find out if she has the same ADHD I was diagnosed with two years ago. I'd show her pictures of Sioux City, Iowa, and even the parents who raised me. A slow way to get to know one another after twenty years apart while planning future Christmas holidays in my new home country.

I've never allowed myself to dwell on the possibility that she might not want to be found, that she might go out of her way to avoid me if she found out I was looking for her.

But that hasn't turned out to be a problem, because right now I can't even find the cousin who, for all practical purposes, seems to have disappeared.

I'm sitting in a little café off Andrassy Avenue, several blocks from Heroes' Square, which I make a point to visit every evening when it's lit up.

I love this place, from its bohemian décor to its small plates. Namely, the foie gras I fell in love with in a little café during a weekend trip to Trieste and the Croatian coast.

I'm eating it in tiny bites with bits of apricot jam—switching between it and the bowl of requisite goulash and glass of red wine—when I realize there's a guy staring at me from the bar. I feel it before I see it; I know that sensation. I had thought the whole staring-at-Audra thing was distinctly American, but turns out, it's universal.

I lift my spoon to my mouth and my middle finger at the same time. I raise my eyes to be sure he got my international message, and end up glancing away.

213

Because he's laughing. Worse than that, he's sexy—from the shape of his mouth to the light brown hair falling over his eyes. All Euro-masculine chic.

I fish thirty-five hundred forint out of my purse, lay it on the table, and prepare to leave.

Too late. Because he's already walking over, a glass of red wine in each hand.

And I'm sitting here with liver breath.

"This is my apology for pissing you off," he says and sets the glass in front of me.

"Apology accepted," I say, getting up.

"Come on. If you don't at least take a sip, it is worse than giving me the finger."

I sigh. Sit back down, pick up the glass.

"*Egészegedre*," I say.

He raises his glass and laughs. "You know when you pronounce it like that, it means 'to your full ass.' "

"Oh. Well, if the toast fits . . ."

He smiles, and acquiesces. "*Egészegedre.* But, if I'm going to toast to this, then perhaps I should know your name."

I briefly consider lying. "Audra."

"Audra," he says, sitting down across from me. "I'm Luka."

University has started, and I'm out with several new classmates at a ruin pub on Kazinczy Street—a funky bar built into a derelict building

214

with an eclectic mix of reclaimed furniture in the Jewish quarter just down the street from an honest-to-God *mikvah*. We're sitting in an old Communist-era Trabant that looks like it was cut open with a can opener before it was converted to seating in the middle of the courtyard. Stefan is telling some story, but I am checking my phone. It's been three days since I've heard from Luka.

Not that he has any reason to call me. I insulted him three times before I gave him a vague indication that I ate in the area most evenings. I deliberately switched to a more obscure café the following night . . .

. . . and he found me.

So we toasted our asses and ate foie gras together as he talked about growing up in Croatia and coming to Budapest for university. That night I let him walk me along Andrassy past Heroes' Square.

"Do you know who they are?" he says, gesturing to the semicircle of statues on their columns.

"No. Not really," I say.

"Neither do I." He laughs. "But they're impressive guys, right?"

I excuse myself, move along the back wall past a seating area of converted bathtubs-turned-sofas to the restroom near the back alley.

The sensation hits my entire body like a wave rolling in from sea. I actually stumble, catch myself against a wall. I can't possibly be that drunk, having had only a couple of beers.

From the corner of my eye, I see a group of shadows pass through the alley beyond. All midnight leather and black buckled boots, flowing crimson kimonos and soundless stilettos. The girl in the Frankenstein-green shearling coat swivels her head as she passes, fixes me with a glittering gaze. The others glance at me sidelong. One of them—the guy with a black harlequin diamond painted around his eye—winks as they pass out of sight.

I hurry down the corridor to the restroom.

When I emerge, the girl in the green coat is blocking the hallway. The others wait in the alley beyond.

"Who are you?" she says, stepping in close. Purple lashes framing wide-set eyes take in every inch of my face. She's wearing yellow lipstick.

"No one," I stammer.

"I doubt that." She smiles. "What is your name?"

"Audra." I don't know why I tell her, except that I feel an instant affinity for this colorful creature. Which is ridiculous, given that I have as much in common with her as a pony has with a unicorn.

"Audra," she says, rolling it over her tongue like wine. "Where did you come from, Audra?"

"The U.S. I—I should get back to my friends."

"You just found them," she says. "My name is Katia."

21

My life has unraveled to bare threads. But for the first time, I see the pattern in it. For the first time, it makes sense.

And no sense at all.

"You are one of *us*," Katia said the night I met her after I abandoned my classmates and went with Katia and her companions to a secluded basement pub.

I laughed at her, openly, though the moment she said it something in me knew she was right.

"What do you mean?"

"You might as well have that," Katia said, pointing to the shot I ordered. I noted not one of them was drinking anything stronger than coffee. Nothing *but* coffee, actually.

"We have a story to tell you."

Within five minutes, I was convinced she was high. Manic, strung out on something. But her eyes were the most lucid blue I had ever seen.

Of course I didn't believe her. How could I? A four-hundred-year old vendetta. Descendants of the Blood Countess.

I don't even like history.

"The minute we got to the alley, I knew someone was here. You, Audra. And you felt it, too."

But that could have been anything. Curiosity.

Envy. Fascination. They were, after all, mesmerizing to look at.

Which did not explain their fascination with me.

I didn't miss the way they exchanged glances when I told them about the search for my mother. The cousin I'd gleaned from the genealogy site. The silent alarm that passed between them.

"Look it up, if you like," she said, handing me her phone. "But, Audra . . . You need to know you're in danger."

I meet them at the ruin pub again the next night. That is the first time they take me to the underground court in Budapest. But not directly. We stop at Katia's flat, and I laugh when her teenage friend Claudia appears with a blue powdered wig, brief bustled skirt, stockings, and a golden mask.

"You're kidding, right?"

Turns out, she's not.

I sense immediately that Claudia resents sharing Katia's attention. Still, I laugh as I put on the costume. I take out my phone for a picture, but Katia seizes it from me.

"No," she says, shaking her head as though I were a wayward three-year-old.

That first night at court, the frenetic pulse of the music in that cavern amps my adrenaline, burns it like rocket fuel. A strobe stutters over frenetic bodies, their frozen masks and glowing tattoos spiking my vision in a burst of snapshots—teasing my photographic memory before obliterating it. Pushes me beyond anxiety to the supreme thunder of white noise, and serenity.

Katia's right. I may not have found my mother, but I have found my own.

"This is your family, Audra!" she shouts over the pounding music.

And I know that I am home.

I withdrew from university three days ago. I'd been unable to make the morning classes for weeks, sleeping till afternoon. No longer caring about art history, about art at all. About anything but returning to the endless miles of tunnels beneath Castle Hill.

That, and Luka.

He hasn't questioned my story about needing time off from university, helps me move into a sparse apartment on the bottom floor of a house near Buda Hill. The nights that I don't crash at Katia's, he comes to visit in the afternoon. Sometimes we go to the market. Sometimes we eat pâté or fisherman's soup. He talks at length about European politics, sports, and I smile.

"You're not listening to me, are you?" he says one afternoon.

"No," I say. "But keep talking." Because I like watching his mouth.

We make out in alleys behind nightclubs and on the banks of the Danube. I am high from his kisses, his fingers like a drug, touching me until I go crazy.

"This is a horrible mistake," he murmurs one night as his lips trail across my shoulder.

So horrible neither of us stop.

We leave Hungary to visit the Zagreb court, where Katia and her twin brother, Piotrek, have friends. I don't want to go, if only because I'm not ready to be separated from Luka, even for a few weeks. But Katia and her lover, Andre, insist that I need to meet Ivan.

The way they talk about Ivan, I expect superhuman stature, piercing eyes—something. But he's just a guy. Granted, a guy who fills the room with a vibe I can't *not* sense, like a tuning fork that won't stop vibrating.

He sucks in a soft breath the minute we walk in.

"Amerie," he whispers.

Do I imagine it, or does Katia pale?

Luka comes to Zagreb as he promised. But he's quiet and distracted, and I wonder if something's changed. If he came just to say that it's over.

And I don't want it to be.

"I was wondering how you'd feel if I took a flat here for a while," he says. "So we can be together. I want us to be together." But he seems troubled saying it, like he's worried I'll say no.

"You'd do that?" I say as relief washes over me.

"I'd do a lot more than that," he says.

That night he tells me he loves me.

Ivan has given me something—a packet of papers. I'm uncomfortable with the way he stares. I've been around staring people—men and women—for years, but he looks at me as though there's someone else behind my eyes.

"This is for you," he says. "It is why I will protect you with my life, as I did her."

I don't understand.

Until I read them that night.

I know now who I am. Where I come from. What I am.

Luka calls five times, texts asking if I'm all right. I was supposed to be at his flat hours ago. I don't answer.

I have read for ten hours straight and I am stunned, lost, found.

My mother's name was Amerie Szabo. Progeny, like me. But, according to Ivan, she was far more than that.

He gave me something else of hers as well: the Bathory crest. A gold dragon pendant.

221

· · ·

We've been in Budapest long enough for Katia and the others to start climbing the walls. I feel it, too. The nomadic pull of this adrenaline-fueled life that is less bohemian than I thought and more a life simply addicted to the shadows, and being on the run.

They look at me differently now. Even Claudia, who wavered for the briefest instant about whether to follow Katia on to Bucharest or stay in Hungary with me.

I tell her to go. Somehow I think she will be safer.

Nikola wants to talk.

I've taken nothing but some money and my documents, leaving my life, my tears behind.

Nothing is what I thought it was. No one is who I thought. Not even Luka.

Especially him.

For the first time since the lake accident, I miss Iowa. A place that might as well belong to an alternate universe. That can't possibly exist in the same world as this one.

Audra.

Hidden away in Germany, I am in awe. I am afraid. I miss the court, with its thunderous beat.

But I don't trust Nikola.

Ivan texted an hour ago: *Why have you*

run? Come back. There are things you must do. I will help you do them. This is your destiny.

Ivan, such a believer. But I am worried about one life now, and it isn't my own.

I stare out at the Bavarian countryside. I'm journaling, writing letters to myself. Because one day, I will be more lost than I am now and I will need them.

By nightfall, I know that I am reckless. I have always been. Ivan would not approve. Neither would Tibor, who doesn't trust me. I see through him, the protective younger brother. And though I don't know her, I miss my mother.

Amerie.

There's something I don't understand about her letters. Came here to figure out. She left a cache of information in Croatia.

I know where it is, but the rules of this life dictate that I can't go and get it, let alone lay eyes on it myself. I can't know the things, the people I know. Can't love those whom I love. Don't dare die with a full soul.

I've returned not to Hungary but to Croatia. To Zagreb, where I've taken a flat. I've carved the Glagolitic symbol into the doorframe. Three. For the claws of the dragon, slain by St. George—the Bathory coat of arms. Three, for the Scions, the Progeny, and their silent partners, the

Franciscans. For Ivan, my mother, and Nikola, who should have saved us.

Now others are looking to me to save them, and I want to, but there is a life inside me that I have to put first. That I will put first.

I am not the person I thought I was. I am not Audra Ellison. I am not a normal person—even for the Utod.

Luka shows up before midnight at the address I texted. He holds me so tight I can barely breathe. He is crying, and I am, too. For us, for the baby, for the world—the real world, as we know it. The only one.

He gets on his knees. "Marry me," he says. I refuse.

"Marry me," he insists. "I'll protect you—and our baby—the rest of my life."

"And if I don't?"

"I will regardless. I've renounced the calling. We run, live, and die—together."

We're married the next night. The bride and groom both wore jeans.

But there's something else I haven't told him about.

Audra!

We leave the next day for Spain. Go on from there to Italy.

We chose the hospital carefully—through the help of the good brothers on Cres Island, who know the place.

Luka and I take turns holding her through the night. Memorizing the sounds she makes, her tiny fingers. The smell of her hair like down against my cheek.

We leave Eva in a warm incubator set into a wall, with a little door on each side—one for leaving her . . . another so others can take her.

And with that, a part of me has died.

The minute we've gotten a safe distance away, I collapse, and Luka doesn't have the strength to hold me up.

No one speaks when you enter the Center for the final time. There's no need. You've gone through the counseling, tests, and a checklist of preparations to get the plastic bracelet you wear the day of treatment. The one that saves a life.

They don't need to know why you're doing it anymore. Or that you lied about it all.

A nurse takes me into the room, and I lie down on the table. I give her the sealed packet, the only thing I brought with me.

And I think of Luka, already waiting. I told him I knew I'd love him again.

I will.

They say your life flashes before your eyes when you die. But they don't tell you that every detail comes screaming back to life. That you taste each bite of every meal you savored, feel

the shower of every rain you walked in . . .
smell the hair against your cheek before that last
parting kiss.

I will come back for you.

That you will fight to hold on to memory like
a drowning person gasping for poisoned air.

Then everything you knew is back. And you
are alive. Again.

22

"Audra."

An instrument blips from somewhere nearby, incessant as a heartbeat.

"Audra, can you hear me?"

Fingers brush my cheek. A hand squeezes mine.

I want to go back. Stop, suspend it forever. Because for an instant between deaths, I was with her—with them both.

And it was heaven.

But heaven slips away, too quickly . . . is gone.

It hurts to breathe.

"Audra," a fierce whisper over me. I open my eyes.

Luka, unshaven, a bandage above his brow.

"What happened to you?" I croak out. My throat hurts. Everything does.

Luka kisses my hand, which has a plastic tube taped to the back of it, presses my fingers to his cheek.

"You remember me," he says with unmistakable relief. He gets up, kisses my forehead. "Stay here."

Like I'm going anywhere.

"She's awake," I hear him say to someone outside the room.

My gaze drifts from the monitor and IV stand to the ornately tiled ceiling. Lingers on an oversize piece of art. Beside my bed, the curtains have been thrown back from an eight-foot window. Green garden beyond the balustrade outside.

This is no hospital.

I try to shove up. Pain shoots through my chest.

A woman comes in, followed by Luka. At my grimace, she strides to my bed, eases me back into what have to be one-thousand-thread-count linens.

"You won't want to do that," she says.

"I noticed," I grit out.

"Do you know who you are?"

"Yeah." What I don't know is who she is.

I look at Luka as she takes my vitals. A few minutes later she produces two pills from a bottle and hands them to me along with a cup of water from the dresser.

"For the pain."

"I can do that," Luka says, taking it from her, holding it for me to sip.

"Where are we?" I demand as soon as she leaves.

"France."

"France?"

His brow furrows. "Audra, do you remember . . . what happened?"

I search his eyes, not sure what answer he's looking for.

"We were driving to the airport in Slovenia," he says. "We went off the bridge . . . into the river."

I stare at him, and as I do, it comes back in flashes. The SUV, rolling through the air. The weightlessness . . . the cold. Luka, frantic to free me.

"The window quit working. I couldn't get the door open, had to wait for the car to fill up."

Luka, talking to me in my dazed state as he held my chin up above the rising water. Telling me to breathe deep, even as the cold stole the breath from my lungs.

"You nearly drowned," he says.

But what he really means is, I did.

Because I remember floating, and not just from the water. I *saw* him stagger onto the bank, limp form in his arms. *Heard* his jagged breaths as he worked over my body with trembling arms, pounding it once—twice—in desperation as sirens sounded in the distance.

"When was that?" I say, panic rising in my chest. Because that's more than a five o'clock shadow on his cheeks.

"Two days ago."

"Two days?"

"We were on our way to meet Serge Deniel. This is his place."

Adrenaline shoots straight to my heart.

"Who knows we're here?" I say, reaching, this time, for help. He slides an arm beneath my shoulders and props several pillows behind me.

"No one," he says, quietly. "I didn't want to

risk trying to contact the others from here, and your phone is somewhere at the bottom of that river. Serge offered to have someone take me to town, get anything we need, but I didn't want to leave you and I don't trust any phone I don't buy myself."

Two thoughts collide in my mind at once. First, that it's too much to take in. I don't want to hear about phones, about Serge Deniel, about the river. The constant need for secrecy and security, to move unseen. The supreme effort it takes to stay alive in this life. To simply *live*.

Second, that Jester, Claudia, and Piotrek have got to be freaking out.

Claudia. Now I remember the girl she was at sixteen. The way I entered her friendship with Katia, whom she idolized. Claudia's jealousy.

It's like waking up from Oz and realizing they were all there—including others like Andre, who seemed untouchable in his dark leather the night I met him, black diamond around his eye. Now, no longer alive.

And then there was Luka, new to me two short weeks ago, but with whom I've already lived a lifetime of passion, loss, and grief.

I lay my hand on his, but it slides away as he reaches toward the nightstand.

"Check this out," he says, holding up a small tablet. He touches it on, brings up a news site.

It's a breaking story about allegations of

corruption and murder against Hungarian Supreme Court Judge Lazlo Becskei.

"It broke," he says, looking at me. "It's out there."

I lift a finger, scroll down the page. Evidence simultaneously leaked by Cryptileak, InvestIGate, and Anonymous Alley, and subsequently published by eleven similar sites. A video clip of Lazlo himself, avoiding reporters.

"She really did it . . ."

"And this," he says, paging to another headline: NEW EVIDENCE IN IMF CHIEF FRAUD CASE.

"This is awesome," I whisper, impulsively reaching for Luka, and then grimace.

His eyes are tired as he clasps my hand, but there's a hardness around them I've never seen before. "It isn't everywhere. Not yet—"

"But it's enough to send the others scurrying to cut ties with them," a form says from the doorway.

I recognize him instantly from his online photos, which must have been taken a few years ago because he looks closer to forty-five in person. He's dressed in a pair of slacks, the sleeves of his button-up shirt rolled to the elbow as though he's just taken a break from his office to go wash dishes or change a tire. A working man's kind of billionaire.

He shuts the door behind him and moves toward my bed. Luka lowers the tablet. The headline blares from atop the wool blanket beside me.

"They are all wondering, Who is next? Is it me? Because they know their sins. No high-ranking Scion will sleep well tonight." He stops to consider me, and for a minute I'm afraid he'll do the European thing and try to kiss me, in which case I'm glad I have the worst breath in the world. He extends his hand. "I am Serge."

I watch myself take and briefly shake it. Cannot reconcile the image of our hands locked—in alliance, if not friendship.

I was this close to moving beyond the boundaries of loyalties, of history, of time. And now here I am, remarking on something as unlikely as a handshake, bound by all of them again.

He gives an uncomfortable laugh, which is the last thing I expect. "This is very strange, no?" he says, sitting down in the chair Luka abandoned in favor of my bedside.

"No. I mean yes. I suppose I should thank you." Because I'm pretty sure that had I landed in a hospital, I would never have had the opportunity to wake up. And a part of me is still undecided how I feel about that.

He clasps his hands loosely together in front of him and shrugs. "It is obviously in my interest to protect you, given what you know about me. Which is why you should know you are safe here. These grounds have every security, including an underground escape, which I have shown your husband in case the occasion should arise."

My brows lift at the mention of my husband, and I glance at Luka, not sure if that's something Serge learned on his own or Luka volunteered. Either scenario is awkward given that I'm having this conversation in a—admittedly high-quality—hospital gown. I pull the blanket a little higher, and Luka takes my hand.

"How do I know we're not your prisoners?"

"You are free to go, any time. My chauffeur will take you any place you like. My pilot as well. After all, you made it very clear that I am the one . . . at a disadvantage. Which is why, now that you are awake, I would be very relieved if you made a call to let your associates know you are safe."

I know I need to—not for Serge's sake, but for theirs. But like Luka, I don't trust any of the electronics in this place. Nor do I trust that the rooms aren't monitored.

"We will, soon," I say.

"Until then, I believe you are safest here, in the home of your . . . enemy?" he says, ironically. "Though I believe you may find me to be a very useful friend."

23

"Speaking of friends, what exactly did Tibor tell you?" I ask, eyes narrowed.

He leans forward, gaze leveled on mine. "That we both want the same thing: To end the day of the Historian."

"I know why I would want that," I say slowly, glancing from Luka's unreadable expression back to Serge. "Why would you?"

"This war—this vendetta—what use is it to us anymore? We have our power. We have had our revenge. It was always about revenge, if not on Lady Bathory herself, then on her descendants. To take from them all that they gained on the backs of our forefathers and mothers."

"I thought it was revenge for the killings."

"Do you truly believe there were killings? Over six hundred of them? That she *bathed in the blood* of innocent girls?" he says with a laugh.

"No. I think she was smart, independent, and rich. Which would have been fine except that she was also a woman. One the crown owed a lot of money after her husband died. No one wants to owe a woman who can't be controlled. Don't you think?" I say with a slight smile.

"What I think is that it doesn't matter except to those obsessed with her story."

"Kind of hard not to be obsessed when you're being hunted."

"I was speaking of the Historian, whose job it is to be consumed with Erzsebet Bathory's sins, real or imagined. So that, unlike her, they never die. But four hundred years later, what do they matter? This vendetta was never between you and me, but between people buried now for centuries. Any wrong done by Erzsebet herself has long since been paid for. We have won. But we have not evolved."

"You haven't won. You've just become the exact thing you accused her of being."

Serge sits back, lifts a shoulder. "I am ashamed to say that we agree."

"And yet your freshman class keeps killing us."

"Yes, there are those of us who did as we were told. Who damned ourselves in the eyes of God for the Historian's unholy mission. And for that, we were rewarded. But what reward is this?" He spreads his hands. "When we know hell waits for us?"

"Obviously plenty of you think it's a pretty decent trade-off."

"I never wanted this for my children. Thank God, they never have to make that decision. They died in their innocence. They are in the bosom of God.

"What I am saying is that even if we were utterly convinced of Erzsebet Bathory's guilt, what need do we have today, to kill? We are a fraternity committed to the advancement of our brothers and sisters—and we have been wildly successful! What point is there to kill? If you ask me: none. If you ask the Historian, though, it is an edict straight from God as alive now as it was the day the twelve founders formed their alliance. The Historian is no equalizer, but a terrorist." His hand slices the air between us. "I want no part of it, anymore!"

"How convenient, now that you have your . . . what is it? Billions?"

"Look around, Audra! No man in my position possibly believes that money makes him happy. After you have spent your first million, and lost your next five, and your wife has left you, and you become twenty times more wealthy than before but lose your children and no longer know who your friends are . . . you learn this."

"Or you just know it because you have principles," I add.

He acquiesces with a shrug. "What I am saying is that for the Historian, this is a religion. One I have lost."

"If it isn't about the money or power anymore, then go. Walk away."

"That is the thing. There is no walking away! Don't you understand? The Historian has damning information on all of us—often in our own voices and written by our own hands. A full and complete list of our sins."

"So do we," I say. "So what's the real reason you want the Historian gone?"

"Do you know why the Scion head is called the Historian? Because it was the office responsible for keeping the genealogies of the Progeny. So that we would know when the day had come that we had eradicated the last of Erzsebet Bathory's heirs. But also, so that we would have a record of the flourishing of our own descendants. We might as aptly have called him the Genealogist."

"Makes sense." Especially given that others—from the Franciscans with their Progeny Book, and the Progeny who created and passed down the far-too-incomplete Scion map—have attempted to do the same.

"The Historian kept, by way of the memories reported to him and a Progeny genealogy rumored to have been stolen from the Franciscans, the most accurate record of the Progeny in the world. And a full listing of those with rights to the Scion inheritance. Because of that jealously guarded record, handed down from Historian to Historian, he possessed sole power over the appointments of new hunters, and the deaths of discovered Progeny. Until about forty years ago, when power shifted with technology."

He looks down at his hands and sighs. "I own, among my holdings, the parent company of the world's largest genealogy and ancestry DNA sites. For that reason, I have been integral to the

Historian's operation. I provided the names of Progeny—yes, even you—and potential hunters from the descendants of the original Council of Twelve with records more complete than the Historian's own. Your husband became a hunter, I am sorry to say"—he glances at Luka—"because of me. I have hated this responsibility more even than the single act of murder that made me a Scion twenty years ago. Last year, I decided I would no longer provide victims for killers."

"Why not?" Luka says.

"The Historian demanded that I sign over full, anonymous access to the database. I refused."

He pulls out his phone, shows me a picture of two golden-haired children, arms around each other. He points to one, and then the other. "My son, Enzo. My daughter, Celeste. A truck struck and killed them eight months ago as they walked to school with their mother."

"I'm sorry," I say.

He clicks the phone off, and the screen goes dark. "It was ruled an accident, as is so much associated with the Scions. The Historian—this current Historian—is not content to exterminate the Progeny of Erzsebet Bathory, but wants only absolute power for the office. A monster willing to murder his own to achieve it."

I close my eyes. Not just at the story of the children, which hits closer to home than I'd like, or at the revelation that the Historian would pursue a traitor from the Scion ranks. But because of the pronoun *his*.

Which means Serge doesn't know who the Historian is.

Unless, of course, he's testing me.

"I take it things weren't always this way," I say.

"No. Our forefathers believed fervently in our cause. They would sooner die than betray it. But the time of the Scions is past. We are a relic, as is the Historian himself."

"You said this 'current' Historian . . ."

He nods. "No one knows for certain when the Historian's office is handed down. It is meant to make him seem ageless. Eternal as wrath itself. But I have believed for months that a new Historian came into office soon after several of us agreed to separate ourselves from the fraternity. Three of those men are now dead. The rest of us are slaves to the power we craved. To the office we created!"

If I said I didn't take some satisfaction in the irony in that, I'd be lying.

I also know two things he doesn't.

First, that what he's saying about the new Historian is true. Even as I sit here, I can conjure the image of the Scion map rediscovered in my Vienna bank box last week. The circles down the right side of the page—the succession of the Historian's office. A few containing names. Some, only a year. Can see the last circle drawn in crisp, black pen on the crumbling paper, empty except for a year—this one.

Second, that the map left to me by my mother via Ivan—though scrupulously never viewed by him—was compiled by those heretic monks like Rolan. I know this, because I now recall burning the note to that effect in order to protect their existence so they could, in turn, protect mine.

"It sounds like you have some real problems," I say. "What exactly are you hoping I'll do for you, Serge?"

His face hardens. "Tibor said of anyone, you could find the Historian. I know what you are. That you are rumored to have abilities beyond those of the others. I know the lore of your kind, growing stronger with each generation."

"I don't mind telling you that's true," I say, not knowing if it is.

"Then you know you are the most hunted of the hunted. Not only by the Historian but—if rumor is correct—by many of your own."

I don't answer.

"Find the Historian, and I will end this. There will be peace, at last."

"You have no clue who the Historian is, do you?" It isn't really a question.

"Do you?" he says, startled.

I give a short, painful laugh. "You really think I'd have agreed to meet you in person if I did?"

He shakes his head, but he looks disappointed. No, distressed.

"I have to say, you are the only hope I know to ever find my way out. And it is the same for all three of us, no?" he says, indicating the two of us, and Luka. "It must end for us to be free."

"What do you know about the Historian?" I say.

"Very little. He seems to be surrounded by some trusted few who seem to protect him and his identity at all costs."

"There's got to be a money trail."

"He rarely deals in money himself, instructing others where to send it, sending others when he must to retrieve assets from anonymous accounts."

"How does anyone communicate with h—" I cough painfully, having almost said *her*. "With him?"

Serge expels a frustrated sigh. "Via anonymous coded e-mails. None of my people can trace them—the few I dare ask under guise of trying to track a prankster. One time I received a written message. Without fingerprints or trace! Who knows if it was even written in his own hand? He is a ghost."

"If you can't give me any useful information, what do you even have to offer me?" I say with a shrug.

"I may not know who he is, but I also know

you cannot rescue yourself from drowning or the police or Europol, by whom you are wanted, or the hunters currently deployed to find you. I can give you resources. Money. Safe houses. Transportation. People to protect you. I have powerful friends . . . assuming you do not expose them all. Name what you want, and it is yours!"

His eyes glitter as he says it. The thing I've been waiting to hear.

I let the offer hang in the air between us for several long seconds.

"I need to think about it," I say. "But right now I'm tired."

It's not a lie. I am tired. And a part of me wants to know whether the world behind my eyelids is truly gone.

Barring that, I want to make Serge sweat.

Luka stands, and Serge hesitates, having clearly wanted some demand to signify my consent, some plan of action. A moment later, he nods and gets to his feet.

"Of course," he says. "Until then, I have a gift for you. A show of my good faith."

He excuses himself, and I glance at Luka, who lifts his brows.

A moment later, the door opens.

And there is Rolan.

24

Even now, it's strange seeing the two of them—Luka, Rolan—in the same room. Shaking hands mere weeks after they would have gladly killed one another.

"I can't get rid of you, can I?" I say. He's freshly shaved, wearing a gray button-up shirt. And cologne.

"Apparently not."

"But how did you—how did Serge . . . ?"

"After I left you in that garage, I drove north, to the edge of the city. His men found me just before I reached the checkpoint, took me into an unmarked car. At first, I assumed they were the Historian's men and that I had two choices: kill as many of them as I could, or create some story about how you are more powerful than we knew. Able, even, to persuade our kind."

I wish.

"I didn't know if the Historian would believe it, but I knew if I could make him entertain at least the possibility . . ." He pauses there, and I realize he isn't telling this story for my benefit, but for that of anyone listening in.

"When they took me not to the Historian but to Serge, who recognized from the surveillance footage that I willingly helped you, I told him the truth: that I have wanted out for years and that I helped you escape. He offered me safe haven in exchange for what I knew of the Historian, which, of course, is not much."

"Lucky for you Serge has his eye in the sky," I say.

"Yes," Rolan says, and comes to gently embrace me.

"Which means he's been tracking you all this time," he whispers against my hair.

25

With Rolan there, Luka leaves me the next morning long enough to go into town, purchase new burner phones, and get a message to Jester and the others.

I meet Serge for breakfast in the garden. Breathe deeply. Because this world might be filled with struggle, but it is Eva's world, and somewhere she is breathing the same air I am.

And also because pain pills are the greatest invention in history.

I've exchanged the gown that tied at my neck for a pair of soft pajamas—during which I discovered the faint burn marks on my chest. Each one the size of a defibrillator paddle. The two together having delivered enough voltage to restart a heart . . .

. . . or revive the memories electrically turned off two months ago.

I sip sugar-laden café au lait between bites of the most buttery, flaky croissant I've ever tasted.

And for once, I can make that statement with confidence.

The sun is on my face. The birds chatter from the garden below our terrace beneath the broad expanse of vivid blue sky on a seasonal fall day.

I'm startled to realize it's October.

The last time I sat out like this in the open I was eating lunch on the public dock in Greenville, Maine, with Luka, trying to decide if I'd ever be able to be honest about who I am.

Now instead of eavesdropping on the story of someone else's bear hunt, I'm sitting with a hunter of another kind. Surrounded not by feral ducks snatching up french fries but by three French bodyguards gazing out toward the line of trees. Rolan stands behind me, ever watchful.

"You have thought about what I said?" Serge says, stirring sugar into his coffee. The power breakfast of the obscenely rich.

"I have."

"And?"

"How good is your surveillance?"

"What do you mean?"

"What can you see?"

"Everything. Vehicles. People. Submarines. But you are not looking for a submarine."

"Can you locate a specific person?" I ask. "If I know where they've been—on a certain day, in a certain window of time?"

"Yes. Almost certainly."

I take a long drink of my coffee.

"You want to kill the Historian."

"All you need to do is find him," he says, an expensive watch gleaming from his wrist. "And then walk away. What I do from there, you need not know. But I promise, it will end."

"But it won't," I say, shaking my head. "You said yourself: This isn't just a vendetta. This is a religion. There are hunters who would still carry out their missions just because they believe it's right, even with the incentive of money or power gone."

Serge acquiesces with a tilt of his head. "It is possible, yes."

"So it doesn't end with the death of the Historian," I say. "The Progeny won't be able to just walk out of their hiding places without fear of getting murdered—at least not for another generation."

"But with no Historian, there will be no next generation of hunters."

"Murder the Historian and you risk creating a martyr. Fueling the war rather than ending it. Every hunter who takes a memory with a life also gets instant knowledge of every Progeny his victim knew. What's to stop him or her from going after every one of that dead Progeny's circle out of simple revenge? Or another Scion from trying to take the Historian's seat?"

"Cut off the head of the snake, and the body dies . . ."

"Not so easy with a den of vipers."

"Find him," Serge says. "And walk away. Your hands will be clean. I will establish a trust over the next fifty years for the generation to come, available to anyone with Progeny blood.

Resources to begin a new life. Think of it, Audra! One day the Progeny will know nothing of bloodshed or fear. All that happened before will be nothing but a tale to them, handed down by grandparents who are *alive* to see them grow up and flourish. Because of you."

I'm quiet for a moment. "Okay."

Serge releases a sigh of relief with a smile.

"But I have three conditions."

"I'm listening."

"First . . . no one ever knows that the Historian has been taken out. You tell no one, other than me. I want your fellow Scions to look over their shoulders for the rest of their lives. To wonder what the Historian's silence means. To live in fear."

"Understood."

"Second. In addition to the trust, you immediately and irrevocably relinquish the administration of all GenameBase labs and servers and surrender all data backups for a period of one hundred years to an entity of my choosing."

He studies his cup for a long moment, finger tapping the little handle.

"C'mon, Serge. Do you want out or not?" I say. "How much money are you really making off this genealogy stuff compared to your government contracts and other holdings?"

After a beat he says: "All right."

"Third, when it's all over, I want you to find someone for me."

His blue gaze levels on mine. "You find the Historian, and I will find a hundred people for you," he says.

"One will do."

He sets down his napkin, pushes back his chair. My gaze falls on his spoon.

"I'm going to need some things," I say.

"Of course, anything."

"Names and photos of every active hunter. A plane. Two bodyguards—not Scions. And a makeup artist."

"I'll have them for you by tomorrow," he says, before excusing himself to make arrangements.

26

Luka returns several hours later with three new burner phones and French chocolate.

I knew there was a reason I loved this man.

We walk out into the garden beneath the watchful eye of Rolan and the ever-present bodyguards, avoiding carved benches, ornate trees, and manicured hedges, staying in the open. Once we're a good hundred yards from the house, I dial Jester.

"Oh thank God," she says. "Where are you? We saw the report about an accident in Slovenia. A drowning victim without a name. Claudia cried nonstop, convinced you were dead, until we got Luka's text this morning."

"We're in France."

"France!" she says.

"Please tell me there's no way someone can trace this call."

"It's bouncing around the world as we speak."

"Good. When is the next info leak?"

"Tonight."

"Do you have enough to release two at a time?"

She pauses, and then: "Yes. But why? We are already sending them scrambling, worrying with each day who will be next—"

"If we're hacking away at the Historian's legs,

let's cut them off. Completely. Leave no time for a contingency plan."

"It's risky . . . Audra, what are you doing in France?"

"Less risky than drawing it out. But you and the others need to move every twenty-four hours."

"We have been moving, though not quite that often."

"You have to. You're more important than any of us right now."

A long pause. "You've gone to meet Serge Deniel, haven't you?"

I hesitate. It's all the answer she needs.

"I don't understand you," she says, low. "I believe in you, but, Audra, this is stretching the limit."

"I'm bargaining."

"For what?"

"For our future. For help."

"What help can he possibly offer? We have all the leverage! I'll tell you why he's offering to help: to save his own skin!"

I briefly entertain the idea of telling her everything. But even if I wanted to, even if she would welcome that information—and she might not—I won't do it here.

"I don't like it," she says.

"Trust me, I don't relish it, either."

She expels a sigh. "Listen, Audra, there's something you need to know . . ."

I really hate it when people start sentences like that.

"Tibor's dead."

I pause, silent. Glance at Luka.

"How?" I say, clearing my throat.

"He fell from the bell tower of the Zagreb Cathedral. They found him there, on the ground, bones broken, head smashed in." Her voice catches.

"That's . . . Jester, I'm so sorry."

"They are saying, of course, that it was a suicide," she says bitterly.

I'm unable to shake my last memory of him. Bowed low, like a performer taking his leave of the stage.

"You don't think . . ." I start to say. "I mean, is it possible that he might have really—"

"No. Of course not!" she snaps. "Tibor loved life! He would never have abandoned it—not like that."

I can't help but think of something Nikola said the first time I met him after my memory procedure, when I did not recognize him and knew him only as Brother Goran.

We assign stories to everyone around us out of our own need to feel that we understand . . .

"I didn't know him. Not like you," I say.

"I know you didn't trust him. But he was a good man."

"I believe you."

"Please get out of there, Audra, as soon as you can. I'll rest better knowing you're nowhere near that Scion," she says, spitting out the last word.

"Me, too," I say. "Though I'm kind of stuck at the moment. Drowning really takes a lot out of you, you know?"

"What?"

I click off.

Maybe it's Jester's reservations, or maybe it's just cabin fever, but going back into that palatial château is the last thing I feel like doing. Restlessness has crept back over the course of the afternoon, spiking my blood with shots of adrenaline so that I've found myself pacing, clenching my hands, and more than once *persuading* the nurse to give me a couple extra happy pills. Not that I've taken them all, but it's at least let off some steam during the painfully slow process of giving my body time to heal.

I draw Luka closer under the guise of leaning on his arm even as I begin to walk faster.

"Tibor," I say. I don't need to elaborate.

Luka looks away, shakes his head. He's been quiet since he returned from town. Staying here isn't sitting well with him, either.

"You're speeding up the release on the leaks," he says quietly.

I nod.

"The faster we cut off her resources, the faster she goes down." I don't say that I have no assurance I'll be able to find her. But if we can't take out the Historian, I'll at least turn her into an island. After which, I'll use the leverage we have to get Serge to locate Clare.

And, with hope, Eva.

"What about the remaining hunters?"

I'm quiet for a moment. Because I know what I need to do next. And he won't like it.

I wind my arms around his right one, lay my chin against his shoulder.

"The night we met," I whisper. "I was wearing a black burn-out velvet shirt with wings on the back . . ."

He takes another ambling step and then freezes. Turns to stare at me.

"It was my favorite T-shirt mostly because it fit like a glove. When you brought me that glass of wine, I was glad I was wearing it. After I flipped you off." I laugh, softly.

His lips part and he blinks. "You . . . *remember* that?"

I nod.

He reaches for me, pulls me tight against him.

"Oh my God," he breathes.

"I remember . . . everything," I whisper in his ear.

He pulls away just long enough to cover my mouth with his, to kiss me long and hard. As deeply as the first time on the bank of the Danube while I shivered in his arms.

"You used to leave me notes next to my toothbrush. In my dresser drawers, by the coffee-maker. . . ."

"You remember," he says against my lips, stealing my breath.

"The night I came back," I say, voice thick, "you cried so hard it broke me. You got on your knees . . . you asked me to marry you . . . and promised to get me any ring I wanted. I told you a couple carats would do."

He's laughing softly, brokenly, in the scant space between us, hands cupping my face.

"June fifteenth . . ." I say. I won't speak her name. "Was the most intense pain I've ever felt in my life. The hardest, worst pain . . . And ten hours later, the most amazing, crazy love and the deepest, most horrible grief . . ." I choke out the words. "Worse than losing my parents. Worse than dying. Knowing what we were about to do. What we had to do. *That* was dying."

He tilts his forehead against mine, holds me against him.

He makes love to me that night. Gently, careful of my ribs, which cracked as he tried to save me. He doesn't know that this is me being saved—here, now, as his shoulders shudder above me.

27

The third and fourth Scions debut on the anonymous sites late that night.

"We need to leave," Luka whispers, a few hours before morning.

He's been quiet, though I know he hasn't been sleeping.

"We will," I say. "As soon as I get what I need from Serge."

"Have you considered that all it would take is one call for him to turn you over? He'd be a hero."

"Not with Jester's finger on the button. Besides, we have a deal."

He stares up at the ceiling in the darkness. "The day we leave here won't be soon enough," he murmurs.

Turns out, he doesn't have to wait long.

Jester calls just as the sun slants through the eastern window of our bedroom.

"Audra?" Her voice wavers.

"What's wrong?" I say, instantly awake, pushing up with a grimace from the tangle of sheets and Luka's arms. He reaches past me to the bedside lamp, turns it on. His eyes are rimmed in shadows but alert, and I wonder if he's slept at all.

I hear Claudia in rapid conversation in the

background. A few seconds later, she's drowned out by Piotrek. His voice rises in a torrent of Polish, which ends with a guttural cry.

"Audra," she says, audibly struggling, and I realize she's crying. I have never heard Jester emotional in my life.

"What's happening?" I demand, alarm pricking, cold, along my spine.

"The Bucharest court—"

"Bucharest . . ." I glance at Luka.

"Romania," he mouths.

"There was an explosion in the tunnels beneath the city, where the underground is. It wasn't the biggest court, not like Budapest, but at least thirty people died. They say they were homeless junkies and orphans, living in the sewers. They were Progeny, Audra! Killed! Five more were gunned down by police across town. The news is saying they were armed robbers. They were still wearing their masks . . ." She breaks down, sobbing.

I fall back against the pillow with a slow exhalation.

"Piotrek had friends there . . ."

"What kind of explosion?" I say, dangerously.

"Some kind of gas leak, or so they're reporting . . . but the ones who left early, out in the morning, they posted about it and the shootings on the bulletin board . . . they saw them gunned down by police. They were not robbing! They were not carrying guns!"

"It wasn't a gas leak."

"I would have said maybe, that it was possible. We meet underground. We live underground—we have been driven there through the centuries . . ."

"But what?"

"A text came in to your old phone tonight—just before."

I feel sick. I'm afraid to ask.

"Forward it," I say.

I hand the phone to Luka. Get up from bed.

He talks to Jester in low tones as I pace away, fingers digging into my hair. I turn on my heel, stalk back to the bed as he raises the phone to show me.

We can create leaks, too.

I grab the phone.

"Jester, you need to move."

"We are. We're moving now . . . What about you? What will you do?"

"We're leaving."

"For where?"

"Budapest," I say, not knowing the answer until I hear myself say it.

Someone grabs the phone on the other end. Claudia.

"I want to come," she says. "I want to come with you."

"It isn't safe."

"Nowhere is safe!" she practically shouts at me. "I can't stay here, not like this. Not while they're killing people we know, people Piotrek loved . . . Do you know that he's crying over the fact that he wasn't there to die with them? Because he was here, protecting me!"

"He doesn't mean it," I say. "He's alive, and he feels guilty. You've been through it, too." We all have. "He chose to protect you because he loves you. And you have to stay. Someone has to protect Jester."

I hear the phone, jostled against her cheek. A moment later, she says, "I'm coming. Piotrek will stay with Jester."

"Claudia . . ."

"My place was always with you. Ever since Katia died—"

"Claudia, Katia died because of me." I make myself say it, because Claudia's anger at me, always so near the surface, is the best chance I have of keeping her safe.

"No. Not because of you. Because of *them*. You may be Firstborn, but I am no small person. My father may not have been of the blood, but I, too, have gifts . . . and helped teach you to use yours!"

"I know," I say, closing my eyes.

"I'm coming with you. It's settled."

"You're your own woman, Claudia. You make your own choices."

"Ivan believed in you. I believe in you," she says with conviction.

And my greatest fear is that I will never live up to that desperate belief.

"Meet me at my old flat in Budapest," I say.

She falls silent.

"Do you remember?"

"Yes," she says strangely. "Do *you?*"

"Meet me there. Tomorrow night."

"I will," she says and hangs up.

I glance at Luka, silent all this while.

"You think I'm crazy, don't you?"

"No," he says. "Even if I did, there's no way I'd let you go without me." But as he says it, the faint frown lines around his mouth have deepened.

I climb onto the bed and kiss him. Do I imagine it, or does he hold me closer than the night before, and linger over my lips a moment longer?

After he's disappeared into the bathroom to shower, I wrap myself in a robe and text back that number of the oil-slick voice I will never be able to scrub from memory.

You have made a bad mistake.

I drop the phone on the duvet, barely recognize the fact that I've sent out a mental call for help by the time the nurse and two bodyguards come to the room.

"Get me Serge."

28

By noon, the news station permanently on three screens in the parlor outside my bedroom is consumed with interviews about early associates of Lazlo Becskei and the woman from the IMF and, now, the bank conglomerate associated with her and the president of the EU's Parliament.

Only a tiny blip of news about some gas explosion in Romania. Gang violence in the streets that resulted in five deaths.

They don't say that they were all under the age of twenty-two, and unarmed. That only shows up on the leak sites. Because unlike the political and business giants splashed across the headlines, the victims of the gas leak are, for all practical purposes, nobodies.

I text Jester, asking the names of our next three leak subjects. I'm nervous, pacing, by the time she responds nearly thirty minutes later.

I don't know if this is a good idea anymore, Audra.

I text her back:

No. We shut her down. Completely.

The names come through five minutes later.

I've exchanged the pajamas for a top, leather jacket, and jeans from the wardrobe Serge's people have supplied us with. The makeup artist is here, with a small camera crew.

Luka paces along the back wall while the makeup person exclaims about my hair, and finally takes out a pair of shears to fix it properly before dyeing my roots. I'm impatient with the entire process, ready to be gone. But I also know that looking like an urchin isn't going to serve my purpose.

An hour later, I don't recognize myself.

I glance around for Luka, but he's apparently stepped out. Rolan stands, arms crossed, in his place, but raises his brows when I look at him. And I can't tell if that's approval or he's just weirded out.

It takes me three tries to record what I need. I've already given Serge the list of my other demands: a plane and a non-Scion pilot, money, a car in any city we arrive in. And last, a look at his database.

His technical person is there by the time we finish, the GenameBase database live on a huge monitor.

I scroll through it, clicking from page to page. From the arterial branches of one Scion family to another, marriages and issue branching like capillaries across the screen. But I'm distracted, the sound of Jester's voice, of Piotrek's cry still in my ear.

After forty-five minutes, I stand.

"You're done?" the guy says.

I nod, having seen enough. I don't say that I'll review it later, on the plane, from memory.

Serge comes to oversee our preparations himself, but his brows knit together.

"Something has happened, I think, to make you leave so swiftly," he murmurs, studying me sidelong.

But it doesn't feel swift. It's already late afternoon. Given the chance, I would have been gone by morning.

"The Historian's scared. That's what's happened."

"I'm pleased to hear it. What will you do now?"

"Scare him some more."

He smiles then. "Your plane is standing by."

The sun is setting by the time we arrive at Serge's hangar. Luka, Rolan, and I each carry a bag of clothes. Luka carries an additional knapsack filled with cash. The two men are both grimly silent in the presence of my new bodyguard— a pale-skinned man with broad shoulders stretching the back of his tailored suit jacket.

"I wish you would take more men with you," Serge says, having accompanied us.

"Did you forget?" I say with a dangerous

smile. "I'm Firstborn. I don't need your men."

He glances around and tugs on his suit jacket, but does not ask what exactly that means. And I'm happy to let him wonder.

As we board the private jet, I glance at the two men in the cockpit.

Shame about those bedbugs.

The pilot swipes at his neck as the copilot scratches beneath an arm.

At least Serge has been true, so far, to his word about keeping Scions away from me.

We're wheels up within five minutes. Within ten, we're thirty thousand feet in the air.

Luka gets up and heads back to the galley. Returns a few minutes later with espresso and two plates, sets one in front of me. I wrinkle my nose.

"You need to eat," he says.

"I'm not hungry," I say, sliding low in the white leather seat. My mind is churning, familial trees sinking their branches into the nether reaches of my brain like roots. I'm searching for the three known Historians: Otto Errickson, Attila Bertalan, and Cristian Alexandrescu. And they are there, descended from the original twelve families. Men with parents and siblings. Two of them with wives and children. None of them with the marker that designates them as initiated Scions.

But something else has been scratching at the

264

back of my brain ever since I sat down at that monitor this morning, though I haven't been able to put my finger on it yet.

"You used to love this. Remember?" Luka says, sitting across the polished burl wood table from me. He cuts into the small portion on the plate. Foie gras on brioche.

I give him a small smile. "Yeah."

He holds up a forkful. "Come on. I ordered this just for you."

I eat it to make him happy.

"I didn't realize we had a menu."

"You were busy getting a haircut," he says, rubbing his face. He looks exhausted, but when he turns his eyes on me, his gaze is wistful. "Have I told you how frighteningly beautiful you look?"

"Hmm. 'Frighteningly beautiful.' Not sure how I feel about that one."

"No wonder your kind make exquisite super-models."

"Yeah, well, this makeup isn't staying on forever."

"It isn't the makeup."

I eat more after that, stomach growling to life after that single bite. All the while, I'm twisting familial trees like three-dimensional holograms, combing through the branches and stripping away leaves.

Not the initiated Scions. Not the hunters—and

apparently not all of them managed to make it to full Scion-hood, several of them having died in their twenties through the centuries. Missed marks, lost kills.

I'm also seething. For the nameless, faceless Progeny who lost their lives this morning. For those no doubt injured, burned by the blast. There had to be some survivors, surely. Serge has said he will put out an inquiry for any burn victims admitted to hospitals this morning in Bucharest. But he knows as well as I do they'd have to be dying—in enough agony to *want* to die—to show their faces there.

My leg bounces against the table, the jitters having returned in full. Sitting here like this, I can't keep the thought at bay: *Did I bring this on? Is this my fault?*

I'm the one who told Jester to speed up the leaks. And I stand by my conviction to go after them all—as many as we can, as fast as we can. But I also wonder if those deaths in Bucharest are at least in part on me.

"You knew there'd be repercussions," Luka said in private to me earlier. "That it couldn't possibly be bloodless."

But that's the thing. I hoped—had allowed myself to believe, somehow—that it might be.

I get up, pace past the sofa where Rolan dozes, a magazine over his face. Stare out the window, wish I had run a lap around the hangar before boarding. Because right now, given a parachute, I'd gladly jump.

I've drained three more cups of coffee by the time we touch down in Brussels. My phone chimes as we taxi into the hangar.

You are the one who is mistaken. You have bitten the ankle of a giant. And now others will be crushed for your actions.

My thumbs move furiously across the screen.

All I see is a coward scurrying around in hiding like a rat.

I search for and send a gory picture of a bloody, dead rat along with it before removing the SIM card.

I call Serge from Luka's phone as we deplane.

"Where's our guy?" I say.

"He's left the office," Serge says. "We've got him going into a dinner meeting on Rue de Rollebeek," he says. "I'm sending the address."

"I don't suppose you'd mind putting in a call there for me—about a birthday boy?"

Serge actually chuckles as he gets off the phone.

But as we get into the black car waiting for us and our bodyguard slides behind the wheel, Luka takes me by the wrist.

"What are you doing? Is this really necessary?" he says.

"It is to me."

"Then let me do it," he says.

"No," I say, slipping on a pair of oversize sunglasses despite the fact that it's dark. "I need to do it."

Which isn't true. The fact is, I *want* to do this.

"This isn't a joke, Audra!" Luka says.

"You're telling me? We just lost at least thirty of our own!" I shout, pointing out the window.

He looks away, jaw twitching.

My phone pings with a photo. A European guy with a long face and neatly trimmed beard. Salt-and-pepper hair.

We arrive outside the restaurant twenty minutes later. I get out of the car the moment it pulls up at the curb, before Luka can stop me. And then he and Rolan are out and following me into Sartre's bistro at a rapid clip.

I step past the maître d', gaze roving over the well-dressed elite dining on fine bone china. I spot him at a power table in the corner, in deep conversation with another man.

Blaise Garcon. Interpol Deputy Special Representative to the European Union. A young guy—about thirty-five—for such an important position.

But then again, he's been a Scion for about ten years.

He glances up at the three of us as we arrive, a pleasant enough expression on his face—

Until I take off my shades.

"I'm guessing you know who I am," I say. His companion, meanwhile, has gotten to his feet with a surprised smile and effusive French.

Garcon sits back very slowly, hand lowering toward his jacket.

"Uh-uh," I say with a smile. "I'm only here to give you a message. Besides . . ." I glance around us. Heads at every table have turned. Fifty witnesses to our encounter. "Your friend and all these people seem to think I'm some famous French actress."

I drop a folded paper onto the table in front of him.

"What is this?" he says, looking at it like it's a piece of filth.

"Special delivery."

Garcon's face turns white when he flicks it open and reads.

You're next.

I step away as several waiters come carrying a dessert with one lit candle and begin to sing.

"Many happy returns," I say, before we slip out.

29

By the time we land in Budapest early the next evening, we've paid visits to Italian Senator Giada Borghi and the office of the German financial conglomerate Gerald Schelert.

Or rather, Borghi's chauffeur, since I never actually saw the senator but *persuaded* her driver to give me a ride around the Palazzo Madama in her black Mercedes. I left the message taped to the back of the front seat:

Send my regards to the Historian.
A.E.

It's the same note I delivered to Schelert's assistant, which was admittedly harder, given the security of the financial group's twin skyscrapers. It was a concession to Luka that I didn't attempt to deliver the message to the man himself.

"I can promise you they've never heard of a Progeny passing for a specific person before today," Jester said, when I checked in with her earlier in the evening. "Using her *persuasion* and *charisma* together at once. I wonder if I could do that, or if that is a Firstborn thing."

"Dunno," I said. Because I honestly never

270

thought of doing it until today. "Did you get somewhere safe?"

"*Oui.*"

"And Piotrek is with you?" I'm sad about the prospect of Claudia and Piotrek separating like that. I wish they hadn't, though it's imperative someone protect Jester.

"He is."

"How is he? Piotrek, I mean."

She sighs. "Not good. None of us are. But what can you expect after knowing we have lost so many of our own—whether you even knew them or not?"

Which is why I'm going to make sure it can never happen again.

Budapest sparkles like an onyx and amber brooch from the sky, separated by the dark ribbon of the Danube. Buda Castle, the jewel among it all. How many miles of undiscovered tunnels wind beneath the Buda Hills? How many Utod rave in her caverns under the jurisdiction of Nikola, the traitor prince?

The only time I ever came face-to-face with the Historian was there, within those caverns. I wonder if it's possible her killers are in those tunnels now, preparing to deliver the Progeny population another crushing blow.

But no. Nikola's allied with her. Assuming he's managed to mitigate her anger at my failure to deliver the so-called diary, his court will be the last one standing.

And if he hasn't . . . everyone in those tunnels is in danger.

My heart has begun to race by the time the car pulls up to the long mismatched buildings that run together like row houses along Donáti Street at the foot of Buda's Castle Hill. The hair rises on my arms as I glance out at the buildings—some of them restored, painted butter yellow or pale blue with statues and stonework on their façades . . . some pockmarked and leprous where their paint and plaster has crumbled away.

"Keep going," I say. Luka glances at me but says nothing, well aware this is not my former street, that I've deliberately passed our turn.

I direct the driver to a neighborhood several blocks away, where I ask him to stop at a persimmon-colored residential building. We get out, and the driver lowers his window.

"Get a nice dinner," I say. "Treat yourself to a good hotel. We'll call you tomorrow when we're ready to leave."

And remember you dropped us a block east of here.

"That house up there," the driver confirms.

"That's right."

Because ally or not, I have no desire for any Scion to know the actual address of the flat I used to rent under an assumed name.

I back up and turn toward the persimmon building, walk straight up to the front door, which is just starting to open.

A woman in her sixties ushers us into her apartment as if we're old friends.

I go to her window, peer through the edge of the curtain until the driver is gone. When I turn around, the woman looks surprised. But of course she does; she's just let three strangers into her living room.

"If Serge checks surveillance to confirm the address the driver gave him, he'll know you *persuaded* him to hide where you really went," Rolan says.

"And he'll see us coming here, and think he's onto me," I say.

"I take it this isn't the house," he says wryly.

"No."

The woman chatters in Hungarian as she dresses me in one of her housecoats, gives me a pair of her worn black boots. She ties a scarf on my head before leading me out the back door.

"Go," Luka says, taking my bag. "We'll follow in an hour."

The walk behind the building is lined by a retaining wall, a steep drop from the next building farther up the hill.

I school my steps to the arthritic hobble of someone far older. All the while, my heart— which stopped just three days ago—is pounding so hard I think it might burst through my aching ribs. I disappear beneath the dark umbrella of a tree. Hurry up a flight of stairs between buildings to a path roof-level with the building below.

My skin prickles as I near the corner of Donáti. Just a little farther on, it turns into Csónak Street, where I entered a broken-down house and made my way through the cellar tunnel to the underground nearly two weeks—a lifetime—ago to confront Nikola and the Historian.

I drop down over an iron railing to the back of my old building as one of the residents comes to let me in.

Thirty seconds later, I'm knocking at the door of my old flat. For an instant I wonder if I've beaten Claudia here. If the current tenants are out. If I'll have to jimmy my way in.

But then that familiar sense rushes toward me. The door opens, and Claudia throws herself into my arms.

A moment later, she steps back, hands on my shoulders, and looks me up and down, nose wrinkled.

"Audra, what *are* you wearing?"

"What, you don't like this look?" I say, pulling the scarf from my head.

She actually gasps at my haircut, the makeup I forgot I had on—which has somehow weathered the afternoon and early evening.

"Audra, you've changed so much! You're . . . so chic!"

"Gee, thanks."

I don't remember her presence feeling so overwhelming. Wonder if it's a product of the steroid shot the nurse gave me before we left, or just of dying . . .

Until Jester and Piotrek appear in the kitchen doorway behind her.

"What?" I say with an incredulous laugh. "What are you two doing here?"

"You didn't think we were going to let you have all the fun?" Jester says, coming forward with her uneven stride to embrace me.

"You're supposed to be somewhere safe!" I say, bemused but so glad to see them as Piotrek wraps me in a hug and then kisses me on both cheeks. "Seriously, though, you're the least expendable of any of us."

"No one is expendable," she says. "We're all we have. Every time we lose someone, the only good that comes of it is that we remember how precious life is. And those we live it for."

Claudia murmurs agreement.

"But where is Luka?" Jester says. "And the other one?"

"Rolan. They'll be here in a bit."

I glance around the flat. It is exactly as I remember it, except that the furniture and wall art has changed. A colorful rug sprawls across the wooden living room floor, occupied by an ultramodern red sofa and matching love seat.

A tiny table and two chairs sit in the window alcove. But the black glass chandelier is the same.

"What happened to the current tenants?" I say, looking around us.

"We *suggested* they find somewhere else for a while, effective immediately," Jester says.

At least they kept the place tidy and don't seem to be smokers. I wander into the kitchen, pull open the short cabinet above the stove and discover a stash of white coffee mugs. American-size.

"Claudia said that you . . . ah, seem to remember some things?" Jester says behind me.

"You mean like the fact that the very first time we met, you were done up like an exotic flower and wearing green tights . . . but not your fake leg?" I say, turning, mug in hand. "So that you actually looked like you had a single stem?"

Jester breaks into the first laugh I've heard from her in over a week and hugs me.

"How can it be?" Claudia says. "When three weeks ago you remembered nothing? You didn't even know your name!"

I rummage around the small pantry for coffee.

"Here," Piotrek says, taking my mug, having already gotten the French press and electric kettle out across the small galley.

"I'm chalking it up to drowning. Or the

defibrillator. Or both," I say, leaning back against the counter.

"But it's okay. Because you have now found the thing you were protecting anyway, yes?" Piotrek says, spooning coffee into the press.

More than he realizes.

"So now what?" Claudia says.

I shed the floral housecoat and reach into my back pocket for the thumb drive I brought with me from France.

"Now we work on saving our own."

30

Claudia narrows her eyes as Jester comes to take the thumb drive.

"Saving our own, how?"

"By going back to court," I say.

Claudia purses her lips into the shape of a little heart, and then laughs. "You're crazy, you know that, don't you?" And then, more soberly: "No. You cannot. You know Nikola will *kill* you."

"He'd have to know I'm there," I say innocently.

She's weighing my words, her eyes like caged things behind her lashes. Of course they are; she and Piotrek have both paced for over a week behind Jester's screen, cooped up, hands tied, in hiding as the Zagreb court disbanded.

"Nikola's called for a celebration of remembrance in honor of Bucharest," Jester says. "A weeklong Bathory ball."

Piotrek spits out a string of Polish at that.

"Many of the surviving Romanians have already fled here. Bucharest's loss is Nikola's gain. Nikola has already added most of the Zagreb population. Others have come from Paris, Berlin—are coming from as far, even, as Moscow. Flooding Nikola's court with the greatest concentration of Progeny ever in one place." She looks meaningfully from me to the others.

The color drains from Claudia's face. "Oh my God," she whispers. "The night you met with Nikola. You said he brought hunters into the court, that they had access to its tunnels . . ."

"Yes," I say. "Which is why we have to shut it down. And why Rolan and I are going in alone."

Because for all I know, a "gas leak" could take out the underground tonight.

Which means Luka, too, stays behind.

One of you has to survive.

"No," Claudia says, shaking her head. "Absolutely not."

"She's right," Piotrek says. "We didn't come to watch Jester at her computer anymore. Sorry, Jester."

"Then Luka will stay with Jester—"

"I'm going, too," Jester says. "Because for this one, you'll need me."

"No. You can't," I say, panicked. "You have to get the contents of that drive out to the other courts! You're the only one who can keep leaking the evidence against the Scions."

"The contents of this drive will go up on the board within the hour. No. We are Progeny. Our blood was made to boil. Not simmer behind a monitor. You are not going without me."

If I said a part of me wasn't relieved, I would be lying. But the recklessness I felt coming here—

even up until ten minutes ago—has crumbled, giving way to new caution I can't afford.

"No. It's too dangerous. Anything could—"

"It is wrong," Piotrek says, "for us to sit in safety while others are in danger. We have hidden all our lives. We have run as long as we have been aware of what we are. You can't take the opportunity to fight away from us."

He takes me gently by the shoulders, ducks his head to gaze into my eyes. His are a far deeper blue than I realized. Not the winking sapphire that I've watched charm unsuspecting men and women alike, but the color of the sea ten thousand feet deep.

"This is not your decision, Audra. Your hands are clean, whatever happens."

"You realize you're trying to persuade a Firstborn," I say, with true affection.

"Yes. Is it working?" He smiles and kisses my cheek.

The three of them study the file from the thumb drive I brought with me on Jester's laptop in sober silence.

"This . . . this is something, Audra. Truly fantastic," Jester says, turning to look up at me. "We only have one problem: I'm certain there will be extra security. In the past, a Progeny guard was all it took to know that those coming in were Utod. But Nikola has every justification he needs now to require anyone coming in to show his or her face."

Claudia grimaces, and I understand that for a longtime member of any Progeny court, it's practically a human rights violation.

"And why wouldn't he? It's a handy way to take census of his growing court . . ."

"And keep an eye out for me."

She nods.

"As far as Nikola knows," I say, "my two priorities are keeping Luka safe beyond the reaches of anything associated with the Historian, and protecting the new contents of my brain—ostensibly by staying away myself."

"That is what a sane person would do, yes," she says wryly.

"What entrance are they posting?"

She glances at her screen. "One four blocks from here, on the other side of the hill."

"Well, I happen to know there's a house that leads to the main underground grotto, just down the street." I don't mention that I wasn't supposed to live to retain that information.

"You don't think they'll be using it for VIPs or something?" Claudia says.

"She is a VIP!" Piotrek says, gesturing at me.

I shake my head. "The tunnel was too long and winding to usher any kind of traffic. For all we know, it's the same entrance the Historian used herself."

I actually pause, considering that.

"Have you tried getting into Serge's surveillance systems at all?" I say.

Jester shakes her head. "The last thing we can afford is a digital trail or single mistake when we're leaking the things we are. Why risk it if you've got Serge in your pocket?"

"Excuse me. Back to a practical matter," Claudia says. "What are we going to wear? Housecoats and babushkas?"

"Come here," I say, going into the bedroom.

I shed my jacket, drop it on the bed. Cross to the closet and slide the pocket door open. It's full of the tenants' dresses, blouses, and men's tailored shirts. I shove them all to one side, get down on my knees. Reach to the dusty floorboards along the back.

"Is this *Prada*?" Claudia says behind me. I glance back to find her searching for the label on my jacket.

"It's all yours," I say, digging my nails beneath a piece of wooden molding.

Piotrek comes to stand in the doorway, steaming mug in one hand. "Audra, my dear. What are you doing?"

"She's lost her marbles," Claudia says, sliding my jacket on.

"It wouldn't be the first time," I murmur. "Claudia, how many times have you been in this room?"

"Thirty-two."

I glance back at her, weirdly. She shrugs. "It's true."

"And I used to think I was strange." Though I note I haven't resorted to my old habit of comparing anyone's ears to eggs in days.

"Does this room look different to you?" I say. An instant later, the molding rips from its nail and I fall onto my butt.

Claudia comes to peer into the small space and gasps. "I didn't even notice!" she exclaims. "Your memory is better than mine. How is that possible?"

"I remember patterns and you have OCD?" I say, tugging a chunk of drywall free.

Piotrek hands his mug to Claudia. By the time Luka and Rolan arrive, he has torn most of the closet's back wall open.

"Do I even want to ask what's happening in here?" Luka says, walking into the bedroom.

I take one look at him and laugh hard enough to hurt myself. He and Rolan are both dressed in housecoats and head scarves, and while Luka makes an almost pretty little old lady, I have to admit, Rolan looks positively hideous.

At first I think that's what causes Claudia and Jester to stand off and stare. But then I realize they've never met Rolan in person. And despite his obvious aid to me through the last several weeks, they have no reason to trust him.

Rolan seems to sense this, too, as he slides the scarf from his head.

"This is Rolan," I say, wiping my hands on my designer jeans and standing. "But I guess you got that."

Silence from the others. And I know what they're thinking: Two full-blown hunters stand mere feet away from four Progeny. A single one of them could go to the Historian with everything she has ever wanted from my memory alone. How many Progeny lives could they expose and destroy from the knowledge contained in our four memories combined?

The answer: all of them.

Piotrek is the first to step forward and shake Rolan's hand, before giving Luka a more comfortable clap on the shoulder.

And tense and strange as this scene might be, it gives me hope for a future beyond this one.

If we survive the night.

31

By ten o'clock, the closet is open. And by "open," I mean that the entire back and one side have been ripped away to reveal a space nearly six feet deep and twice as wide.

I reach inside to flip the second switch. As the interior comes to life, Claudia steps over the ruined back wall through what might as well be an invisible looking glass.

"Ah . . . I wondered what happened to this one," she says, lifting out an abbreviated ball gown dripping bullion fringe. The tapestry of the bodice showcases the image of some French medieval emperor. Embroidery covers the sleeves. And though the costume is breathtaking, I know the reason she sighs is that it belonged to Katia.

Claudia slides down the rack, fingering one garment after another, talking about the time so-and-so wore it, how much better it fit someone else. How that one used to be so plain until some Progeny girl inherited it—and completely made it over so that everyone else wished they had it . . . and this one tore when one of Katia's crazy friends leapt from a fifth-story window onto one of the ornate statues outside a building near the opera house.

"She was killed two days later. Drella, we called her. Her real name was Giselle. The last time I saw her, it was morning. She turned one way down the street, and I went another. When I looked back, she did, too, and waved. Her shoes were in her other hand."

"When was that?" I say, stepping in after her past an entire box of wigs, and another filled with ostrich feathers, pink plumes, and ornate masks.

"Nineteen months ago," Claudia says softly. "Four days . . . eleven hours."

I stand there for a quiet moment, realizing that despite my claims, I *have* discounted her. For her youth, her love of beautiful things. Her moodiness. "A court of savants," Nikola called us, the second-to-last time I saw him. Misunderstood genius in every form. How many deaths has she counted, and how many hours since those she knew expired? How many good-byes has she clung to, realizing each one was the last?

Even genius is its own form of pain.

Claudia shakes me out of my reverie with a flash of gold. Holding up an elaborate Asian dress, she says, "I claim this one."

"Whatever you want," I say, as Piotrek comes in to rummage, and Rolan stands warily back, to stare. I have a different reason for wanting to get in here.

I fish through an oversize hatbox of stockings, and then its twin, filled with gloves.

"What about you, Audra?" Claudia says.

"You'll see."

Piotrek holds up one hanger and then another. "Firebird or gypsy queen?"

He's been around Claudia way too long.

I find what I've been looking for, push back onto my heels, and stand. Look around for Luka. Find him changing into a clean shirt in the spare bedroom.

"Luka . . ."

I've been waiting for his flat refusal to let me go to court alone. To my surprise, he shakes his head when I start to explain.

"You're right," he says. "You have to go. You're Audra Ellison. Audra Szabo." He lifts his gaze to me.

It's the first time I've ever heard that name—mine, my mother's surname—used together.

"Audra Novak," I say.

He gives me a small smile.

"I promise this isn't about protecting you. It's about—"

"I know what it's about." There are new circles beneath his eyes on top of the bruises.

I nod, look down between us.

"If I could do this for you, go as you, I would. And I know I can't." He closes his eyes, breath escaping in a whisper as he says, "I hate this entire thing."

I wrap my arms around him and kiss him, and

I can *feel* how tired he is. But it's the slump of his shoulders—the defeat in them—that actually scares me.

He's only twenty-three. No one should look so beaten down that young.

"Do me a favor," I say, stepping back.

He looks at me.

"Sleep tonight. I'll be back by the time you wake up, lying right beside you."

I hope.

He nods and takes one of my hands. "What's this?" he says.

"This "—I hold up the purple lightbulb—"is in case you can't sleep."

He lifts his brows.

I unlock the door, pull him from the bedroom across the narrow hall into the flat's only bathroom, and shut the door.

"What does this remind you of?" I say.

"The night we found the tattoo on your back in Graz?"

"I think this was actually the inspiration for that," I say, reaching up to unscrew the three bulbs across the top of the light fixture, taking the middle one out completely. The bathroom goes black.

"What am I going to see lit up this time?" he says.

I replace the middle bulb with the purple one, tighten it into place.

The walls come to life in the dark light.

They are the scribblings of a woman obsessed. A savant indeed, who needed to process. Who didn't dare keep a journal.

At least, not yet.

Me.

Names of new friends. Their relationships. The stories they told. They line the eastern wall. My mother's name is there.

On the western wall, the names of hunters, of Scions, by generation. Twelve original names near the top of the wall, just beneath the crease of the ceiling. Farther down: the three known Historians, in their family lines, circled. All taken from the envelope of notes from my mother.

To the right of the mirror: the names of foundling hospitals and locations of baby boxes. Of monks from various monasteries.

To the left: possible baby names. Amerie, my mother. Emily, for my high school best friend. Amy, for my adoptive mother. Eva, for Luka's. Barbara, the alias my mother lived under.

Luka turns in a slow circle, taking in the scribbles so much like the product of a manic episode. A wild garden of ruminations that exploded onto the walls over the course of months—during the day, before dressing for court at night, in the morning before collapsing into bed. As though worried I might forget some detail if I didn't see it with my eyes.

"Welcome to my brain," I say with a small laugh. "But this is what I wanted you to see." I point next to the mirror, to the first thing ever written on these walls:

Luka and Audra . . . (Luka's name, with a heart around it) . . . *Audra Novak* . . . *Mr. and Mrs. Luka Novak* . . . *Mrs. Luka Gerard Novak* . . .

Eva Amerie Szabo Novak.

"How middle school can you get, right?" I say. "But look." Beside each line is a date.

The date we met.

The date we became lovers.

The date I first wondered what it would be like to marry Luka . . .

The date he asked me.

The date, on the last line, that we married.

The date Eva was due, if not born.

She came two weeks early.

"I just wanted you to see—to know—that I had already thought about marrying you before you ever asked." I turn and take his hands. "That I loved you. I loved you first." I smile in the purple light.

"No way," he says, shaking his head, something pained about his expression.

"Way. And when you asked me to marry you, after I came back, and I said no . . ." I whisper with a smile. "What I really meant, was *yes.*"

I pull a marker from my pocket and add two lines with two new dates:

The date I met him again in Maine . . .

And two days ago, when I woke up, remembering everything.

I cap the marker, set it on the sink, and then slide my arms around his shoulders.

"And I did fall in love with you again. Exactly like I thought I would. Well, not exactly like I thought it would happen," I concede. "None of this really went as planned."

"But," he says, kissing me, "I loved you before I told you. And wanted to marry you before I asked you. You should see *my* bathroom wall." He laughs softly, but it ends in a broken sound. He pulls me tighter against him, and then lifts me up onto the edge of the sink. I wrap my legs around him as he buries his head in my neck.

"I love you," he says roughly, hands sliding up my sides. "Never forget that. Get back safely. Come back alive." But there's sadness in his voice.

32

It's nearly midnight, quiet except for the bark of an occasional dog, conversations of late-night couples out for a walk two blocks over. The distant sounds of the river walk. But the bright lights of this city are reserved for the Pest side of the capital, where ruin pubs and raucous hostels are just shifting into full swing—at least for those above ground level.

Jester walks ahead of us in a blue peacoat, the blunt cut of her blond wig bouncing over her shoulders. I'm not sure how she got all her dreads under there.

We steal up the back path between two residential buildings. Double back beneath a tree-lined walk to the house on Csónak Street. I pause, point soundlessly to the camera above the gate's stone arch. Piotrek bends down and lifts Claudia onto his shoulders just out of sight of the camera. She pulls a creamy tube of purple lip gloss from her pocket, squeezes a glob onto her finger. Reaches up, smears it across the lens.

Jester consults her phone, taps out a brief message. A moment later, the gate unlocks with an audible click. She pushes it open, gestures us inside like a butler, which makes me shudder;

the last time I was here, there was indeed a masked butler who answered the door.

A large plum tree obscures most of the small, overgrown courtyard, including the front stoop badly in need of paint.

Piotrek moves up the step to the door, glances back, shakes his head no, and looks at me.

But I don't sense any Progeny within, either.

Rolan moves up beside him, clicks the safety off his gun. Piotrek pries open the door. The frame gives way with a crack that sounds far too loud in the darkness.

Phones become flashlights inside the decrepit interior. And it's as I thought: empty, the house's innocuousness its best security feature.

I point to the back of the house, and Rolan pushes me behind him. We follow him down two flights of stairs to the small chamber I remember. The tunnel is boarded shut. Once again, Piotrek and Rolan set to work with crowbar and hammer.

Twenty minutes later, I'm leading them through the broadening tunnel into a series of corridors.

Claudia glances at me, and I can tell she's nervous. There are stories of Progeny wandering beyond the boundaries of this court and never being seen or heard from again—even as recently as five years ago. It would be all too easy to make a single wrong turn, get lost in these underground passages forever.

For anyone else but me.

We emerge in a cavern shored up with ancient brick. Rolan tilts his head, and I know he has heard the faint drum of that industrial pulse amplified by the series of grottoes farther on. And even Claudia takes a half step back at the sheer presence of the Progeny mass in this underground hive.

I nod toward a smaller tunnel as dark as the one we just came from.

They emerge like strange butterflies from chrysalises: Piotrek, the gold and crimson matador, sharp in his "suit of lights," his full face mask featuring a patch over one eye. I teased him earlier about apparently not being a very good bullfighter—or having a run-in with a pirate.

Rolan, the duke who could not be persuaded even by Claudia to get into the pirate getup. Who actually looks very stately in his powdered wig, midnight blue velvet coat, and buckled shoes.

Claudia, the Chinese empress, a rainfall of gold cascading from her black, upswept wig. She turns toward me, the crimson lips of her full face mask a near-perfect imitation of the way her lips look when she purses them in real life.

Jester removes her peacoat and blond wig, pulls the skullcap of her bodysuit over her dreads. Transforms into a black bird woman with gold-tipped feathers and gilded claws, glittering beak on her mask.

"Hurry up," she says, reaching to help me with my cloak, pulling it carefully from the ruff standing out from my neck.

I adjust the beaded headpiece holding the long, black wig securely on my head. The red velvet dress is heavy; its sleeves fall to my knees. Claudia has loaded my neck with jewels, but there is one feature of this costume that stands out beyond them or the chandeliers hanging from my ears . . .

The giant embroidered gold dragon with its three talons snaking down my shoulder.

I've come as Bathory herself.

"Are . . . are you sure you want to wear that?" Claudia said at first, chewing her lip. "There will be other Countess Bathorys there, right?"

"Of course," Jester said. "And Nikola would never expect it of a fugitive Firstborn. A bit too on the mark, no?"

But that's exactly what I'm hoping he'll expect.

A part of me wishes I had my gold pendant, left behind in Zagreb, though it might be too much of a dead giveaway.

Literally.

I reach toward my left arm, for the single accessory chosen not by me but by Rolan: a knife, the sheath of which is strapped, upside down, to the inside of my upper arm.

My breath feels hot behind the full face mask as we skirt into the first grotto. I pause to gaze down a dimly lit corridor.

"What's down there?" Piotrek whispers.

From here I can just make out the pillars, the roughly hewn carved heads that top each one of them, vacant eyes staring at everything and nothing at once.

"That's where we were," I say.

Jester grabs her mask by the beak, holds it out from her face. "Let's see the court itself."

I know the direction from my nightmares. Would know it anyway, from the sound.

I lead them through the bright eye of the next grotto and down a tunnel increasingly filled with glittering others.

Kings, princesses, barons. Egyptian gods and gypsies. Indian maharajas, Siamese princes, and czars. Swans, phoenixes, and firebirds. Color and gold everywhere. Driven by a relentless electronic beat tinged with Bulgarian rhythms. Drowning out words. I feel, more than hear, Claudia suck in a breath. Even Jester stops cold.

There have to be four hundred Progeny here.

The ceiling rains gold light like coins. But it's not the light or the music fueling the frenzy . . . rather the sheer density of the others like us.

The strobe shutters, goes black. The cavern erupts in a roar. Daggers and dragons and serpents appear where jewels and velvet once were. Twined around wrists and throats. Streaking down bare backs. Tearing at shoulders. Skeletal teeth glowing on red-rouged lips. The dark story behind the glittering gold. On the far cavern wall: the Glagolitic number three, at least a story tall.

The strobe flashes. Shocks the cavern to erratic black-and-white life. A film jerked out in frames.

Claudia's eyes are wild. Piotrek's chest rises and falls, too rapidly, in his glittering suit. Like addicts confronting a drug they cannot overcome or quit, and don't know when—if—it will ever be available again. And I feel it, too, crawling along the base of my skull, dictating the rhythm of my heart, tugging at my skin.

In a flash, they are gone.

Jester gives me a quick last look and melts into the fray.

And it's all I can do not to run after them.

Rolan stays close, but he's staring.

"Your mask!"

I don't understand what he's saying, reach up to touch it, make sure it's in place.

"It's a skull! A crowned skull," he says, as the cavern explodes in crimson light.

How bizarre this all must seem to him! Meanwhile, this is the closest I'll ever come to one of those awkward extended family reunions.

A golden-haired king crowned with a headpiece like a stag sweeps in front of me, grabs my hand. Rolan starts but holds back as the stag bends over my fingers, barely brushing them before melting into the melee.

I watch Rolan's eyes flick this way and that over the crowd. Wonder if he's trying to find the others . . .

And realize he's looking for Nikola.

He has to be here. If not in the cavern itself, then somewhere else, watching. He called this celebration. There's no way he'd miss the opportunity to watch his kingdom swell.

I glance around but can't see past the riot of silk and gold, more regal than the Zagreb court and more feral. A hooded cobra to Zagreb's frenetic rattlesnake.

I move into the cavern, looking for Piotrek, Claudia, and Jester. When I don't see them, a new surge of adrenaline floods my veins like fear.

I begin to push my way into the glittering throng.

The mob melts away.

Just ahead, a Baroque baron does a double take, removes his hat, steps back, bows low. Farther on, a gilded courtesan with a deadly-looking fan of knives drops into a curtsy.

Heads swivel, their masks animated only by eyes.

I glance at Rolan, thinking this is hilarious,

Progeny bowing to the duke who isn't even one of them!

Until I realize he's standing on my other side.

They aren't bowing to him . . . they're bowing to me.

Panic seizes my heart.

Rolan grabs my hand. Leads me forward on an invisible carpet. The music forgotten, the throng parts like a sea.

Colors blur around me into a gilded mass. I try to remind myself that the prince bowing his feathered turban low is probably just some kid. That the chick in the gold star crown is a college girl from the States for all I know.

Maybe her name is Emily.

Like that, the golden costumes are lost on me. I see, instead, a glittering company of souls that deserve to live. With royal blood—gifts and legacy—in their veins. I want to touch them, and I do, fingertips drifting over foreheads and cheeks, clasping hands with those farther back, who reach for me.

I know they don't see me. Not Audra from Sioux City, Iowa. But *her*. The devoted mother history made a monster, from which a multitude of orphans and misfits were born. Savants and geniuses. Derelicts and outcasts. Too strange to call anyone but others like them family, too hunted to be allowed to live. Too fragile and strong at once to survive the embers of jealousy that should have burned out centuries ago.

Rolan falls away, and when I look back at him, he is staring at the strange enactment taking place. I want to tell him that this isn't how it is. That they don't know who I am—that I am Firstborn and nobody. The most hunted and least among us all. That it's just the costume . . .

Claudia was right; she taught me what I am. That love is not earned but bestowed—even as I watched her struggle to learn to give it.

I can't remember if I told her I loved her. If I've ever told Jester, or Piotrek, or Katia, or Andre . . .

So I tell these others instead.

I love you. I love you.

I see you.

Tears run from beneath a courtesan's mask. I kiss her hair.

The strobe flutters, flashes to the music, goes black. Breaks the spell, as the serpents and dragons emerge again.

And then the music dies.

The giant Glagolitic three—the same symbol I carved on the doorframe of my flat in Zagreb—disappears as another image takes its place. A giant projection, as tall, nearly, as the cavern itself.

Me.

Rolan stands protectively behind me as

celebrants glance at one another. *What's happening? Who is that?*

"Hello," the giant image of me says. It is the product of a talented hair and makeup artist who labored for two hours. But on the cavern wall like that, she is fiercely striking, deliveringa message with all the charisma of the Utod.

"My name is Audra Ellison. I am the daughter of Amerie Szabo."

Subtitles appear beneath my face in three different languages.

A murmur ripples through the assembled crowd. Exclamations erupt from farther away. An insult, hurled at my projected face.

"You have heard of my mother, who is gone. And you have heard, quite possibly, of me. But not all that you heard is true. I am no traitor. I am no savior.

"Like many of you, I am an orphan. I am also Firstborn. And so are you. Firstborn to someone. Loved, even if you don't know it. And wanted. By the parents who were lucky enough to raise you. By the parents heartbroken to have given you up."

A cry issues from somewhere near me. A broken sob, farther down.

"I recently discovered a cache of damning information about the Historian's most powerful Scions that we are in the process of leaking to the world. Good news to those of us who want to live free.

"The work we are doing today to take down the strongest pillars of the Historian's citadel has just begun and may take years. The convictions—if they take place at all—may take decades. The hunters assigned to you are zealots committed to their cause. But the killing can end. It will end. And it does end, with you."

A brief smattering of cheers. The rest are struggling to understand, or to keep up with the translations.

"With luck and God's grace, this will be the last generation of Progeny hunters to ever walk the earth."

A woman beside us bursts out weeping.

"There are those of us who have devoted ourselves to finding and ending the Historian. Her days are numbered."

A ripple of shocked shouts from the crowd.

"Soon, she will have no money to support or reward her hunters. No incentive for her hate. No means to hunt!"

A rising roar, deafening our ears.

"Until then, we give you the best tool we have: information. These are the names and faces of the hunters assigned to those Utod known to the Historian. Perhaps you, like me, will recognize your hunter's face. Have even made his or her acquaintance. Guard yourself. Protect yourself. Save yourself.

"I wish you life. I pray for us mercy and the hope of tomorrow."

Silence, as the screen morphs to the first face. A man in his twenties who might be any kid in grad school or working the mail room of a Fortune 500 company, his name listed across the bottom of the screen. A woman, also in her twenties, who could be a collegiate athlete. A kid who looks like he's in the military.

I glance at Rolan as the faces continue to flash across the wall. Ten of them. Thirty. Seventy. The montage goes on and on. Cries erupt at some of them. Murmurs at others. A scream at one.

This time, no one notices Countess Bathory as she makes her way to the far edge of the giant cavern.

No one, that is, except for Nikola.

33

I know him the moment I see him, even robed and masked.

His costume has not changed.

The same black robe of death. The same white, expressionless mask as before. Incognito to anyone expecting a prince clad in more finery than the devoted have worn here tonight.

He waits until the video has ended. Anticipates—expertly—the cries and applause and cheers that go on and on. I wonder if he saw the deference shown me earlier, though no one else could have known that I'm *her*.

But he knows.

I made sure of that.

The lights come on, full force. Blaring and too bright and unforgiving at once, as Nikola takes a small stage near the front.

And then he takes a page from my own playbook.

He tears off his mask.

The place goes frantic, and then wild.

He holds out his hands to quiet the mob.

"Progeny. Utod," he says. He's miked, and his voice booms through the massive sound system. "I know you are confused. I called the daughter of Amerie Szabo a traitor. I said the rumors of her being Firstborn were untrue. Let me explain."

He pauses to translate into Hungarian, then continues.

"What you have not known—what I could not share—is that Audra has been working for me. For us. For life! And she has delivered," Nikola says. "It's true. We are behind the leaks hitting the news, even now, tonight!"

He's taking credit for Jester's work?

But I've left him no other card.

I glance around, wonder where she is. Fight back a surge of fear. If Nikola's out here after she managed to get the presentation to play from his control center, what's happened to her? To Claudia? To Piotrek?

Nikola continues:

"To this end, the Historian had to believe Audra Ellison was a traitor. So I condemned her— loudly—as a Progeny consumed with her own desire for power at any cost. What the Historian did not know is that Progeny do not betray their own!" he shouts. "One mother! One blood!"

The refrain echoes from the back and ripples toward the front.

One mother! One blood!

Nikola raises his hands for quiet.

"We have worked for the freedom of generations to come. Justice will not be swift. But the end to our persecution is in sight. We will decide our future. Not the Historian. Not the

Scions. Not the hunters. And one day soon . . . we will be free."

The cheers become a rolling roar.

By now I'm actively pressing my way through the crowd. Have to nudge my way past those caught up in the frenzy. After the video and the revelation of the hunters, Nikola's appearance and rousing speech have galvanized them more than any frenetic rave.

Several people turn and take notice of me. Turn to hail—not me, but the giant gold dragon snaking down my shoulder. Reach to touch it. To take my hand.

I slip through them like water, do not stop on my way to Nikola's dais. I want to kill him with a murderous outrage I have never felt before—for pretending to help those he'd gladly sacrifice. For manipulating those he should protect.

His head turns, gaze fixed squarely on me. I have forced him into this spot, this new alliance, and he is angry. But every reservation I felt returning to this place has long melted away. He doesn't dare move against me in front of what is no doubt the largest gathering of Progeny in history.

But also because I've offered him a better public ally than the one rapidly losing key resources and hiding in her rat hole at this very moment. And he knows it.

Twenty feet from the stage, a loud murmur

begins and passes through the cavern. The crowd parts before me. Nikola hesitates onstage.

I pull off my mask, drop it behind me.

"It's her," someone whispers, and then shouts: "It's her!"

An excited murmur ripples through the crowd as masks swivel, blank-faced, toward me. My name rises up like a startled flock of birds.

Nikola's voice returns at last. "On this night of remembrance and new beginnings . . ." He extends a long arm. "I give you our own Audra Ellison!"

An aisle opens to the stage as cheers explode through the cavern, deafening me.

And then something stops me momentarily in my tracks. Ahead of me, a gilded Greek goddess slowly removes her mask.

Beside her, a maharaja does the same—revealing himself as a towheaded blond. Farther on, a young woman as dusky-skinned as Jester, and a man with distinctly Eurasian features.

The boy can't be more than twenty. The girl ahead of me, no more than eighteen. She should be finishing her senior year somewhere, dressing up for prom—not for this.

The girl grabs my hand as I pass. Lets it go reluctantly as I reach the stage. Nikola pulls me up beside him.

I turn to look out at the Progeny gathered around us, as one by one they remove their masks. My gaze falls on a girl standing near the front. A waif dressed as a white swan, a delicate tiara on her head.

She can't be more than sixteen. The age Claudia was when Katia found her digging through trash cans for food.

It isn't Claudia that she reminds me of, though, with her huge eyes and sparrow's bones for wrists. Not Claudia . . . but Ana, who died just two weeks ago.

Suddenly I'm not sure I can do what I have to next.

34

Nikola grabs my hand. I try to twitch away, but his grip is too strong. Crushing my fingers in his, he raises my arm into the air.

"Behold the newest royalty of the Progeny nation. The new Prince—Princess—of Zagreb!" he shouts triumphantly as his eyes bore into me like drills.

He reaches up with his other hand, taps off his mike. The next instant, the overhead lights black out, plunging the dais into darkness. The music thunders back to life.

Nikola hauls me from the stage straight toward the back wall—which turns out to be not a wall but a panel of cleverly painted fabric obscuring a tunnel.

"The others are looking for me," I shout as he drags me after him. The passageway is lined with a simple row of industrial lanterns set in brackets, electrical wires hanging between them.

And no fewer than six guards.

"I'm sure they are," he growls.

"They'll notice if I don't return. As will the entire *Progeny nation* out there."

"Oh, you will return," he says dangerously. "You will return, you will thank your new subjects that I have so *generously* given you, and you will also thank me." He turns down an unlit side passage, yanks open a heavy wooden door, shoves me ahead of him, and slams the door shut behind us. Once inside, he throws away my hand as though it were a piece of garbage.

We're in a surveillance room. Screens line the expansive back wall, most of their cameras trained on the cavern, where the strobe is setting off a new series of epileptic fits throughout the court. Gone, the frozen masks, replaced by flesh-and-blood faces upturned in frenzied rapture. Two screens monitor tonight's entrance, which is attended by at least four guards that I can see. Three more flicker among varied tunnels and grottoes, including the colonnaded passage to the room where I met the Historian and the house on Csónak Street—or at least that's what I'm guessing it to be by the dark smear across its lens.

Music blares from a set of speakers, broadcast from the cavern system itself.

Nikola storms away from me, hands going to his head, looking for all the world like he might bash it into the stone wall. A moment later, he grabs one of several remotes from the table in front of the monitors and turns the volume down.

"Do you know . . . what you have done?" he says quietly.

"Yes. I've told the truth."

"You have put a price on my head now as surely as it is on yours. But not just mine . . ." He gestures to the bank of screens. "On all of theirs as well!"

"There was always a price on their heads, Nikola!" I say. "Or have you forgotten what it means to be hunted?"

"This was the one safe place left to us. You have cost all of us our only sanctuary!"

"You call this hole safe?" I shout. "When the Historian herself has been in these tunnels?"

"We had an alliance," he says, closing his eyes, as though I were too stupid to begin to understand.

"I noticed—when you handed me over to her!"

"A small price, the life of one for many. Would you not sacrifice yourself for the welfare of your kind? Does it matter who makes the choice for you, if the result is the same?"

"How is delivering *more power* to the Historian a sacrifice for many?"

He turns away to sit on the edge of the desk in front of the monitors.

"The way you are with them . . ." he says faintly. "The way you stand out from them. You have no idea the power you hold over them, do you?" His voice hardens. "I wanted to kill you less than an hour ago."

"You've always wanted to kill me."

"That's not true." He shakes his head. "It is

the furthest thing from the truth. I have wanted many things for you. Things you have not always seen fit to envision for yourself. But—" He waves his hand. "You have no memory of that anymore. You see me as some villain, having no context of our history. Yours and mine. We were allies, once. And now, we will be again."

"I lost my memory, Nikola. Not my mind."

"You owe your life to the swift speech of your friends. You realize that, don't you? Your friend Jester got caught in our media room. I nearly shot her," he says lightly.

I go very still as a chill pours down my spine—cold, and then hot.

"Until she explained that you had come to bring a very valuable service. To me, she claimed, in an effort to save your life."

"What have you done with Jester?" I demand.

"I have detained her. But I am not unreasonable. And I have seen merit in what she said, for us both."

Urgency rises up in me like panic. Unlike everyone else out in the cavern, I have burned none of the frenetic energy about to explode through my pores, fear and shock having done little to remove its raw edges.

"Nikola . . ." I say as evenly as I can. "She has nothing to do with this. It was me. I need to find the Historian."

"Truly, Audra, you are such a confused girl. Railing against me one minute for having brought you to the Historian before. And now you want to find her?"

"Yes."

"She'll kill you."

"That's not your problem."

"But I'm afraid that it is."

"Please, Nikola. Let Jester go and tell me how to find the Historian."

I don't want to beg. I meant to come in every position of strength that I could. But I am—begging.

He looks disgusted. "Just like your mother, throwing your life away."

"She didn't throw her life away. You took it!"

"Do you really think anyone who loved Amerie could have killed her? No matter how much she might have deserved it—how much it might have needed to be done?"

I stare at him. "If you didn't, then who did?"

"She marched to her own destruction. As you are doing now."

"What's it to you? If I die, I become a martyr. And the Historian gets what she wants. Either way, you win."

He glances down with a small smile. "You know, there was a time that I aspired to be a martyr. To live on in the minds of our kind after my inevitable, and no doubt early, death." He looks at me. "And then I realized I'd rather not die at all. That I'd rather live, even without my gifts, and find another way to power when they were gone.

"Besides, there is one problem with martyrs among the Utod: They take down a portion of the population with them. You, however, without your memory of before . . . you would condemn only those you know and love most. You truly want to find the Historian even though you will die and lose all that you worked to find?"

"Yes," I say softly.

His hand lashes out, slaps me hard enough to spin me into the wall.

"Do not lie to my face!"

I stagger, clutch at a chair.

"Don't you see? Everything's changed! You want to kill her! You think, in your arrogance, that you can? Well, if that is how you choose to die, who am I to stop you? *This* is how you find the Historian: You go out there." He points in the direction of the cavern. "You *thank* me for the princedom I have bestowed on you, and then *publicly* relocate your court to Budapest and my protection. Do *that,* and I will tell you how to find the Historian."

Can I do that? Pretend this underground court is safe for just one day in the name of finding my daughter?

I close my eyes, summon the image of Eva. But it is replaced by the swan girl standing in the crowd.

How did she keep from getting trampled all this time? This court, these rough-hewn caverns, are no place for a girl that age. She should be in a mall with her friends, trying on lipstick. In the freshman hallway, laughing by her locker. Skateboarding down the sidewalk.

Just like Ana should have been.

But Ana, too, found her way here after slipping away from the rest of us in Graz. To bargain with Nikola after Nino was taken.

And Nikola killed her.

It's my job to protect Eva. But does that girl— any girl or boy out there—deserve to live any less?

"I can't do that," I whisper.

"You can. You will, if you want to save your friend."

Nikola comes toward me, and I flinch away, but this time his hands are gentle as he wraps an arm around my shoulder. I stumble and clutch at the front of his robe.

"Poor, lost thing," he sighs, holding me against him. "If you had only come to me, this could have been different. But you force my hand instead."

"No court is safe anymore," I say. "Not even yours. Especially yours. The Historian knows these tunnels—could walk in with her hunters, kill everyone, at any moment! You have to send these people away."

He drops his arm, stares at me as though I'm insane.

"It has been safe *because* I've given her access. Because she *knows* she rules it at her pleasure, through me. It's the reason there will never be an attack on Budapest. Because of *me,* and *my alliance* with the Historian. My willingness to hand you and whatever you've found over to her was the *price* of this sanctuary! And now you've ruined it. Especially now that you've released the names and faces of her hunters to the masses! Made them believe they're *empowered.*"

"They are."

"When is an animal raised in captivity ever able to survive in the wild? Let them out of this cage, and what will they do? I'll tell you: look for a new one. They don't *know how to be free!*"

"Speak for yourself."

He straightens to his full height, glowers down at me. "I have lived long enough to know what it means to make choices."

"You've lived long enough to lose your gifts. The only power you have left is whatever the Historian is willing to let you keep while she picks a few Progeny out of the herd for her hunters whenever she needs new Scions. Which keeps the Utod afraid and coming back here, to you."

"Better that a few of them die," he spits. "They don't know how to function in the world."

"It's called living, Nikola," I say. "And everyone has to figure it out."

"You could have been a god to them. Didn't you see the way they looked at you? Like the embodiment of Bathory herself. You may be willing to throw that away, but I am not. Kill the Historian if you can, but the hunters will survive for a generation without her. It's enough time for me. I will be prince for as long as I live. After that . . . what do I care?"

I step toward him. "You will close down this court. Or they will know how you killed Ana and Nino, and the way you handed me over to the Historian for my mother's documents—"

"They were to be mine! *I* was her sibling. *I* protected her!"

"She knew better than to leave them in your power-hungry hands. And so did I. I told you a year ago I'd never give them to you for that reason. Which is why you tried to kill me the first time."

His eyes widen.

"*Remember,* Nikola? *Because I do!*"

"That may be," he says dangerously, and then points to the monitors behind him. "But you will never survive to tell them."

I glance up at the screens.

"I don't need to. You already have."

He stares at me and then turns.

The image on every one of them is so static as to seem frozen, each figure in that crowd gone still.

"The Historian's hunters know this place and can return any time," I say loudly. "You are not safe here!"

As my words echo from the speaker, Nikola glances down at his robe, looks for his mike.

I lift my hand, the tiny red light flashing in my palm.

With a savage roar, he lunges for me as panic breaks out in the cavern.

35

I shout Rolan's name. But nothing can be heard over the chaos in the cavern, the skirmish in the corridor outside.

The mike has fallen from my hand, skittered away. Nikola drives me into the wall, hands around my throat.

His thumbs lock over my windpipe, and my lungs turn to fire. Lightning shoots behind my eyes as he pulls me toward him, spittle spraying from his lips onto my cheek.

The next instant, his eyes go wide. He blinks, expression confused. I grab his forearm, punch him in the throat for all I'm worth. Shove my knee into his groin. But it's the knife between his ribs that sends him staggering back.

I'm on him in a flash, tackling him into the table, falling with him to the floor. Crazed from pain and unspent adrenaline. By the lives at risk in the ancient subterranean hunting grounds. At the prospect of all he has cost me.

My mother. My daughter.

"Tell me how to find her!" But I no longer know which "her" I mean.

He throws me aside, and I launch myself at him again. Grapple for the knife hilt glinting between his fingers, red as the bloody velvet of my dress as he tries to pull it free.

Nino. Ana . . .

A wheezing grunt erupts from his mouth as I shove the hilt deeper, up toward his ribs, hitting bone.

Tibor.

I scream for Rolan.

Nikola lets out a wet, broken laugh.

"Looking for someone . . . to finish the job?"

"No," I say, jerking the hilt of the knife free. "Just afraid you'll bleed to death before he can get here."

I drive the knife into his stomach, my entire weight behind it, hair dangling in his face.

"You see," I whisper near his ear. "I brought my own hunter into your court."

"I was . . . finished . . . when you showed up here," he hisses from the pool of his robes, smeared like a bloody mop on the floor.

"Tell me how to find the Historian! Let it come from your lips instead of your memory."

He smiles, gums bloody.

"Where is she?" I demand. "Where do you meet her? Who's her lackey? What's his name?"

He looks away.

"I'm offering you a shot at redemption, Nikola!"

"I lived as a prince . . ." he says, eyelids beginning to sag. "I die . . . a prince."

"Oh no. No, you don't!" I push to my feet, stagger across the room to tear open the door.

"Rolan!" I run down the corridor. The guards are gone.

Mayhem from the direction of the cavern. Sounds of an all-out brawl from the next tunnel.

"Rolan!" I scream.

A few seconds later, he comes running into the corridor. He's lost his hat and mask, though not his velvet coat.

"Audra!"

"Hurry," I say, turning on a slippery heel.

I don't think about the fact that I have become a killer. That witnessing this final act will make me no better than the hunter I've asked to complete it.

I am thinking of one person now, and one person only.

I tear back down the corridor, into the surveillance room. Come up short on the blood-soaked stone.

The room is empty.

"Where is he?" Rolan says, behind me.

I run out into the corridor, in the other direction, toward the unlit tunnel.

"Audra, wait!" Rolan says, rushing after me.

He's got his gun in one hand, pulls out his phone with the other, hands it to me, flashlight on.

We run twenty yards into the tunnel before it

abruptly ends. Stop, stymied, before doubling back. Rolan nudges me, points down the floor of a narrow side corridor. Droplets of blood.

We duck into it, winding one way and then another, until the blood disappears and the tunnel dead-ends.

I go back, retrace our steps. Feel my way along the walls in case one of them is another painted hoax. Retrace our steps again.

But Nikola is gone.

36

By the time we return to the cavern, half the population has taken to the tunnels for the surface.

And I have just lost my single tie to the Historian.

"How could he just vanish?" I shout.

But I know how. The Budapest princes have owned the city's only survey of these caves since the late 1800s, when it disappeared.

They know this subterranean maze better than anyone.

We emerge into the dwindling chaos. Progeny stand around in groups, some of them pointing toward exits, some bobbing as though the music were still going, unheard by everyone else. A few of them crying, comforting one another.

I make my way along the perimeter of the cavern, looking for Jester's bird or Piotrek's harlequin, Claudia's Chinese empress.

Someone says my name. It echoes up to the stone ceiling, and then around the cavern itself in hushed tones as a few of those who remain move toward me.

"Is it true, what Nikola said? That wasn't staged—it was real?" the Grecian girl asks in a German accent. Her male counterpart stands beside her in a matching white toga. Her gaze falls to my hands, caked in drying blood.

"*Mein Gott*," her sibling whispers. "Are you all right?"

No. I'm not all right. I wipe my hands on my dress. "Yes, it was real. Nikola escaped."

The maharaja is there, along with what could pass as a cast of Baroque nobles straight out of a period movie. They look different beneath the harsh glare of white light. Everything that was beautiful and glittering before looks cheap, gaudy as gold rickrack.

I glance past them to the next group of stragglers, and the one beyond that. Find myself looking for a white swan, but she's nowhere to be seen.

"This place isn't safe. You have to get out. You can't come back."

"My sister, Melia," the toga guy says, pointing to the girl beside him. "She saw her hunter's face. She knows that face. She is afraid to leave."

"You stand a better chance up there than in here," I say. I raise my voice. "Get out of Budapest. Be careful."

I wish there was more I could do. Someplace I could tell them to go. But there is no crisis center or church shelter for Utod, and after tonight, any place associated with me is no safer than this cavern.

"Everyone out!" I yell. For all I know, Nikola

has contacted the Historian and told her to send in a squad. Tonight. Now.

Ten and then twenty and forty more drift toward the tunnels with a last glance back. And I wonder if I'll ever see any of their faces again.

A figure summons me from across the cavern. Claudia.

I find her with Piotrek and a badly shaken Jester. Jester's hood is gone, only a black skull-cap covering her hair, her costume askew.

Piotrek grabs Rolan by the shoulder, and they hurry away down a tunnel.

"What's going on?" I say.

"Piotrek," Claudia murmurs.

"What about him?"

"He killed someone," she says, lower lip trembling. "One of Nikola's men."

"What'd they do to you?" I ask Jester.

"Nothing. Thanks to him."

I stalk several steps away, consider going after them. Rethink that.

A knot of some seventy Progeny remain in the center of the cavern. I run toward them, waving my arms like a person trying to scare away a flock of birds.

"You have to leave! There's nothing for you here!" Some of them turn to stare. Several more reluctantly drift away. Others continue urgent conversations, planning, perhaps where to go from here. And a few loiter near them, eyes shifting from one group to another, as though unsure whom to follow.

And I can't help but think of what Nikola said about animals released into the wild.

Piotrek and Rolan come jogging toward us a few seconds later, both of them paler than before. With a last look around, we make our way out through the grotto.

We strip out of costumes, down to jeans, black slacks, and bodysuits. Throw peacoats and robes over our shoulders, wigs and hoods over our heads.

And then we are hurrying out the way we came, flashlights shining on the path before us. Rolan with the safety off his gun.

37

We return in wary silence, let in by a neighbor I *persuade* from sleep to admit us.

We gather in the front room to keep from waking Luka. It's still early by Progeny standards—just past 4:00 A.M.

Rolan paces before the window, studying the street. Piotrek is somber. Claudia watches him in short, stolen glances. And Jester's expression has hardened to stone.

I want to ask her if she's dug up any more on Serge. Wonder if the leverage we have on him is enough to secure his help. It has to be.

Eva has never felt so far away.

"Audra, what's on your hands?" Jester asks.

"I stabbed Nikola," I say dully.

"I hope he's dead."

"He got away."

"This isn't how I thought it would happen," Claudia says faintly.

"What did you expect?" Jester says. "Did you think it would be bloodless? We *disbanded* our largest court rather than let the Historian rule it. The *Progeny nation* now knows Nikola is a traitor! More important, they know the names and faces of their hunters. Did you hear them?" she says. "The way some of them cried out? They recognized them! And now that they know who they are, they may live."

Claudia looks up with dull eyes. "Easy for you to say! There's no blood on your hands." She glances at Piotrek. "How will he get to heaven? How are we any better than them now?" Claudia says, glancing at Rolan, who doesn't turn.

"We aren't," I say.

"How can you say that?" Jester says angrily.

"Because we aren't," I say, looking up. "For four hundred years this entire thing has been about making wrongs right, and taking revenge and saying who's better and who deserves what for being innocent or guilty. Looking for a *diary* to prove who's wrong. The *entire thing* is wrong!"

They all stare at me in disbelief.

"Don't you get it? No one is only good or bad or Progeny or Hunter or"—I point at Rolan—"monk or Scion. Innocent, guilty, right and wrong got lost in this a long time ago. That's the whole point!

"We think we're better because we're told that. Because we don't *live* long enough to be more than victims. Nikola was right about one thing. We don't know how to be free. To deal with a lack of black and white. With this." I raise my hands.

Claudia looks away, and I realize it isn't just

328

the deaths tonight that have shaken her. She, too, has lost the only safe haven and structure in her world. The gilded court was all that was shining and safe and good to her for years. The best manifestation of what it meant to be Progeny. The one constant in a life defined by loss of loved ones.

I let out a heavy breath and wish Luka were awake. He's dealt with similar demons. I remind myself to ask him to talk to Claudia later.

I glance around. "What happened back there anyway?"

"I found the media room. Went in like I belonged there," Jester says. "Said I had brought new music . . . by the time they caught me, I had the file loaded, it was already in the queue. One of the guys called Nikola on a radio. He was there in seconds. I talked fast. I told him that with the Historian's support system failing around her and the rest of the leaks already programmed to break, this was the best thing that could happen to him."

She looks skyward, shakes her head. "They took me to some other room and locked me in. I assume Nikola went to find you. I heard fighting . . ."

"We had lost Jester earlier," Piotrek says. But saw them moving her. Claudia went for help. I got Jester out. But I . . ." He trails off as Claudia begins to weep.

"You did what you had to," I say. "Rolan, were you able to . . ." I don't even know how to ask the question about harvesting a memory. In all this time, Piotrek has studiously avoided looking at him.

The older man turns, the lines around his eyes more pronounced than before, lips pursed as though he's got a bad taste in his mouth.

"Enough to learn Nikola comes and goes from there unseen," he says. "There must be another way in—one only he knows." He glances up at me. "Probably the way he got out."

We sit in silence after that, and though I know our actions tonight will unquestionably save lives, I feel defeated.

Jester defaults to her laptop, and I finally get up to look for some meds or even a shot of something for Claudia. Progeny don't drink because alcohol dulls their gifts, but right now, I'm not sure it matters.

Piotrek comes into the kitchen, and I pull him aside. "Are you okay?"

He shakes his head. "Rolan put his hands on that man's head and was quiet for a minute. That is all. But it was like . . . it was worse than watching someone die."

"Knowing that's how it could have been for any one of us?" I say.

"No. It was like watching *Rolan* die. You should have seen the terrible look on his face.

As though he absorbed something horrible. You're right," he says, gaze level. "Everyone suffers from this war. Even them. I wish I could take back asking him to do it."

I stare at the glass in my hand, half-filled with a couple shots of some kind of brandy. I asked Rolan to do the same for me once. I realize now I had no idea what I was asking and wonder if it's anything like reliving my own life, the two times I have.

"Audra," Jester calls from the front room.

I hand Piotrek the glass for Claudia and go out to the table where Jester's set up shop.

She points to the screen.

"Gerald Schelert—the Scion you delivered the message to . . ."

"The one we leaked last night," I say.

She nods. "He committed suicide yesterday."

I lean in and read the news article translated from German. Gerald Schelert, father of three.

"He jumped off one of the company towers," she says and silently closes the page.

I think of Serge and his kids. Their mom, who may or may not have been a Scion. Who no doubt enjoyed the fruits of his pact with history . . . and certainly would have given it all up to keep her children safe.

I tell myself we never made the decision to jump for Gerald Schelert. God only knows how many Progeny orphans the Scions have created over the centuries. But thinking of those three children makes me want to weep.

I glance at the clock on Jester's screen: 5:07 A.M. I told Luka we'd be back by morning. What I didn't say is that I hoped to bring good news: a way to the Historian, which we would exchange for Serge's help in finding Clare . . . The knowledge that we would see Eva again.

In a couple hours, I'll call Serge.

But right now, I want—no, need—to curl up with Luka.

I kiss Jester's cheek and excuse myself, slip silently into the dark bedroom. Inside, the last of my unspent energy seeps out of me as I sag onto the edge of the bed. I lie back and turn toward Luka, reach for his warmth . . .

And find only the pillow.

"Luka?" I murmur, sweeping an arm across the comforter. But he's not there.

I push up in confusion, cross to the light switch, and flip it on.

The room is empty.

Luka is gone.

38

I hurry from room to room in rising panic.

"I thought you were lying down?" Jester says.

"Luka's gone!" I say.

She blinks. "He was supposed to wait for us. Where would he go?"

"Someone took him. Nikola must have come back and taken him!"

"We don't know that," Jester says, moving into the bedroom. She scans the bed, the floor, the items on the dresser. "There's no sign of a struggle."

"Maybe he went to get something to eat. Or to look for us?" Piotrek says from behind me.

"No. He wouldn't just leave without saying something." *Would he?*

"Call him," Jester says, holding out her phone.

My hands shake as I tap out his number, wait for the connection, the ringing on the other end like torture. Too much like the night I called the monastery over and over, so that I can't even stand the sound.

Please answer. Please answer.

It rings and rings. I hang up, dial again, fingers digging into my hair.

No answer.

I search out my own phone. Text him swiftly:

But for all I know, he doesn't even have his phone on or with him. Or he's disabled it in favor of a new one.

"Jester, can you find his phone?"

"I can . . . but I would need some help." She chews her lip.

I dial Serge.

He answers on the second ring, alert as though he's been awake for hours.

"Serge?"

I've schooled my voice. Even so, the minute I say it's me, he says, "Audra? What's wrong?"

"Luka's missing."

"What do you mean, 'missing'?"

"We went to court here in Budapest last night to release the video. Luka stayed behind . . ."

"Where's your bodyguard?"

"I sent him away," I say with an inward curse.

"Audra! I sent him for your protection!"

"Not everyone wants a Scion-provided body-guard around, Serge, commoner or not!"

"Yes, you're right. I understand," he says, as though talking to a crazy woman, which he is.

"It's retaliation—I don't know if Nikola survived, but he had to, or got a message to the Historian . . ."

"Audra, you're not making sense."

334

"I closed down Nikola's court when I exposed the Historian's hunters in the video!"

"Closed it down . . ."

"Yes! And I—" I can't try to explain the entire night. "I stabbed Nikola."

"You *what?*"

"He got away, and I'm afraid he came after Luka. Listen, I know this isn't part of the deal . . . I can't find the Historian with Luka missing. If he's not all right."

"It's fine, Audra, I'll help if I can."

Jester holds out her hand.

I give up and hand her the phone. Turn away, fingers over my eyes as she begins a conversation about protocols and cell towers and some device she needs to access.

I wander out of the living room to stare at the bedroom that used to be mine. That was ours a lifetime before.

Rolan and Piotrek are in there, checking the closet space and under the bed, saying nothing's been disturbed. The window is locked, shade down against the morning sun. The comforter isn't even that rumpled where he lay down on it, fully dressed, as we said good-bye.

My gaze catches on something sticking out from beneath the edge of the pillow, that looks like it slipped off the smooth top of it when I jostled it earlier. I slide my hand beneath it, and come away with a fluorescent pen.

I shove up, heart drumming against my ribs so hard they ache, and hurry to the bathroom where the loose purple bulb still sits in the center socket of the light fixture. Lock the door. Overturn the trash can, step up onto it to close the high window's slats against the morning light. Tighten the purple bulb and unscrew the two on either side. Lean over, flick on the light switch.

The walls come to manic life.

Scrawled on the bathroom mirror in Luka's handwriting is a message:

SORRY.

39

There's a smaller line beneath that horrible word:

*GOING TO TRY TO FIND AN END TO
THIS. WAIT FOR ME.*
—L

I search around me, at the frantic scribbles
of the nineteen-year-old Audra trying to make
sense of her life. Having entered my story,
it's only right that he write here on the mirror
beside the time line of our relationship, the last
entry made by me just last night.

But this is his story, too. Not just here but
scrawled on the west wall in a morbid progression
of ambition and murder.

I search for a postscript—anything to say where
he's gone and for how long.

But there's nothing else.

At first, I'm angry. That's it? That's all he
leaves for me? His lover—his wife!—the mother
of his child? *"Sorry"?*

He doesn't answer his phone or return my
text—sneaks off after I kissed him good-bye . . .
as he lay there fully dressed on the bed.

I know that trick.

And what they say about karma is true.

Despite the fact that I probably had this coming, I know he hasn't acted out of spite.

A knock on the door. "Audra?" It's Claudia, the earlier rift between us mended by this latest crisis. "Are you okay?"

Do I tell her?

No. He wrote his message here, left the marker in the bed for me alone to find.

"Yeah. I mean no, I don't feel good."

"Need me to come in?"

"No. No, I'll be out in a few. Thanks."

I back up and sit down on the edge of the tub.

Luka left the message for only me. Then how did he expect me to explain his absence to everyone else when I can't explain it to myself? Why leave a message, why not wait, tell me in person this morning?

Because he didn't want me to stop him. Or try to go with him.

He was protecting me.

Wait for me.

It's more than I ever said to him when I left.

He, at least, plans to come back.

I scan the three lines again. Too few words.

Sorry.

An apology. For what—leaving? It's more than I gave him the time I abandoned him in Bratislava. But I never felt guilty any time I thought I was protecting him. Regretful, yes. Heartbroken—of course. But even though it ripped me apart, I never felt apologetic once. Why does he?

Going to try to find an end to this.

An end to what?

I press the heels of my hands against my eyes. He can't have thought he'd leave and just try to end four hundred years of killing on his own. How? What can he possibly do that hasn't been done? That we haven't tried already? He's lost all ties, been declared a traitor.

A chill passes up along my spine. Would he offer to turn himself over?

No. He wouldn't have told me to wait. Besides, Luka's not Progeny. There are no secrets the Historian can glean from his brain other than any information he gives up willingly. He's a loose end, not a prize. But the cache systematically being used to bring down the Scions is.

I unscrew the bulb, tighten the others, and unlock the door.

"Jester!" I say, striding from the bathroom.

She's off the phone and staring out the window. Turns, chewing a fingernail. I've never seen her look pensive before.

"Is anything missing?" I say.

She blinks and begins to look around, to sort through her bag and take a quick survey. And it occurs to me just how much valuable information we left behind—in Luka's care—when we left nearly six hours ago.

"Where's Piotrek? Where are the others?" I say, noticing that we are alone.

"He's gone searching in case Luka's on foot. Claudia and Rolan heisted a car."

She checks her satchel and lifts her hands with a shake of her head. "Nothing's missing," she says. "It's all here. Why?"

"I just— I'm paranoid, I guess. What did Serge say?"

"He's trying to locate Luka's phone. As well as the one I couldn't trace earlier—the one belonging to the Historian's creepy lackey." She's somber as she says it, and I wonder what she's not telling me.

"That's good, right?"

"Maybe," she says, brows drawn together.

I pick up my phone and text Luka again.

Please call me. I'm freaking out.

"Audra," Jester says tentatively.

"Yeah," I say, pacing to the window.

"What's really going on?"

"What do you mean?" I say, craning my head, willing Luka to appear. To come walking back with coffee, saying he couldn't sleep.

"There's something here I don't know. And I am not one to ask, because it is not our way.

'Better to die blindly than having seen too much,' the old saying goes. Because when your memory can be harvested, not asking *is* the safer option. But there is something here that does not make sense. Ever since you took off from Munich even though Brother Daniel was already dead. The way you went to Serge—how you even knew to go to him . . ."

I chew the inside of my cheek. All this time I haven't wanted to hurt her. And all this time she's been operating on faith—in me. But if there is a true savior of the Progeny, I know it isn't me.

It's her.

And she deserves the truth.

I turn away from the window. "I knew because Tibor told me."

She studies me with a frown.

"When?"

"In Munich."

Her brows lift. "I see."

"He gave me Serge's name. Said there was a rift in the Scion ranks, and that he was at war with the Historian. Which he is. He hates her for killing his children after he told her he no longer wanted to supply the names of future hunters and Progeny victims."

She walks several steps away.

"I see," she says quietly, again.

But she doesn't, and I hate it. Because right

now, I wish I had a friend I could confide in. It's the one luxury a Progeny can never quite afford, the unspoken rule that maintains enough walls between the progeny of Elizabeth Bathory to keep them isolated even when they're together. And I realize looking at her right now that though I've always considered her closer to my age than Claudia, I don't know how old she is.

I don't even know her real name.

"Don't get mad at me for asking this," she says slowly.

"I won't," I say, already knowing what she's going to ask.

"Is it possible that Luka's gone to someone?"

Okay, I was wrong.

"What do you mean? Like . . . another woman?" I say with a short laugh.

"Like a Scion. Or even . . . one of the Historian's lackeys."

"No. Why would he?"

"I'm saying, is it possible that he's betrayed you? Us," she says, trying to soften the question. "Betrayed us."

"What? No!" I shake my head. "Absolutely not."

She crosses the floor and lays her hands on my shoulders. "I know you don't want to consider it. I'm just asking. Is it possible? A hunter will go to many lengths. Many extremes."

"No. He would've killed me by now."

"What if he doesn't need to? He's been such a part of your life that he knows everything! You have no idea what Serge could have convinced Luka of while you were unconscious. Something must have happened there or in the last few days—"

"Yes!" I say. "He wanted to leave. He hated it there. He hates that I took the extra risk of dropping in on Interpol's deputy to the EU in Brussels and Senator Borghi in Italy. I was reckless, and he didn't like it, but he wants this to be over as much as I do."

Her gaze bores into mine. "Is it possible he went to warn Nikola or the Historian about our going to court?"

"No!"

"I know you want to believe he loves you—"

"He's gone to try to end this."

"You don't know that! And it wouldn't make sense even if it were true. There is no way to end this other than what we are already doing! And if it's true that there is a rift within the Scions, then Luka's leaving looks even worse."

I close my eyes, attempt to tamp down panic. Because I don't know what Luka is trying to do. But I also know I can't find him without her help.

"Come here," I say at last, gesturing her to follow.

I lead her to the bathroom.

"What are we doing?" she says.

I screw in the bulb, reverse the others, and close the door.

She sucks in a breath.

"I just found this," I say, pointing at the mirror.

"But . . . why would he put this here? And what is all of this?"

"This is . . . more than you ever want to know. And if you don't want to know it, then it's time to turn the light off."

But instead of moving toward the light switch, she scans the length of one wall and then the next, exclaiming under her breath. Cursing softly.

"There's something else," I say.

I pull my sweater off, turn my back toward the light fixture.

"I remember this tattoo," she says, a light finger tracing down my spine. "You decoded it in Graz to get into your safety deposit box. Here—the logo of the vault that I located for you," she says, tapping the bottom cipher.

"I didn't decode it all. Not until I went to Košljun," I say, looking over my shoulder into the mirror. "The top three numbers are the date I married Luka."

She closes her eyes briefly, and I know she is braced for my sake. For Luka's ultimate betrayal of me.

"The next three . . . are the date our daughter was born."

Her eyes fly open and she stares at me in the purple light.

I pull my sweater back on. Point to the wall beside the mirror.

"Eva," she reads with soft wonder.

I nod and unscrew the bulb. The room goes black. I tighten the other bulbs to life, and all the writing—my old life, my daughter, and Luka's message—is gone.

Jester's face is ashen.

"Brother Daniel was the last person who knew where she was," I say, feeling my diaphragm tighten. "I told Serge if I delivered the Historian I needed him to use his surveillance network to find someone. Last night I begged Nikola to tell me how to find the Historian. But he wouldn't help me unless I turned over my new court to his protection and let them believe they were safe in Budapest. I couldn't do that."

"I'm . . . I'm speechless," she says. "You poor thing. I'm so sorry. So very sorry," she says, wrapping her arms around me.

I accept her embrace, but I'm numb.

"Oh my God," Jester says and steps back. "You're not the only Firstborn!" she whispers, eyes wide.

"No."

"*Mon Dieu!*" she says, walking from the bathroom, hand to her head.

"But your baby—is half hunter . . ."

I give a small nod, and then go to take her hands. "Jester . . ." I say urgently. But there are no words adequate to say how much I am entrusting to her.

She squeezes my fingers.

"I will never betray your secret," she says. "We never say among the Utod 'your secret is safe with me.' But, I assure you . . . it will be."

In a normal world, they are pretty words shared between friends. In ours, they are a far graver promise.

I let her go, but she's staring at me.

"No one has ever trusted me so much with their life."

"No one has ever protected mine more. Other than Luka," I say. "This is why he wants to end it. I just don't know where he's gone."

"And so," she says. "We have to ask ourselves now: What does he know that we do not?"

40

It is by now nearly 6:00 A.M. I've lost track of the number of times I've tried to call Luka. Have cursed myself and repented over and over for the time I left him in Bratislava.

Serge calls back to say that they are working on it, but he has no news.

I close myself in the bedroom, haunted by Jester's question.

What happened in France?

Luka hadn't slept for nearly two days. Was quiet, off and on since I woke up, anxious to leave.

I press my fingers to my brow, searching the room at the château by memory. Reviewing the times and hours he was gone. One, to buy phones, text Jester, buy chocolate . . .

Again, as I got my makeup done. Where had he gone?

He didn't trust his privacy in Serge's house. Wouldn't have said anything even if he could have . . .

Something else is bothering me: an itch at the back of my brain ever since I sat down in front of the GenameBase monitor.

Twelve original Scions of the Dispossessed. Twelve families, branched out into tiny and ever-multiplying capillaries like roots. Roots, sunk into the soil of commerce, politics, the military, the nobility. Rarely intermarrying between the twelve families in four hundred years—choosing to marry into power, when they could, instead.

Three known Historians: surnames Errickson, Bertalan, Alexandrescu. Errickson was first, a descendant of one of the original twelve surnamed Samsa.

Bertalan was second, two generations later, from the original family of the same name.

Alexandrescu, from the original family of Tolvaj.

The twelve strands dangle before my eyes, twisting like DNA in a hologram.

Samsa. Bertalan. Tolvaj. They are listed in a separate genealogy of the twelve original Scions Serge directed his administrator to show me—in that same order, with two and then three names between them.

My mental gaze skips down the hand-drawn Scion map I discovered in Vienna, to the progression of Historians. The row of circles, most of them empty. Two circles between the Historians descended from families Samsa and Bertalan. Three between Bertalan and Tolvaj.

The same number of names between them at the top of the GenameBase file.

They're going in order. Taking turns in the office. The new Historian appointed in the next family by the acting leader of the last, in prescribed order.

I flash back to the spheres of progression on the Scion map. Four empty circles after the last known Historian.

Back to the GenameBase listing. Shift over four names. Family name Me'sza'ros.

The lineage of the current Historian.

"They're going in order!" I say aloud and get to my feet.

I tug open the door, go into the living room, where Jester is gazing at her laptop screen.

She's already begun to pack up her things. Despite the fact that it hasn't been twenty-four hours, we both know the risks of staying here after last night. But there are other considerations now: namely, that Serge knows she was here.

After all, if his testicles are on the chopping block, she's the one holding the knife.

Time to leave.

"I know which family it is," I say.

She glances up, startled. "Then you know who the Historian is?"

"Not exactly," I say, lamely. "Given that there are a few thousand options alive. Divided roughly by two, since we know she's a woman. Which doesn't help."

"Serge just texted you," she says and hands it to me.

Lost Luka's phone around Gyor. Does this location mean anything to you?

I glance at Jester. She turns her laptop screen around. There's a map up on it.

"Here," she says, pointing to the city west of us, barely within the Hungarian border. I frown.

"He's going to Bratislava," she says.

"Why? Why would he go to Bratislava?"

"You tell me," she says, shaking her head. "But Gyor is directly between here and Bratislava."

I text Luka:

> *We traced you to Gyor. Where are you going?*

I start to send it, stop, and then send it anyway. But if he's destroyed his phone, he'll never get it.

"I need to go," I say suddenly. "And so do you—in the opposite direction. Where are the others?"

"I just called. They're headed back."

"Will you be all right until they get here?"

"You can't go without at least Rolan!"

I go to take her hands. "Jester . . ." I pause, tilt my head. "What is your real name?"

"Chantal," she says softly. "Chantal Allard. Though I haven't been called that name in years."

"It's beautiful. Chantal," I say, gripping her

hands. "The Progeny nation is on your shoulders. You need Rolan more than I do. I know you may not trust him, but I do. He's solid. And he will protect you."

I dial Serge's bodyguard. Ask him how soon he can pick me up at the house down the street.

"Twenty minutes," I say to Jester. "I'd offer you a ride, but . . ." I don't need to say that the bodyguard might be a commoner, but he's still Serge's man.

"No thank you," she says with a tight smile.

I grab my coat, leave the Prada jacket behind for Claudia. But I have a parting gift for Jester as well.

"What's this?" she says, as I hand her the carefully wrapped item.

"Serge's sugar spoon. I thought it might come in handy," I say, as a wry smile crosses her face.

"Audra, be careful. This is a dangerous game. The minute you're no longer of use or the Historian loses her power . . . Serge will come after you."

"No. He'll come after you. Which is why you need to get out of here as soon as you can."

She hands me a new phone. "I'll be in contact on this one and able to track you."

I want to ask where she'll go and know I can't. For the first time in my life, I'm panicked at the thought of leaving. After watching so many Progeny from the Budapest court go their separate ways last night, I can't help but wonder when we'll meet up again.

"I'll be in touch. We'll find him," she says, and then adds: "I hope you don't regret telling me what you did."

"No. Never." And I don't. Because if Jester goes down, we're all screwed anyway.

I kiss her on both cheeks and hug her tightly.

"I love you," I say. Because that's what family does.

41

I slip out just in time; I can sense the others returning even as I leave.

My phone buzzes immediately with a text from Claudia:

I can't believe you left by yourself.
Without saying good-bye!

She texts again:

Found the jacket. I forgive you.
At least tell Rolan where to meet you.
Don't go after Luka alone.

I text back only:

Take care of my jacket.

I get someone to let me in the building down the street, hurry past the smell of someone cooking curry. Stop by the babushka lady's door, where I leave the pile of her things and the equivalent of a couple hundred dollars.

Out front I slide into the car as it pulls up, barely giving it time to stop.

Rolan calls. I don't answer, but text him only:

Will meet up with you soon as I find Luka.
Keep Jester safe. She's everything now.

I call Serge on the way to the airport, wondering if he found anything on the other number—the one belonging to the oily voice of the Historian's mouthpiece.

"No," he says. "Unfortunately, not yet. Are you sure it's still in service?"

"As far as I know."

"Let us worry about it."

"What about Luka?"

"The last location we had was just south of Gyor. There are only two logical places to go from there—Vienna or Bratislava."

"I thought you had all this world-class spy stuff!" I say. "What about your government surveillance—your satellites?"

"We tracked him on the highway in a car. We lost him in the city. It can happen—especially when someone is working hard to evade surveillance. I hate to say it, but he learned from the best. Don't worry. We'll find him again. Gyor is big city with many electric eyes. Where are you now?"

"In your car headed to your plane. Some direction would be helpful."

"You know Luka better than anyone. Use your best guess. He's not going anywhere that isn't a plane ride away, right? If we learn anything, I'll contact your pilot. And if Luka contacts you, let me know right away."

I sigh as I hang up, sink low in the backseat of the car. Watch the city go by.

"Where should I tell the pilot we are going?" the bodyguard, whom I've mentally nicknamed Bruno, says.

He's gone to try to end this. End this how? The Scions have deep interests in both cities.

But Jester said Slovakia.

"Bratislava."

I receive a text from Jester that they've left the house, are safe. That much I can be glad for. Though it also makes me feel more alone, because I have no idea where they're headed.

Nor will I ask.

At the airstrip, I board the plane, glance into the cockpit to find the same pilot and copilot as before, apparently on standby this entire time.

I'm anxious as we take off, wishing I had run a lap around the hangar before boarding. I unbuckle my seat belt the minute we're in the air and pace the aisle.

I drink three cups of espresso during the twenty-minute flight. Realize, as we descend into Slovakia, that I have no clue where to go from here. That, for all I know, Luka has doubled back into Hungary.

My phone chimes as we land.

Jester: Serge's on the move. My money's on Bratislava.

And a text from a number I do not recognize:

Call me.

I hesitate over this latest as we taxi into the hangar.
A moment later, I dial it back.

42

The other end rings three times before it's picked up.

"Hello?"

Luka.

"Oh, thank God," I exhale. "Where are you? Why did you leave like that?" I say, fear oxidizing to anger in my voice.

"Audra, I'm sorry."

"Just tell me where you are."

"I can't."

"Can't what?" I say, impatient.

"Didn't you get my message?"

"Yes." *All three lines of it.* "Thank you," I say more gently. "Please. Whatever you're doing, don't do it alone."

"I have to." His words drift from the phone as though he's looking around him. I panic, afraid he'll end the call.

"No. It'll get you killed! Listen. I know you've gone north. We lost your phone somewhere in Gyor . . ."

"'We'? Who's 'we'?" he says with audible alarm.

"Jester . . . Serge." Mostly Serge, though I don't say so.

"No. Not Serge. You have to stop communicating with him. You need to leave Budapest with Jester and the others."

I glance at Bruno the bodyguard, who is waiting for me to deplane.

Get out.

I cup my hand around the phone. "The others are already gone. I'm by myself, looking for you!"

"Where are you?"

"Bratislava," I say as Bruno lets down the stairs and ducks through the exit.

Silence.

"Luka?"

"You have to leave Bratislava."

"Luka, you're scaring me. You have to tell me what's going on!"

"We promised no more secrets . . ."

"That's right," I say. But my stomach twists.

There's a choking sound on the other end of the line. "There's something I haven't told you . . ."

"Whatever it is, we'll work it out."

I can practically hear him rubbing his face, his forehead.

"When you . . . When we were in Slovenia and went over that bridge—"

"We fell in the river. You saved me."

"You were drowning. I tried to keep you breathing for as long as I could. And then the car filled up with water." His voice breaks.

358

"I kept talking to you. I told you I loved you. I held your head up . . ."

"I remember," I say, though a dark dread has begun to fill me.

"I couldn't get the car open. The windows wouldn't work. I couldn't get the door open! Not until it filled up and the pressure equalized. I held your head up until there was nothing left to breathe."

"I know," I whisper.

"And then you were choking, jerking in the water. You were dying."

I stare at the table in front of me. Burl wood. It has always looked uncannily like weird, smoky souls with ghoulish eyes to me. Ghosts, drifting up from the netherworld.

"I didn't know if I'd get you out in time. If I could get myself out . . . the car was full. I kept kicking the door, out of air. My lungs were bursting, I thought I was gone." He pauses. "And at the last minute, the door opened. I remember thinking it was some kind of miracle. It opened. I grabbed you by your shirt and pulled you out. Swam for what felt like forever."

"I know," I say faintly. But I don't. Because I wasn't there. Not anymore.

"When we got to the bank . . . you were blue. Your skin was so cold! I tried to revive you."

"You did, Luka."

"No. You were gone. I tried everything. You

wouldn't come back. And I couldn't deal with the idea of living without you!"

I close my eyes.

"I had to have some part of you. I'd never done it before, didn't know if it would even work . . . I put my hands on your head . . . Audra. *I took your memory.*"

A tear skids from the corner of my eye, down my cheek.

"I'm glad," I whisper.

"But I didn't just take it. I *lived* it. Right there, on the bank. For however long it was—maybe just minutes. Maybe seconds. I lived *you*. I *was* you. Fishing with your dad. I saw your parents," he says with a broken laugh. "Your school. Piano lessons. Swimming. High school . . . your first kiss. I have to admit, that was kind of weird."

I give a soft, broken laugh.

"Your friends were so mean to you. I hated them. I felt bad for them. It was so senseless. And I understand, finally, why you have that shell around you. You deserved to be prom princess."

I stare without seeing. I've never told him about that.

"I know why you chose that name now, when you erased your memory. Emily Porter. She was the best friend you ever had . . ." He swallows audibly.

"Your parents. You told me last year how they

died, but I never knew what it *felt* like. Until that moment. How easy it is to get angry, even if it's not at them. But what I wanted to say was that the night I met you . . . I didn't know how much I really bothered you."

"You bothered me plenty."

"I guess I knew a little when you flipped me off. But I didn't know that you were actually attracted to me. You *were*," he says with wonder. "You *wanted* me to call you. And I did, because I was crazy about you."

"Yeah?" I say, breathless.

"I felt it, Audra. I lived it all!"

"I'm glad!"

"I *felt* you fall in love with me. How I made you feel. How mad you were when I didn't call you right away. How you wanted to be together . . . But more than that, what it feels like to be *you*. Progeny. At court with so many other Progeny around. God.

"I heard what Ivan said to you the night he gave you your mother's things. I . . . read your mom's notes to you. Her letters. With your eyes. Felt how defiant and determined you were. To end this all. To live. And then how scared you were when you found out you were pregnant. What it felt like to feel Eva move inside you. A whole new life beginning. So incredible. Amazing."

"Luka," I whisper. "Tell me this in person. So I can see your face."

"I know how painful, how hard it was to bring her into this world," he says as though not having heard me. "And I lived through letting her go all over again.

"And then the weirdest thing. It's like I watched it all flash by when you went in for the procedure . . . lived it all for a second time. And woke up without any of it. Scared. Alone with Clare. I was such a goof when I met you in Maine."

I sputter a laugh, tears sliding down my cheeks.

"I know how much you didn't trust me. And still, somehow, you learned to love me again. And I know, too, why you left me in Bratislava. I finally get it. Felt a love—your love—so deep and intense it almost hurt."

"Then you know what I feel like right now."

"You were trying to save me. And when you went to the underground in Budapest to bargain for me . . . you marched in without a costume or a mask. Because you knew none of that mattered when you went to see Nikola. And the Historian was there."

My heart is thudding. Loud—too loudly—in my ears.

"And then the Historian came in and you heard her voice. When she told me to say hello through the phone, her voice was disguised. But I heard it through you."

For a second, all I can hear is the sound of his breathing.

"She had me, and you were screaming. You were horrified. And I was horrified with you. Because I *know that voice!*"

Chills spread across my back and down my arms.

"No you don't," I whisper.

"I do." His breath is ragged, and he's shifting, moving around, and something clicks on.

"Luka, what are you doing?"

"Is this her?" he demands. "Is this the voice you heard?"

Something starts to play. A machine of some kind. A recording.

" 'Happy birthday, Luka! Have you been practicing your English? I have, too. I practiced just for you so I can visit you in the States when you transfer university. I miss you, my dear. Nineteen. I can't believe it, my little boy, so grown up. Happy birthday, my love. I'll see you soon.' "

No . . . no, no.

A cold sweat has broken out across my back. I squeeze shut my eyes. But the family tree is floating before me, rotating in the darkness behind my lids.

Family name Me'sza'ros. The original member of Luka's Scionic family. Intermarried with merchants of increasing wealth through the centuries, including Austrian banker Franz Novak—then Nowak—four generations ago.

I can hear him on the phone, sobbing on the other end. I lift it to my cheek.

"That's her, isn't it? *Isn't it?*" he says.

I'm too sick to answer. Unable to lie. Unwilling to voice the truth he already knows. The Historian is Eva Novak.

His mother.

"All this time, I wondered why the Scions didn't kill me when they had me. You asked me what they did. They tried everything they could to *remind* me of my duty. I begged them to kill me, but they wouldn't—and now I know why! Because everyone else has failed or betrayed her, and I'm the only way to *you*."

"Luka, where are you?" I say, looking around me at the interior of the plane, seeing none of it, trying to picture where he might have gone. Why Slovakia? If indeed he's still in Slovakia at all.

"I'm going to find her."

"Luka, no!"

"I have to. I have to end this. Which is why you have to stay away. Because she'll kill you. And then she'll have everything she ever wanted."

"Don't—"

"I love you."

The call clicks off.

43

"Luka? Luka!"

But the line is dead.

I redial, again and again, but I already know he won't answer.

He's gone to find his mother.

All this while, I've been trying to find her. To deliver her to Serge in exchange for Eva's whereabouts . . . Eva, who's *named after her!*

I could tell Serge. Tell him and let him go to the trouble of finding her and do what he wants and wash my hands of it. I will have found him the Historian. He will owe me Eva.

Except Luka's there, too. And I don't trust Serge to hold his life as sacred as I do. In fact, I don't trust him at all if he knows Luka's the Historian's son.

I still have leverage over him in the form of everything Jester's prepared to leak. But at this point I don't know what he cares for more: staying out of prison or killing the Historian.

One offers far more immediate gratification.

I dial Jester, already dreading the words I'm about to say.

"Audra."

"Please tell me you can trace a call to Luka from this phone."

"Did you hear from him?"

"I did. He called. I called him back on this phone. Jester—" My voice breaks, and I know I'm about to lose it.

"Audra, what's going on? What's happening? Be careful what you say and where you are when you say it."

"He's gone to find her!" My throat tightens around the words.

" 'Her'?" Her voice lowers. "You mean . . ."

"The Historian!"

"How?"

But I don't dare say it out loud here. I trip my way down the stairs of the plane. Run across the tarmac toward the nearest hangar.

"How can he find her? Audra! What's happening?"

I run into a repair shop of some kind. *Persuade* the mechanic who comes to yell at me to turn on his heel and walk away.

"His mother," I pant.

"What about her?"

"The Historian is *his mother!*"

"What? He kept this from us all this time? What has he been telling her—what information has he been feeding her?"

"No! He met her, vicariously, through me— through my memories when I drowned. He's going to confront her. I don't know where. But he's alone and I don't trust her! She's already had him kidnapped and beaten. Even put a hunter—Rolan—on him when we were in Maine!"

I can hear Jester reeling on the other end. Claudia in the background, alarmed, asking what's wrong.

"All right," she says, more flustered than I've ever heard her. "All right. Let me—*merde*. Let me think."

"You have to trace him. Follow him. Serge can't know."

"Audra . . . Serge has been following you for months. Following Luka for months. There's a whole marker here on you."

Those words make my skin crawl.

"He's left France, I'm almost certain. I promise you, he's taking more interest in this than he appears."

"That's— No. For all he knows we had a fight. Some lovers' quarrel."

"He's too smart for that. He knows what Luka is. If you know what family Luka's from, he does, too."

"Then why have me find the Historian, if he knows?"

"He hasn't made the final connection. As soon as he does, you're both expendable."

I grimace. "And I asked Serge to find Luka!"

"Do you have any idea where his mother might be?"

"No. None," I say. "She left his dad when he

was a teenager. Family name Novak. His grandpa had some kind of farm . . ."

"I'll log in to Serge's network and see what I can find on both of them. I can do quite a few things thanks to the fingerprint you brought me. Let me do some looking, I'll call you back."

The minute we hang up, I don't know what to do with myself. I have no direction. No idea where Luka's gone.

I try him again. This time, the phone doesn't even ring but goes through to an automatic message in another language.

I jog back out and across the tarmac to the sleek private plane with Bruno waiting like some lone Secret Service guy at the bottom of the stairs.

"Stay," I say and run up into the plane. I retrieve my first phone, the one known to Serge, and dial him.

He answers on the second ring.

"Serge," I say.

"Audra, did you land?" he says.

Some kind of sound in the background, of a vehicle or something. He isn't at the château.

I play along.

"I did. I'm in Bratislava. But I don't know where to go from here. I can't find him. He's gone."

"Yeah, we've also had a tough time."

"What about the other number Jester gave you?"

"We're still waiting."

"Serge, you have to give me something here."

"I'm sorry, Audra, it isn't magic. I'm willing to help you as a sign of goodwill, but you know that I have far larger concerns. Unless this has something to do with our mutual purpose . . ."

"It does."

"I'm listening."

"It does in that I'm not going anywhere, finding anyone, or doing anything until I locate Luka!"

"I'm sorry, but that wasn't our agreement. You promised me the Historian. I gave you the names and faces of the current hunters so you could warn your kind. I've given you resources, access to the GenameBase database. But what have you brought me?"

"Did you think I'd just find you someone you've been looking for all this while—in a few days? You said yourself it's not magic."

"I'm afraid we need to renegotiate. Because I'm not here to help you chase your husband across Europe. I'm a businessman."

"Oh, I know all about your business," I say. "And I'd be glad to share it with the world if I think for one minute that you're not giving me your best self, Serge."

"Be careful with idle threats," he says softly.

"There's nothing idle about it. I can push the button on you any time."

"I don't believe you will."

"Try me."

He sighs. "Audra, I wasn't completely truthful with you, I'm afraid. All that I said about finding myself at cross-purposes with the Historian is true. What I did not say is that we only recently parted ways. Because that is the way to throw off your enemies—by holding them close until you are ready to betray them. You're young. You'll learn. I tracked you and Rolan to Košljun, where I believe you found your useful information, as I hoped you would. And that's when I realized that I had no desire to hand over your locations, though I did give the Historian that of Brother Daniel once he reached Pristava. So be grateful that I wanted you to live. To escape. To do exactly as you have, and use what you found against her."

I go very still.

He called the Historian "her."

"As far as finding her, however, I'm afraid Luka has proven more useful than you. Which isn't to say we cannot renegotiate."

"I have nothing to negotiate with you," I say quietly.

"Are you sure? I never told you that my doctors found something interesting about you during their initial examination. It seems at some point—in the last year, even—you had a child."

I don't even breathe.

"I would like very much for her to stay alive. Though I'm afraid it will cost you Jester."

44

The call ends before I can even attempt a response.

I drop the phone.

It takes a moment for me to realize that the second phone is ringing on the table.

Jester.

I answer wordlessly.

"From what I can tell, Serge's people got a location on that number for the Historian's lackey as early as a half hour after you gave it to him," she says. "Some Vladimir Kysely."

Souls writhe along the burl wood edge in front of me.

Jester and Eva. One life for another . . . What kind of hell have I just fallen into?

"Audra. Did you hear what I said?"

I swallow, glance out the plane window.

"Jester?" I say softly.

"What?"

"Remember that thing I told you?"

A pause, and then, "*Oui*."

"Can you look?"

"Yes, I will. Of course."

"Can you soon? As soon as we find Luka."

I tell myself that for Serge to threaten Eva means that she's alive.

She's alive.

And right now so is Jester.

"I promise," she says.

"Where's the number coming from?"

"Nové Mesto, Slovakia."

"Where's that?"

"East of you. Near Cachtice."

Cachtice. One of the ancestral holdings of Elizabeth Bathory—most famous for being the place where she was walled up in her castle the last years of her life and where she died. Of course the guy with the creepy voice would have to be from there.

"Okay," I say slowly, trying to process. Forcing Eva and Jester both to the edge of my mind. Just for now.

Because Luka is out there somewhere. And right now he's in the most immediate danger.

"Small area in the White Carpathians."

"I know. I've been there." I can now recall driving there and back in my previous life—in the search for the cache I eventually found in Košljun.

"You sure that's the Historian's lackey?" she says.

"Yeah."

"Here's the other thing: One of Serge's planes left Paris around six this morning. You'll never guess where he's going."

"Nové Mesto?"

"Well, technically they don't have an airport. But there's one in Trencin nearby. If you can call it that. It's just a regional strip mostly used for skydiving."

"So who's Serge following—Luka, or the Historian's lackey?" I say. But it's hard to think when you've just been dealt a blow.

"My guess is both."

"When's Serge supposed to land?"

"In a half hour. But that doesn't mean he doesn't already have guys on the way."

I stride to the cockpit, peer in at the pilot.

"I need to get to Trencin," I say. "Now."

To Jester I say: "What about *her?*"

"If the lackey's there, I'd bet money the Historian's nearby. It's *Cachtice,*" she says.

And I admit, there is a certain morbid poetry there.

"Audra, are you okay?"

"I'm on my way."

45

Except that I'm not.

"What's the problem?" I demand, standing outside the cockpit.

"Trencin is saying they have higher traffic than usual," the pilot says.

"What, two planes in one day?"

"We have wheels up in fifteen minutes."

"It's only going to take twenty to get there!"

I claw at my hair and then take out my new phone, text Luka, and pray he'll receive it:

Serge knows. He's coming.

I turn my gaze toward the cockpit.

Get us in the air. Now.

The plane's engine rises to a smooth whir a moment later. After a beat, I switch to my old phone. Dial a number I know far too well.

It rings twice before the inevitable answer.

"*Da.*"

"It's me," I say.

"Well, hallo, Audra." He even sounds pleased.

"Serge's coming for your mistress."

A pause.

"And you know this how?" he says.

"Because I've been working with him."

"You'll understand if I don't believe you."

"Then she's going to die."

"She is prepared for that eventuality. Her successor is already appointed."

"Yeah, and how's that happen? Who informs the new Historian—you?" I say, as the plane begins to taxi.

"I may have the papers of succession, if that should happen."

"Well, I guess that explains why he's coming for you first."

"Rest assured he doesn't know where to find me."

"Doesn't know where specifically in Nové Mesto, you mean?"

Another pause.

"Put me in contact with her, *Vladimir*," I say.

A sharp rap sounds somewhere on the other end, followed by rapid footsteps.

"Put me in contact with—"

The call clicks off as we pull onto the runway.

46

Jester calls as we touch down. Craning against the window, I can see another private aircraft already on the lawn.

"Please tell me you know where Luka's gone and that it's somewhere close," I say.

"There is a piece of property under the family name Nowak—"

"That's it," I say. I grab my other phone as Bruno opens the exit, lowers the stairs.

"It's just south of Visnove, right by Cachtice."

I shudder, all too familiar with the area's rolling fields dominated by Cachtice castle. Can remember peering through the stone window of that ruin—one of the few left standing in what has been reduced, in other areas of the stronghold, to rubble. Recall walking through the remains of the room where Elizabeth Bathory spent her last days peering down, perhaps, on the village as I did that March afternoon. I wonder how many of the Scions' original twelve labored in the shadow of Cachtice castle, emerging finally in their slow march of power throughout Europe.

"Stay here. Stay ready," I say to the crew, leaving Bruno behind.

And then I'm running toward the air club,

throwing out a plea as I go and wondering if it'll carry far enough. We're practically in the middle of nowhere.

Just as I reach the building, a man comes out through the hangar and hands me a set of keys. He points to an old Zafira.

I get in, dial Jester, and thirty seconds later, I'm peeling out from the airstrip. Not.

But I'm winding full-speed to the highway.

"Got you," Jester says from the phone speaker. "Silver Zafira, no? This system's amazing."

"Where am I going?"

"Hold on . . . It seems Luka was sighted twenty minutes ago in Cachtice proper."

"What about Serge?"

"He's ahead of you, but he's made a stop in Nové Mesto."

"I kind of thought so."

I focus on the road. My heart is pounding and I'm not sure why—at the prospect of coming face-to-face with the Historian or with my mother-in-law?

Of saving or of killing her?

I speed south on the 61, send three cars into the other lane as the Zafira teeters on the edge of 120 kilometers per hour. A low whistle in the background. Piotrek.

"We're all here, Audra," Jester says. "We're all here with you."

The simple statement and the image of their

faces makes my vision blur. I swipe at my eyes and nod, though I know they can't see me.

"I know," I whisper.

I drive in their silent companionship for several minutes until a sharp gasp sounds on the other end of the phone.

Jester shouts a curse, and something slams on the table, rattling the speaker.

"What is it?" I say, not sure my heart can take much more.

"The system just shut me out!"

47

Cachtice is a tiny town east of the castle by the same name. You have to take a winding road through the forested hills to reach the stronghold where Elizabeth Bathory spent her last years, imprisoned in its walls.

Unlike Visnova, where the Bathory name is still held in contempt, Cachtice profits from its association. From the sallow wooden statue of the countess in the town square—a ghostly girl emerging from her gown—to the Bathory pizza parlor complete with portraits of the countess and bottles of Bathory wine for sale.

It is the culmination of Elizabeth's life and the birthplace of her bloodiest legacy. The most obvious and therefore least likely place for a Progeny or Scion ever to return.

I remember the first time I came here, in March two years ago. When I gaped at the statue's dour, masklike face and empty eyes . . . and then went and ate the pizza. Claudia and Katia had a lively discussion about whether the countess would find any of this amusing. Katia thought she might be vain enough to be insulted by the statue, but good-humored enough to appreciate the café. Claudia disagreed, calling both horrendous.

Today as I drive into the town presided over by the clock tower with its copper-green onion top and quaint yellow houses, I have to agree.

With Serge only minutes behind me, I careen to a stop on the side of the road. Not bothering to lock the Zafira, I strike out to the center of the town square, hand raised to shield my eyes against the sun overhead. I glance from the church to the statue of the countess to the Alpine-style guesthouse. Last of all, the pizza parlor with the narrow awning and delivery sign posted out front.

"Luka!" I shout. I can't imagine the Historian actually sitting in there, but then again, there's a lot I can't imagine about my life at this moment. The place is full of the lunch crowd—as much of a crowd as this place can conjure between summer's scant tourists and the ski season. Three tables are filled inside. None of them with my husband or a woman with any of his features.

I hurry past a small shop. Run over to peer into the window of the guesthouse office. The two chairs in the foyer are empty, and the dining room appears to be closed.

"Luka!" I shout again, casting a wide-burst *suggestion* for help. An image of Luka, a mental missing person poster.

Pain. My hands go to my head as I whirl around, glance toward the church, in the direction of the museum.

Where would a Historian of the Bathory legacy meet her son, the would-be Scion? A museum means history, doesn't it? But it also connotes antiquity, no longer relevant today. A church? Serge called the Historian a zealot. God knows her father, Luka's grandfather, raised him to wage holy terror against the Progeny.

I glance at the eyes of those I pass. No recognition. They haven't seen him.

I stride up the street toward the coffee shop. But coffee is the Progeny drink of choice. Of the frenetic young. Not of the head of nouveau-riche leaders clinging to their champagne, the puppet master behind the powers that crown and sever heads.

And then I know.

There is no place for the Historian but the best hotel in town. With its crystal chandelier and iron banisters—the finest place Claudia said she had ever been. Where she gasped over the china in the stately old dining room and slipped a silver fork into her pocket.

But more than that, because of its name: Palatin. It was the palatine himself, Gregory Thurzo, who arrested Elizabeth, investigated her atrocities, and collected the testimonies of more than three hundred witnesses. Who made the case for her life, which ended with her getting walled up in the castle a kilometer away from here, her name struck from society as if she never existed.

I race down Malinovského Street toward the Palatin. Shove through the heavy front door, past the foyer, and into the small dining room.

And there, at a table covered in a pink tablecloth, sits Luka with a woman whose back is toward me.

At first, I'm baffled. Teacups sit between them. A few cookies on a plate. A benign afternoon reunion between a young man and his mother. The set of her shoulders is narrower than I expected, clad in a nylon jacket against the threat of rain.

And then I see his jaw, squared with tension. His eyes, the stormy blue I found mesmerizing the first time I saw them up close, are now flat and gray as flint. He glances up as I move toward the table, and those eyes widen in alarm.

I slide directly into the seat between them.

"Hi," I say, turning toward his mother without smiling. "I'm Audra."

Only then does it occur to me that I maybe should've made sure she wasn't holding a gun. But when I flick a glance down at her hands, they're folded in front of her.

My first glimpse of her is bizarre. With her shoulder-length hair the same shade as Luka's—except for some gray—conservative slacks, and quiet eyes, which are a shade darker than his own, she looks like . . . a mom.

Like a normal person who doesn't order

executions, but shops for groceries every weekend and has a library card and maybe rides horses. Because, yeah, she has that athletic look about her, I guess. Her nails are short, and she isn't wearing much jewelry except for a simple silver band on her right ring finger, which I think is weird because she left her husband several years ago—unless her office is like some holy vocation and she's married to the Scion god of money and power like a militant nun.

When she turns her head toward me and takes me in, her gaze is cool.

"Audra." She says it as though we've met before at a social function. As though we were here to discuss wedding flowers. "You look well."

I gaze at her for a short moment and then slap her, hard across the face. Her head snaps to the side. And then she reaches up slowly, smooths her hair from her eyes and where it has stuck in her sheer lipstick.

"I ought to kill you," I say.

Her gaze drifts from me back to her son. It doesn't soften on him. But it does seem sad.

"Come on," Luka says, getting up. "Let's go."

"And what—just leave her here?"

"She's done."

"What do you mean 'done'?"

"She's over. I'm exposing her."

"So what—we just walk away?"

"Do you want to kill her?" he says, pausing and gesturing back at his mother. His jaw twitches, and for a minute I think he might kill her himself.

"Yeah, actually," I say. "I do. Though I hate the thought of having to explain that to Eva. You know." I glance at her. "Our daughter."

She closes her eyes, refuses to look at us.

"Did he tell you about her?" I say. My hands are shaking.

"I have no granddaughter. Because I have no son."

"You don't deserve him," I whisper.

"He lost his calling," she says, looking at him with a faint shake of her head.

I lean over, get right in front of her face. Her eyes are like shards of glass. "This isn't a calling, *Eva*. This is serial murder. How do you justify that? Because as far as numbers go, I think you have Bathory beat."

"How do I justify that?" she snaps. "How good are you at math, Audra? Do you know how many descendants six hundred slaughtered girls would have produced over four hundred years?" She regards me placidly, and I shrug. "Millions. Millions of lives lost."

"How good are you at history, *Historian?* Because it doesn't work that way," I say. "Otherwise let me tell you—you're part German, right? Well, you're in deep over Auschwitz alone."

"Don't bother, Audra. You can't reason with a fanatic," Luka says.

She chuckles at his statement and shakes her head. Looks down at her napkin and folds it.

"Too bad," I say. "I understand you really wanted my memory. Now that I have it back, I thought you might have some questions for me."

She looks at me. "How's your mother?"

I'm up on my feet in an instant, knocking over my chair, and Luka is pulling me away.

"Audra, she's agreed to step down. No Historian can stay in office once she's known to a Progeny. She's done."

"So what? She gets to retire to her cushy house and ride horses for the rest of her life?" I shout.

Eva stands. She's tall.

"Actually, I was thinking we take her in," Luka says.

She begins to laugh, the sound like bubbling water. Like mania.

"They can't arrest me," Eva says, as though he were a child. "And if they did, they couldn't keep me."

"You're right. The police answer to the Scions, which is why I'm taking you to a mental ward." Luka smiles blandly. "A nice Eastern European backcountry psychiatric hospital. I don't recall a lot of Scions going into mental health."

Her head snaps toward him.

"Think you could *persuade* a nice orderly to get her into a straitjacket?" he asks me.

"I think so," I say, nodding.

"You have what you want. Just go," she hisses.

"We don't have anything close to what we want," Luka says. He takes her roughly by the shoulders. Marches her toward the entrance.

I follow as she moves stiffly in his arms. But when he opens the door, she shoves him away with surprising strength. I lunge for her, but she bolts out of the hotel and runs down the street.

We take off after her as an SUV coming the other way squeals to a halt to avoid hitting her.

She turns in the street, something in her hand.

"Audra!" Luka shouts.

Screams from the sidewalk. I drop to the ground.

But the gun she raises isn't pointed at him. Or even at me.

She holds it to her head and shouts: "I will have justice!"

Before it can fire, her chest explodes in a spray of crimson.

Luka staggers back, horror etched across his face, and pulls me behind a parked car.

48

My breath is heavy against the back bumper of the car as I try to reconcile the figure of the Historian—Luka's mother—unmoving on the pavement. The SUV that came to a halt behind her. The shooter, emerging from the driver's side.

I glance at Luka, eyes wide.

He creeps forward around the corner of the car, but I tug him back.

I glance around us, spy a car coming from a side street.

You.

Shots fire. A car swerves.

I lean out in time to see the gunman fire again, in the direction of oncoming traffic.

Meanwhile, a second man gets out of the SUV and walks over to pause before Eva.

Serge.

He tilts his head. Seems to regard her for a solemn moment.

There's something in his hand. A document.

Serge squats down, reaches for her wrist, and lifts it. Her fingers dangle limply as he dabs them in the gore of her own chest and then carefully presses one of them against the page in his hand.

"What is it?" I whisper to Luka.

"Document of succession," he says tightly.

But that can't be. Because the document naming Eva's successor is with . . .

. . . the lackey Serge just killed in Nové Mesto. *No, no, no.*

Serge never meant to abolish the Scions—only the Historian . . . in order to seize her scepter.

He straightens, the page dangling from his fingers, and looks dispassionately back at the body on the ground before raising his head to survey the square.

"Luka!" he calls. "Luka!"

He's calling Luka out as a loose end. Ready to end him now, before Luka can hunt him down for the murder of his mother.

I grab Luka, hold him tight, determined that he'll have to run out there dragging the full brunt of my deadweight if he gets stupid. His muscles tense and bunch against me, ready to spring, but he squeezes his eyes shut, stays still.

Serge takes a last look around, barks a short laugh.

"He's letting his Progeny wife save him," he says loudly enough to carry as he walks back to the SUV. "She won't be able to protect you forever." A minute later the vehicle's doors slam shut.

My legs are screaming at me, muscles petrified where we kneel by the time the SUV backs up and starts to speed away.

And then Luka's running for the form on the ground and dropping to his knees.

"Don't look," I say, pulling him away.

"I'm not. That's not my mother. Not anymore," he says, hoarse. He pries the gun from her fingers.

And then we're racing for the car.

49

I've been in this position before. Skidding onto the highway, Luka at the wheel. Getting shot at.

Except this time it isn't Rolan shooting at us, and I'm actually buckled in.

Luka returns fire, sends the SUV skidding. A second later, our windshield shatters as a bullet punches the backseat. A semitruck pulls onto the highway ahead of us. *You.* Within seconds, it's accelerating straight toward the SUV.

Serge's gunman—Scion, I know that for sure—fires out the window. The semi skids off to the shoulder, into the ditch, and jackknifes. The cab unhitches and rolls.

I shove up in the seat and look back just in time to see the driver open the door.

"I can't keep sending trucks at them," I gasp, my vision blurring.

"No," Luka says grimly. "I know." He falls back five more car lengths, then ten.

"They're going to the airport at Trencin."

"We can't follow—"

"We have to!"

"They'll just keep shooting, and I am not going to lose you. So what if he makes himself Historian? There won't be anything left. Call

Jester. Tell her to hit the button, release the information, now. All of it."

"We can't."

"Why not? He's not going to find Eva for us anyway!"

"He's going to kill Eva, Luka, if we don't give him Jester!"

"What?"

"He knows, Luka. He's the one who told the Historian where to find Brother Daniel. Because he tracked me all the way to Košljun. He knows!"

Luka veers back into the left lane, accelerates.

"Grab the wheel."

I do, and he leans out the window, firing at the SUV.

The gunman shoots back and our front tire blows, sends us swerving. I grab Luka by the belt as he slams against the car door. We're decelerating, a nasty *whump whump* with every rotation of the tires by the time we steer the Zafira off the Trencin exit on fumes and rims.

The car limps along the airport drive, and I point to the tarmac. The first plane is gone, but the one I arrived in is slowly taxiing to the runway.

Luka floors the gas, and we roll past the hangar—straight for the tarmac as the plane begins to turn.

"We're too late," he says, pounding the wheel with a sharp sounding of the horn.

I shove open my door and get out. And then I'm running down the runway. At the other end, the plane is rolling forward, picking up speed as it accelerates right toward me.

"Audra!"

I hear Luka yelling, chasing after me. Shouting, screaming my name.

It comes in a rush—the torrent of air propelled toward me. Hard enough to glide beneath metal wings, to make the implausible happen. To do, beyond reason, what the mind cannot grasp . . . to make ordinary the impossible. To fly.

The plane lifts, soars over my head, wheels folding up. The fierce wake sleeks back my hair as the plane climbs, overhead.

I remember what it is to die. To be afraid. To hate. To want to kill. To compel out of need, or want, or fear. I know what it is to let the extraordinary destroy you. When a gift becomes a weapon and a legacy of hate.

But I also remember what it is to live. To love and surrender. To wonder and believe.

I watch the plane ascending toward the clouds.

Luka runs up to me and grabs me, holds me tight against himself.

"What were you thinking? What were you doing? Audra!"

But I am throwing the heftiest persuasion yet.

Effortlessly. Without pain. And with far more

strength than I've ever summoned out of self, panic, or any face of fear.

It's soft as a sigh. But it feels like a roar.

Luka turns to follow my gaze. And I hear him gasp as the plane banks, too sharply, to the right, careening toward the hills.

The impact shakes the ground beneath our feet.

But my eyes are on the sky.

50

Rolan is restless as he paces in the outer room. He's been different since that night at court three weeks ago, though it's been good for him to locate others of his kind. I've recommended him to the Center in Illinois, told him there's no sin in forgetting. And after all, he knows how to get there.

But he's intent on New Mexico, and studying under one of his idols—some monk famous for his books on second-stage-of-life faith. Not that idols are really allowed when you're a Franciscan.

"You know, you're making me nervous," Piotrek murmurs from where he sits on my sofa. Rolan exhales and sits down after that, but he's staring out the window. He leaves tomorrow,and I know he's anxious to go.

"I'm going to miss you," I say, as we wait for the screen to connect. "But I swear you'll love the Southwest. I'll even come visit you and we can hit some New Mexican restaurants. Assuming, of course, that's allowed."

He's nervous, I know, about reentering the order. Worried about being accepted. As a murderer. A Scion. A sinner.

"That first confession is going to be hell," he said to me last night.

Aren't they all?

"How do you join an order of action *and* contemplation?" Piotrek says. "Isn't that kind of a contradiction?"

"I am a monk of many talents," he murmurs. And I know he's going to be okay.

The chat app blooms, and there is Jester, waving, dreads piled on her head.

"How's life in the Fortress of Solitude?" I say.

"Oh, you know." She shrugs. "The usual. Updates from all over the world."

Luka comes to sit beside me, and she breaks out in laughter.

"Is that a beard?" she says, peering at the screen.

"You don't like this?" he says, rubbing his chin between his fingers and thumb. "I'm trying to be wise. Like Rolan. Since I'm soon to be oldest person here and Audra's giving me so much grief about turning twenty-four."

"Well," Jester says, "I'll have you know that my birthday is next week."

"What? Twenty-nine again?" I tease.

"Twenty-nine, on the dot."

I blink and then stare. "You're joking."

"No, actually," she says. "And I think I'm getting younger. Wait—there's someone coming to join us."

Claudia appears on the screen, a little square in the corner. I squeal and wish I could hug her.

"I miss you!" she says and then pans the camera. She's standing on a steep incline. "Can you tell where I am?" She beams.

Piotrek comes to peer over my shoulder, and she kisses the screen.

"I'm on the Great Wall!" She laughs. "I've never seen anything like it. It's more than I imagined. Bigger than I thought. And steeper, too."

She's wearing my jacket.

Luka blows her kisses, and Piotrek says he'll see her next week. She signs off with a laugh, saying her phone service is costing her a fortune.

"So we've got Senator Borghi and the IMF under investigation," Jester says. The last of the leaks—for now, at least—broke a week ago, and for as much as we thought we'd follow the news, Jester's is the only update we follow.

"There were three hunter murders last week. One Progeny killed," she says.

I look down and then at Luka, who nods.

"In other news, a few Progeny are claiming the Zagreb underground has reopened. What say you, Prince?"

I sigh. "I say I'm out of outfits since Claudia left. Seriously, I don't know where she stowed her stash."

I don't ask about the thing that is on both our minds. But after Piotrek goes to make coffee, Jester leans in toward her camera.

"I'm still trying," she says, her face softening.

"I know," I whisper, as Luka's hand covers mine.

51

The coffeemaker is leaking all over the counter. I glance around for Luka in time to hear him start the shower, and then sop it up with the dish towel. Just like I did yesterday.

He's promised me every day of the six months since we got this flat that we'd buy a coffeemaker to go with our new place. And every morning I plug the old one in and start it up, optimistic as the day before—only to end up staining a dish towel and, lately, getting out Piotrek's electric kettle.

I think of him every time I use it. The way he smiled and acquiesced to every demand of Claudia's and tried to understand our bad jokes.

It's been three weeks since his body was found in London just blocks from the safe house he established there.

Claudia returned from London last week. Four days ago, we convinced her to come stay with us.

It's too late by the time I realize she's up; she comes into the kitchen, takes a look at the kettle, and bursts into tears.

I hold her and rock back and forth against

the counter before Luka and I leave for our jobs at the Children's House of Hungary.

Two days later, Jester surprises Luka and me with a link to a pair of tickets.

Italy, somewhere on the Amalfi coast.

I call her up immediately, not even knowing where I'm connecting to except that her skin is shiny and I haven't seen her in anything other than tanks and camisole tops for weeks.

"What's this?" I say, holding up my phone.

"I call it . . . an anniversary gift." She smiles.

"That's great," I say. "Except that it's not our anniversary."

"One year, seven months, three days? That sounds like an anniversary to me. Besides, did you ever really have a honeymoon?"

We leave two weeks later, spend three days in Rome. On the fourth, we wind our way south along a twisting road overhung with lemon trees. And I desperately want to try limoncello, though Luka claims it tastes more like lemon Drano.

He's aged in the last few months. We all have.

But none of us complain.

We check into our hotel on the terraced slope and wander the town of Positano. As on every day since we arrived in Italy, we end up eating too much pasta, crash out in our hotel that afternoon.

Jester chimes in some time around dinner.

Where are you?
Me: Preparing to eat. Again. Some more.

Come downstairs.

There's a picture attached, and I recognize it as the beach of our hotel.

"Jester's here!" I squeal to a drowsing Luka. "Let's go!"

"Doesn't she know it's bad manners to crash a honeymoon?" he asks. But he's up, immediately awake, and putting his shoes on. We haven't seen her in over three months.

We pick our way along the beach, looking for her dreadlocked head.

But it's the blond one that catches my attention.

The ponytail is longer than I remember, practically past her shoulders. I stare, afraid to move, as though she might be an apparition.

Until I see the small form with her.

She is the image of perfection. The face of love.

I cover my mouth, and stagger to the beach on legs with rubbery knees.

Clare turns, in mid-laugh, a small hand in hers. She lifts the girl up in her arms. She's so big, and it's the first time I have ever heard her giggle.

● ● ●

"Come back and see where we're staying," Clare says. "I want you to meet our neighbor. She has trouble with her memory."

I don't care about neighbors, but it doesn't matter. I will follow that little face anywhere.

We go to the small house on the side of the cliff. The courtyard is filled with lemons. Eva is shy, afraid of holding my hand, but she looks back at us with a smile.

"Give her time," Clare says, and I tell her I don't mind. It's okay to be afraid of strangers.

There's a little gate between their two villas, and Clare ducks through the old stone arch to the adjoining house and raps on the door.

"Barbara," she calls out. "Eva's parents have come to get her. Come meet them and convince them to stay."

A middle-aged woman comes out a moment later, an apron around her waist.

"Isn't this wonderful?" she says, smiling at me and clapping her hands. "And yes, you must stay! I admit, I'm attached to the girl. She's like a daughter to me."

I know that face. Her smile is mine. But she tilts her head in confusion when I start to cry.

"Oh, such happy tears," she says, wiping my cheek. "Come! Come inside. Clare, get them drinks while I finish the dumplings."

We duck into her villa, and I steal glances at them

401

both, and at Luka, whose eyes are red-rimmed.

A half hour later, Eva's peering around the kitchen doorway, no longer shy, and I chase her toddling steps into the small sitting room as I have now three times in a row.

Except this time I slip and bump into Barbara's bookshelf. A thick volume in another language falls flat from its standing position. As I reach to straighten it, I notice a very old book half-hidden behind the others. I pick it up, begin to thumb carefully through the fragile pages . . . and my heart begins to hammer.

"Barbara," I say, as I go into her small kitchen where Luka and Clare regard me from the table. "What's this?"

"Oh, that. I found it in a box of my things, must have had it forever. A family, ahhh . . . what is it called?"

"Heirloom," Clare says gently.

"Yes, at least I think so. Some high-born woman's journal from long ago. Proof, I guess, that if you go back far enough, everyone is related to nobility." She chuckles.

I page to the beginning. The first entry is dated 1576.

I clasp the book and excuse myself to her little courtyard.

A little while later, Barbara comes out with Eva in her arms, finds me sobbing on the bench beneath her lemon tree.

"Poor girl," she says. "Don't you know when you should be smiling? The dumplings are ready. Eva's smiling, aren't you, Eva? Yes, Barbara makes her favorite dumplings." She laughs as Luka comes to lean in the doorway. "But dear, now I've forgotten your name, and that of this handsome man with you."

I wipe my eyes and set the diary aside, leave it on the bench as I get to my feet. Because everything I wanted is here, alive, right now.

"My name is Audra Ellison," I say. "I'm twenty-two years old. This is my husband, and my daughter. And your real name is Amerie." I smile softly and take her hands.

And you are my mother.

Author's Note

With the exception of the St. Francis Center for Memory Research, the locations, sites, and buildings in the Progeny books are all real, and the details about them are true.

Photos of the monastery on Cres Island, the windows in the Nyirbator church, Cachtice Castle, as well as the Bathory crest and portraits of Elizabeth herself may all be found on my Real Life Progeny board at www.pinterest.com/toscalee./real-life-progeny/.

The part about the tunnels beneath Budapest—as well as the missing map—is also true. And while I'm unaware of clinics selectively erasing memories in humans, researchers have been tinkering with turning off and on the memories of lab rodents for years, offering promise for those suffering from conditions such as PTSD in the future.

Who was Elizabeth Bathory?

If you've read my historical novels, you know I'm a big believer in the idea that there's always more to the story. That no person is only one thing or another. In that way, I'm pretty sure Brother Goran got it right when he said that we like to think we learn people when we really only learn their stories.

The Elizabeth Bathory of history and Hollywood is portrayed as a monster, a seductress, a sadistic narcissist with a vendetta against those more youthful than herself. But somewhere between the purported rages and explicit stories of torture suffered at her hands—as well as the blood-bathing that became part of her legend two hundred years after her death—hers is the story of a woman trained in the classics, philosophy, fencing, and art appreciation when women typically received little to no education. A Protestant subject of a Catholic king, she gave money to the clergy, church, students, the poor, and was known to be a doting and caring mother to her children.

As a noble, her pedigree was undisputed. Born into one of the most prestigious families in Europe, her uncles on both her mother's and father's sides were princes of Transylvania, her uncle the king of Poland.

A lifelong learner, Elizabeth Bathory was fluent in Hungarian, Greek, Latin, German, and Slovak and was known for writing her own letters in a succinct, to-the-point style. Her education in the arts was likely furthered at the household of her future in-laws after her engagement to Ferenc Nadasdy at the age of twelve.

It was at her in-law's estate in Sarvar that the thirteen-year-old Elizabeth is rumored to have had an affair, after which she gave birth to a daughter who immediately disappeared to history.

In addition to her extensive learning, Elizabeth was extremely wealthy, having inherited her parents' estates by the time she married Ferenc at the age of fourteen, during which her new husband gave her Cachtice Castle, where she would later spend the last years of her life incarcerated in a set of rooms.

Rumors began during her marriage: that she maimed her serving girls, that she kept secret rooms where she meted out punishment and torture, that she was helped by female accomplices, including her own children's wet nurse and a young man she took into her household.

Did abuse occur? No doubt. Peasants were considered property, along with the land they lived on. Elizabeth and her contemporaries functioned during a time of near-constant war where enemies were roasted alive, sewn into the carcasses of horses, and met other equally barbaric and imaginative ends. Did she ritualistically kill young girls? We don't know. If so, did her victims number in the hundreds? Not likely.

By the time of Ferenc's death as a national war hero, Elizabeth would own thousands of acres and more than twenty castles, making her richer than the Habsburg king who, after years spent fighting the Turks, owed Elizabeth and her late husband more money than his coffers could repay.

It's possible, in the end, that Elizabeth's greatest sin was not her wealth, power, and Protestantism, but her unwillingness to retire from public life and her insistence on directing her own financial affairs, including calling in debts after Ferenc's death—most notably from the crown. It didn't help that her cousins were allied on the side of rising Transylvanian tensions against the king, either.

Perhaps foreseeing that her massive fortune would make a widowed Elizabeth vulnerable to the Turks, the crown, and a long list of debtors with no ability or intention to repay their debts, Ferenc entrusted the protection of his wife and children to Palatine Gregory Thurzo—the most powerful man under the king himself. This was the same Gregory Thurzo who would later, at the prompting of the crown, begin an investigation into the growing rumors surrounding Elizabeth.

Whether Thurzo succeeded is debatable. Owing obedience to the crown's interest but himself a Protestant, Thurzo was in a dicey position. Nor could he have wanted to encourage the torture and execution of a noblewoman—the widow of a national war hero, no less.

After hundreds of dubious testimonies and a

total body count that could not be confirmed but likely ranged from thirty-six to an unbelievable 650 (this second number attributed to a witness named Susannah who claimed Elizabeth kept a diary of her victims), Elizabeth's accomplices confessed under torture. Her female accomplices' fingers were ripped out with hot pincers before the women were burned at the stake. A young man named Ficko was beheaded and burned.

Elizabeth herself was walled up in Cachtice Castle, her existence struck from the record as though she had "never been." The crown's debt was canceled, and the king became Holy Roman Emperor in 1612. Elizabeth's grandson, also named Ferenc, was later executed for treason and her descendants eventually banished to Poland.

Today, Elizabeth Bathory's place of burial is not known; her grave has not been found.

Nor has her diary.

Her story is best known for its morbidity—on par with that of Vlad Dracul, "The Impaler"—and probably made more shocking because its main actor is a woman surrounded by other women. And while some of the allegations against her could be true, the story that rarely gets told is that of an intelligent, independent woman caught in rising religious tensions during the Protestant Reformation and myriad political crossfires.

For those interested in learning more about Elizabeth Bathory, I recommend *Infamous Lady: The True Story of Countess Erzsébet Báthory* and *The Private Letters of Countess Erzsébet Báthory*, both by Kimberly L. Craft.

Probably the weirdest thing that happened to me during the writing of these books was learning of my distant relative Sir Ian Moncrieffe's link to Bathory herself, thanks to my mother's lifelong commitment to genealogy—including the use of DNA testing.

In the end, *The Progeny* and *Firstborn* aren't about history at all, but what it really means to be alive, right now, in the only moment that exists: this one. They're about what we choose to stake our identity on (our experiences? Our jobs, families, culture, education, religion?) . . . and who we are beneath them all.

It's also about genius in all its forms—some more obvious than others. Maybe you, like me, have OCD. Or have contended with something unseen by others, in secret, for years. Maybe you've struggled with it through your life to the point that it's interfered in your daily existence. Whether it's ADHD, addiction, depression, anxiety, bipolar disorder, autism, a chronic illness—whatever it is—I believe it informs your particular genius. The thing that causes you to see the world in a way that others can't. I wrote this book as a reminder that the way you—and

I—see this world is a gift. You are amazing. *You* are Progeny.

Use your powers for good, people.

—Tosca

Acknowledgments

I usually thank my readers first, though I've realized recently that there's a group of people I've neglected in the acknowledgments of my other books: the teachers. So let me correct that here by saying thank you—not just to the teachers who encouraged me to pursue writing (Pat Kaltenberger and Anne Cognard of Lincoln East High, Craig Davis of Smith College, and Daniel Mueller of the University of New Mexico), but every teacher who had the dubious honor of having me as a student, as well as those intrepid souls who get up each morning to shape the lives of young people (and grown-ups) everywhere. You are my heroes.

Thank you to my readers—from your letters to your interactions on social media to the stories and hugs we share when we meet in person, you are such a bright light in my life. I love you guys.

Thank you to my agents, Dan Raines of Creative Trust and Meredith Smith, to Jonathan Merkh, Amanda Demastus, Ami McConnell, Beth Adams, Jennifer Smith, Brandi Lewis, and Bonnie MacIsaac at Howard, president and CEO Carolyn Reidy, and the team at Simon & Schuster.

Thank you to Stephen Parolini, Cindy Conger, Lisa Riekenberg, and Jeff Gerke for keeping me functioning and turning stuff in (mostly) on time.

Nikola Špehar, thank you for your patient answers to my many questions. You are a wonderful ambassador for Croatia.

Barbara Bocz, you are one of the most intelligent and amazing women I know and a wonderful ambassador for all of Europe.

Bryan, you are perfect to me in every way. Thank you for your amazing love, for making me a mother, for keeping me sane, and for holding me every night.

Kayl, Gage, and Kole . . . my favorite adventures are with you. Sorry about the creepy bedtime stories.

And thank you most of all to the Ultimate Author, for loving me to the very last line.

About the Author

TOSCA LEE is the award-winning and *New York Times* bestselling author of *The Progeny*, *Iscariot*, *The Legend of Sheba*, *Demon: A Memoir*, *Havah: The Story of Eve*, and the Books of Mortals series with *New York Times* bestselling author Ted Dekker (*Forbidden*, *Mortal*, *Sovereign*). A notorious night owl, she loves watching TV, eating bacon, playing video games and football with her kids, and sending cheesy texts to her husband.

You can find Tosca at ToscaLee.com, on social media, or hanging around the snack table.

Center Point Large Print
600 Brooks Road / PO Box 1
Thorndike, ME 04986-0001 USA

(207) 568-3717

US & Canada:
1 800 929-9108
www.centerpointlargeprint.com